Hands-On Serverless Computing

Build, run, and orchestrate serverless applications using
AWS Lambda, Microsoft Azure Functions, and Google
Cloud Functions

Kuldeep Chowhan

BIRMINGHAM - MUMBAI

Hands-On Serverless Computing

Commissioning Editor: Gebin George
Acquisition Editor: Shrilekha Inani
Content Development Editor: Priyanka Deshpande
Technical Editor: Manish Shanbhag
Copy Editor: Safis Editing
Project Coordinator: Virginia Dias
Proofreader: Safis Editing
Indexer: Rekha Nair
Graphics: Tom Scaria
Production Coordinator: Nilesh Mohite

First published: July 2018

Production reference: 1200718

Published by Packt Publishing Ltd.
Livery Place
35 Livery Street
Birmingham
B3 2PB, UK.

ISBN 978-1-78883-665-4

www.packtpub.com

To my lovely wife, Priya, who has always accepted me and supported my drive and ambitions.
You are and always will be my loving partner throughout our joint life journey.
My loving daughter, Myra, this is for you.

– Kuldeep

`mapt.io`

Mapt is an online digital library that gives you full access to over 5,000 books and videos, as well as industry leading tools to help you plan your personal development and advance your career. For more information, please visit our website.

Why subscribe?

- Spend less time learning and more time coding with practical eBooks and Videos from over 4,000 industry professionals

- Improve your learning with Skill Plans built especially for you

- Get a free eBook or video every month

- Mapt is fully searchable

- Copy and paste, print, and bookmark content

PacktPub.com

Did you know that Packt offers eBook versions of every book published, with PDF and ePub files available? You can upgrade to the eBook version at `www.PacktPub.com` and as a print book customer, you are entitled to a discount on the eBook copy. Get in touch with us at `service@packtpub.com` for more details.

At `www.PacktPub.com`, you can also read a collection of free technical articles, sign up for a range of free newsletters, and receive exclusive discounts and offers on Packt books and eBooks.

Foreword

Cloud computing has been my passion for years. Ever since I started focusing on this area, advances in automation and software have continually amazed me. This amazement fueled the inspiration for my blog, Cloud Musings (`http://blog.govcloudnetwork.com`). Now in its tenth year, the blog's content has matured from explaining the basics of cloud computing to addressing its advantages from a business standpoint. Now that the second decade of the cloud computing era is upon us, why are the standard IaaS, PaaS, and SaaS models all of a sudden being replaced with serverless computing and the new Function as a Service (FaaS) model? Is this the end of cloud computing as we know it? Is my career as an application developer about to change again?

Luckily for many of us, cloud computing is not going away. Serverless computing, in fact, represents the next stage in cloud maturation. Although a misnomer, FaaS takes technology abstraction to the next level by completely removing infrastructure considerations from the developer's plate. With serverless computing, developers can now develop, deploy, and run applications without needing to think about provisioning servers. Developers don't even need to worry about managing or even scaling the infrastructure. All of these headaches are taken care of by the cloud service provider.

Similar to how the Large Hadron Collider explores and discovers elementary particles, the FaaS approach drives developers toward discovering, and in this domain, creating single-purpose blocks of code. Putting this in another way, just like physicists have abandoned the atom and accepted fermions and bosons as the most elementary particles, software developers must now abandon monolithic applications and microservices to accept the function block.

Hands-On Serverless Computing does not stop at explaining this new worldview. It gives the modern developer much-needed tools for creating and deploying serverless applications to AWS, Microsoft Azure, and the Google Cloud Platform (GCP). In providing his expert guidance, Kuldeep Chowhan goes into depth on development environments such as Visual Studio, Node.js, and JavaScript. He even tackles application testing with Postman.

If you are a developer and want to participate in cloud computing's future, you must accept this book as your serverless computing bible. Ignoring this inevitable change is like ignoring the microprocessor, object-oriented code, and the internet.

Kevin L. Jackson

Contributors

About the author

Kuldeep Chowhan is a Principal Software Developer at Expedia Group. He has been involved in building tools and platforms for the last 5+ years at Expedia. He has extensive experience on using serverless technologies on AWS (such as AWS Lambda, API Gateway, and DynamoDB) through Node.js. He has built a Platform as a Service (PaaS) tool for the automated creation of source code, a CI/CD pipeline, and a fully automated pipeline for deploying Docker containers/AWS Lambda. He is also passionate about CI/CD and DevOps.

I would like to thank my wife, Priya, and my mother-in-law, Durga Rani. I would also like to extend my gratitude to my mom, Durga, my dad and my two sisters – Sudha and Sai for their support over the years.

A big thanks to entire Packt team, Priyanka Deshpande, Shrilekha Inani, and Manish Shanbhag, for supporting me while I was writing the book.

About the reviewer

Siva Gurunathan has over 10 years of experience in establishing and managing successful technology companies and has strong expertise in cloud computing, virtualization, networking, and information security. Having co-founded his first start-up at the age of 21, he had bootstrapped it into a multi-million dollar venture within 3 years. Siva is an alumni of IIM Bangalore and also has a double major in engineering from Bits, Pilani. He currently focuses on hybrid cloud initiatives, bridging public clouds and on-premises data centers.

Packt is searching for authors like you

If you're interested in becoming an author for Packt, please visit authors.packtpub.com and apply today. We have worked with thousands of developers and tech professionals, just like you, to help them share their insight with the global tech community. You can make a general application, apply for a specific hot topic that we are recruiting an author for, or submit your own idea.

Table of Contents

Preface

Serverless computing allows you to build and run applications and services without thinking about servers. Serverless applications don't require you to provision, scale, and manage any servers. You can build them for nearly any type of application or backend service, and everything required to run and scale your application with high availability is handled for you. Building serverless applications means that your developers can focus on their core product instead of worrying about managing and operating servers or runtimes, either in the cloud or on premises. This reduced overhead lets developers reclaim time and energy that can be spent on developing great products that scale and are reliable.

This book teaches the basics of serverless computing and explains how to build event-driven apps using serverless frameworks on three public cloud platforms: AWS, Microsoft Azure, and Google Cloud. This hands-on guide dives into the basis of serverless architectures and how to build them using Node.js, Visual Studio Code for code editing, and Postman. This book teaches you how to quickly and securely develop applications without the hassle of configuring and maintaining infrastructure on three public cloud platforms.

You will learn how to harness serverless technology to rapidly reduce production time and minimize your costs, while still having the freedom to customize your code without hindering functionality. Upon completion of the book, you will have the knowledge and resources to build your own serverless application hosted in AWS, Microsoft Azure, or Google Cloud Platform, and will have experienced the benefits of event-driven technology for yourself. You will apply the fundamentals of serverless technology from the ground up, and will come away with a greater understanding of its power and how to make it work for you.

Who this book is for

This book is intended to be read by developers, architects, system administrators, or any stakeholders working in the serverless environment who want to understand how functions work and how to build them.

What this book covers

This book provides practical guidance and readers will learn about the following:

- Serverless computing, the benefits it provides, and when to use it
- What serverless computing isn't
- Function as a Service (FaaS) and the different technologies that are provided by three public cloud providers: AWS Lambda, Azure Functions, and Google Cloud Functions
- Different triggers that you can apply to your serverless functions in AWS, Microsoft Azure, and Google Cloud Platform
- How to build serverless application across three public cloud providers using code samples
- How to use programming languages such as Node.js and code editors such as Visual Studio Code to set up your development environment to build serverless applications
- Best development practices with serverless computing to create scalable and practical solutions

Chapter 1, *What is Serverless Computing?*, introduces readers to the concept of serverless computing, use cases of serverless computing analysis, FaaS, the benefits of serverless computing, and what serverless computing is and isn't.

Chapter 2, *Development Environment, Tools, and SDKs*, introduces readers to the programming language and the tools that are required to write their serverless applications. It introduces the different SDKs that AWS, Microsoft Azure, and Google Cloud provide to write serverless applications.

Chapter 3, *Getting Started with AWS Lambda*, introduces readers to AWS Lambda, goes into depth about how AWS Lambda works, provides configuration options for AWS Lambda, and explains how to secure AWS Lambda.

Chapter 4, *Triggers and Events for AWS Lambda*, introduces readers to the different triggers and events available for AWS Lambda.

Chapter 5, *Your First Serverless Application on AWS*, teaches readers how to write serverless applications to run on AWS using Node.js, how to deploy serverless applications to AWS, how to test the serverless application, and how to trigger the serverless application using Amazon API Gateway.

Chapter 6, *Serverless Orchestration on AWS*, teaches readers how to orchestrate and manage the state of serverless applications on AWS using AWS step function.

Chapter 7, *Getting Started with Azure Functions*, introduces readers to Azure Functions and goes into depth about how Azure Functions works. It also explains the configuration options for Azure Functions and how to secure Azure Functions.

Chapter 8, *Triggers and Bindings for Azure Functions*, introduces readers to the different triggers and events available for Azure Functions.

Chapter 9, *Your First Serverless Application on Azure,* teaches readers how to write serverless applications to run on Azure using Node.js, how to deploy serverless applications to Azure, how to test serverless applications, and how to trigger serverless applications using Azure API Management.

Chapter 10, *Getting Started with Google Cloud Functions*, introduces readers to Google Cloud Functions, goes into depth about how Google Cloud Functions works, covers the configuration options for Google Cloud Functions, and explains how to secure Google Cloud Functions.

Chapter 11, *Triggers and Events for Google Cloud Functions,* introduces readers to the different triggers and events available for Google Cloud Functions.

Chapter 12, *Your First Serverless Application on Google Cloud*, teaches readers how to write serverless applications to run on Google Cloud using Node.js, how to deploy serverless applications to Google Cloud, how to test serverless applications, and how to trigger the serverless application using HTTP triggers.

Chapter 13, *Reference Architecture for a Web App,* provides a reference architecture for creating a web application using serverless computing on AWS.

Chapter 14, *Reference Architecture for a Real-Time File Processing,* provides a reference architecture for real-time file processing using serverless computing on AWS.

To get the most out of this book

Knowledge of serverless architectures and frameworks, as well as Node.js, would be an advantage. Sufficient information will be provided to those new to this field.

Chapter 2, *Development Environment, Tools, and SDKs,* has the installation instructions for the software that you will need to develop serverless applications on your workstation. Please make sure to go through it.

Download the example code files

You can download the example code files for this book from your account at
`www.packtpub.com`. If you purchased this book elsewhere, you can visit
`www.packtpub.com/support` and register to have the files emailed directly to you.

You can download the code files by following these steps:

1. Log in or register at `www.packtpub.com`.
2. Select the **SUPPORT** tab.
3. Click on **Code Downloads & Errata**.
4. Enter the name of the book in the **Search** box and follow the onscreen instructions.

Once the file is downloaded, please make sure that you unzip or extract the folder using the latest version of:

- WinRAR/7-Zip for Windows
- Zipeg/iZip/UnRarX for Mac
- 7-Zip/PeaZip for Linux

The code bundle for the book is also hosted on GitHub at `https://github.com/PacktPublishing/Hands-On-Serverless-Computing`. In case there's an update to the code, it will be updated on the existing GitHub repository.

We also have other code bundles from our rich catalog of books and videos available at `https://github.com/PacktPublishing/`. Check them out!

Download the color images

We also provide a PDF file that has color images of the screenshots/diagrams used in this book. You can download it here: `http://www.packtpub.com/sites/default/files/downloads/HandsOnServerlessComputing_ColorImages.pdf`.

Conventions used

There are a number of text conventions used throughout this book.

`CodeInText`: Indicates code words in text, database table names, folder names, filenames, file extensions, pathnames, dummy URLs, user input, and Twitter handles. Here is an example: "The actual event data is available within the `data` property of the event object."

A block of code is set as follows:

```
function handleGET(req, res) {
    res.status(200).send('Hello from HTTP Google Cloud Function!');
}

function handlePUT(req, res) {
    res.status(403).send("Forbidden, you don't have access");
}
```

Any command-line input or output is written as follows:

```
curl -X POST https://<YOUR_REGION>-
<YOUR_PROJECT_ID>.cloudfunctions.net/<FUNCTION_NAME> -H "Content-
Type:application/json" --data '{"name":"Kuldeep"}'
```

Bold: Indicates a new term, an important word, or words that you see onscreen. For example, words in menus or dialog boxes appear in the text like this. Here is an example:

"Select the trigger type as **Cloud Pub/Sub topic**."

Warnings or important notes appear like this.

Tips and tricks appear like this.

Get in touch

Feedback from our readers is always welcome.

General feedback: Email feedback@packtpub.com and mention the book title in the subject of your message. If you have questions about any aspect of this book, please email us at questions@packtpub.com.

Errata: Although we have taken every care to ensure the accuracy of our content, mistakes do happen. If you have found a mistake in this book, we would be grateful if you would report this to us. Please visit www.packtpub.com/submit-errata, selecting your book, clicking on the Errata Submission Form link, and entering the details.

Piracy: If you come across any illegal copies of our works in any form on the Internet, we would be grateful if you would provide us with the location address or website name. Please contact us at copyright@packtpub.com with a link to the material.

If you are interested in becoming an author: If there is a topic that you have expertise in and you are interested in either writing or contributing to a book, please visit authors.packtpub.com.

Reviews

Please leave a review. Once you have read and used this book, why not leave a review on the site that you purchased it from? Potential readers can then see and use your unbiased opinion to make purchase decisions, we at Packt can understand what you think about our products, and our authors can see your feedback on their book. Thank you!

For more information about Packt, please visit packtpub.com.

What is Serverless Computing? 1

Before we start creating serverless applications to run in **Amazon Web Services** (**AWS**), Microsoft Azure, and the **Google Cloud Platform** (**GCP**), let's learn about what serverless computing is. We will learn about how it is being used, and about **Function as a Service** (**FaaS**) and the benefits that serverless computing provides. Readers will also learn about what serverless computing isn't.

In this chapter, we will cover the following topics:

- What is serverless computing?
- Use cases of serverless computing
- Unpacking FaaS
- What serverless computing is not
- The benefits of serverless computing
- Best practices to get the maximum benefits out of serverless computing

What is serverless computing?

Serverless applications still require servers to run; hence, the term is a misnomer. Serverless computing adds a layer of abstraction on top of a cloud infrastructure, so developers need not worry about provisioning and managing physical or virtual servers in the cloud. Serverless computing gives you the capability to develop, deploy, and run applications without having to think about provisioning and management of servers. Serverless computing doesn't need you to provision, manage, and scale the infrastructure required to execute your application. The cloud provider automatically provisions the infrastructure required for your function to run and scale your serverless application with high availability.

In most cases, when people think of serverless computing, they are likely to think of applications with backends that run on cloud providers, such as AWS, that are fully managed, are event triggered, and are ephemeral, lasting only for the invocation that runs within a stateless container. While serverless applications are fully managed and hosted by cloud providers, such as AWS, it is a misinterpretation to say that the applications are completely running serverless. Servers are still involved in the execution of these serverless applications; it is just that these are managed by cloud providers, such as AWS. One way to think about these serverless applications is as FaaS. The most popular implementation of FaaS at the moment is AWS Lambda. However, there are other FaaS implementations from Microsoft Azure called Azure Functions, from GCP called Cloud Functions, and from the open source serverless platform from Apache called OpenWhisk.

Serverless computing is all about the modern developer's expanding frame of reference.

What we have seen is that the atomic unit of scale has been changing from the virtual machine to the container, and if you take this one step further, we start to see something called **function—a single-purpose block of code**. It is something you can analyze very easily. It can:

- Process an image
- Transform a piece of data
- Encode a piece of video

The following diagram depicts the difference between Monolothic, Microservice, and FaaS architectures:

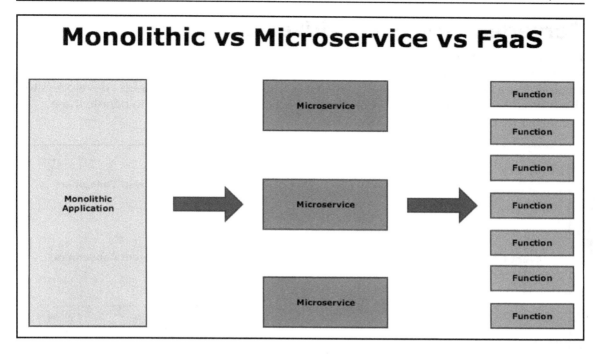

Monolithic versus Microservice versus FaaS

Developing serverless applications means that you can focus on solving the core business problem instead of spending time on how to operate and manage runtimes, or compute infrastructure, either in on-premises, or in the cloud. With this reduced overhead, developers can reclaim the time and energy that they would usually spend on developing solutions to provision, manage, and scale the applications that are highly available and reliable. I will touch upon this more later in the book.

The real goal of the serverless computing movement is to provide a high level of abstraction of the compute infrastructure so that developers can focus on solving critical business problems, deploy them rapidly, and reduce the time it takes for business ideas to be marketed, as opposed to the time it takes if you use traditional infrastructure for your applications.

Serverless and event-driven collision

Event-driven computation is an architecture pattern that emphasizes action in response to or based on the receptions of events. This pattern promotes loosely coupled services and ensures that a function executes only when it is triggered. It also encourages developers to think about the type of events and responses a function needs in order to handle these events before programming the functions:

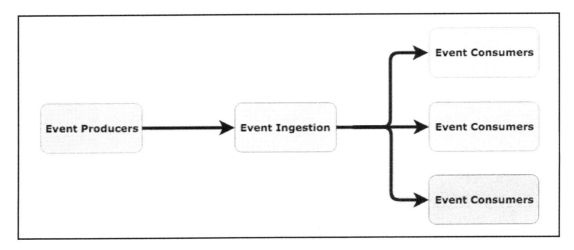

Event-driven architecture example

A system built with event-driven architecture consists of **Event Producers** that produce a stream of events that are ingested using **Event Ingestion**, and then **Event Consumers** that listen for the events, as shown in the preceding diagram.

Events are delivered to consumers in near real time so that they can respond immediately to the events as they happen. Event producers are decoupled from the event consumers. As they are decoupled, the producers don't know which consumers are listening to the events that they produce. Event consumers are also decoupled from one another, and every event consumer sees every events produced by the event producers.

Serverless applications are usually built by combining multiple functions (FaaS) using offerings, such as AWS Lamdba or Microsoft Azure Functions, together with external backend resources, such as Amazon S3, Amazon DynamoDB, and many more solutions to manage the state between invocations. The architecture that ties these multiple functions (FaaS) is event-driven architecture. By combining tools, such as AWS Lambda and Amazon S3, you can develop applications without having to think about the provision and management of the infrastructure. As this is a shift in architecture compared to how you might have operated so far, you would also need to change how data will flow through your application, which is made up of functions.

In this event-driven architecture, the functions are event consumers because they are expected to come alive when an event occurs and are responsible for processing it. Some examples of events that trigger serverless functions include the following:

- API requests
- Scheduled events
- Events in object storage
- Events in databases
- Notification events

What is FaaS?

I've mentioned FaaS a few times already, so let's dig into what it really means. Serverless computing involves code that runs as a service on an infrastructure that is fully managed by the cloud provider. This is automatically provisioned, based on an event, and is automatically scaled to ensure high availability. You can think of this as FaaS that run on stateless, ephemeral containers created and maintained by the cloud provider. You might have already come across terms such as **Software as a Service (SaaS)**, **Infrastructure as a Service (IaaS)**, and **Platform as a Service (PaaS)**. Let's look at what they mean. SaaS is a form of cloud computing in which software is licensed based on a subscription, hosted centrally, and is delivered remotely by the provider over the internet. Examples of SaaS are Google Apps, Citrix GoToMeeting, and Concur. IaaS is a form of cloud computing where the provision and management of compute infrastructure resources occur over the internet, scales up quickly, and you pay for what you use. Examples of IaaS are Azure Virtual Machines and AWS EC2. PaaS is a form of cloud computing where the software and infrastructure that are needed for application development are provided over the internet by the provider. Examples of PaaS are AWS Beanstalk and Azure App Services.

Let's also look at AWS Lambda to learn more about FaaS.

AWS Lambda helps you run code without supplying or administrating servers. You pay only for the total time you consume—no charge is applicable when your code is not running. Using Lambda, one can run code for virtually any type of application or backend service—all with zero administration. We need to upload the code and Lambda looks into everything required to run and scale your code with high availability. You can set up your code to automatically trigger from other AWS services or call it directly from any web or mobile app.

Let's look at features that AWS Lambda offers that fit into FaaS paradigm:

- Essentially, FaaS runs code without having to provision and manage servers on your own and is executed based on an event rather than running all the time. With traditional architectures that involve containers or physical/virtual servers, you would need the servers be running all the time. As the infrastructure is used only based on the requirements, you achieve 100 percent server utilization, and cost savings are also huge as you pay only for the compute time you consume when the function/Lambda runs.
- With FaaS solutions, you can run any type of application, which means there isn't a restriction on what languages you need to write the code in or on particular frameworks to be used. For example, AWS Lambda functions can be written in JavaScript, Python, Go, C# programming languages, and any JVM language (Java, Scala, and so on).
- The deployment architecture for your code is also different from traditional systems, as there is no server to update yourself. Instead, you just upload your latest code to the cloud provider, AWS, and it takes care of making sure the new version of the code is used for subsequent executions.
- AWS handles scaling of your function automatically based on the requests to process without any further configuration from us. If your function needs to be executed 10,000 times in parallel, AWS handles scaling up the infrastructure that is required to run your function 10,000 times in parallel. The containers that are executing your code are stateless, ephemeral with AWS provisioning, and destroyed only for the duration that is driven by the runtime needs.
- In AWS, functions are triggered by different event types, such as S3 (file) updates, scheduled tasks based on a timer, messages sent to Kinesis Stream, messages sent to SNS topics, and many more event type triggers.
- AWS also allows functions to be triggered as a response to HTTP requests through Amazon API Gateway.

State

Functions, as they run in ephemeral containers, have significant restrictions when it comes to management of state. You need to design your functions in such a way that the subsequent run of your function will not be able to access state from a previous run. In short, you should develop your functions with the point of view that they are stateless.

This affects how you design the architecture for your application. Considering that functions are stateless, you need to use external resources to manage the state of your application so that the state can be shared between runs of the functions. Some of the popular external resources that are widely using the FaaS architecture are Amazon S3, which provides a simple web services interface that you can use to store and retrieve any amount of data, at any time, from anywhere on the web, caching solutions, such as Memcached or Redis, and database solutions, such as Amazon DynamoDB, which is a fast and flexible NoSQL database service for any scale.

Execution duration

Functions are limited in how long each invocation is allowed to run. Each cloud provider has different time limits for their FaaS offering, after which the function execution will be terminated. Let's look at the different timeouts provided by each cloud provider for functions:

- AWS Lambda—5 minutes
- Azure Functions—10 minutes
- Google Functions—9 minutes

As the execution of the functions are limited by the time limit set by the providers, certain architectures with long running processes are not suited for the FaaS architecture. If you still want to fit those long running processes into a FaaS architecture, then you would need to design the architecture so that several functions are coordinated to accomplish a long running task, as oppose to in a traditional architecture where everything would be handled within the same application.

Understanding cold start

What is cold start?

Cold start = time it takes to boot a computer system

What is cold start in FaaS?

When you execute a cold (inactive) function for the first time a cold start occurs. The cold start time is when the cloud provider provisions the required runtime containers, downloads your code for the functions, and then runs your functions. This increases the execution time of the function considerably, as it may take more time to provision certain runtimes before your function gets executed. The converse of this is when your function is hot (active), which means that the container with your code required to execute the function stays alive, ready and awaiting for execution. If your function is running, it is considered active and if there is certain period of inactivity, then the cloud provider will drop the runtime container with your code in it to keep the operating costs low and at that point your function is considered cold again.

The time it takes for cold start varies between different runtimes. If your function utilizes runtimes such as Node.js or Python, then the cold start time isn't significantly huge; it may add < 100 ms overhead to your function execution.

If your function utilizes runtimes such as JVM, then you will see cold start times greater than a few seconds while the JVM runtime container is being spun up. The cold start latency has significant impact in the following scenarios:

- Your functions are not invoked frequently and are invoked once every 15 minutes. This will add noticeable overhead to your function execution.
- Your functions will see sudden spikes in your function execution. For example, your function may be typically executed once per second, but it suddenly ramps up to 50 executions per second. In this case, you will also see noticeable overhead to your function execution.

Understanding and knowing about this performance bottleneck is essential when you are architecting your FaaS application so that you can take this into account to understand how your functions operate.

Some analysis has been done to understand the container initialization times for AWS Lambda:

- Containers are terminated after 15 minutes of inactivity
- Lambda within a private VPC increases container initialization time

People overcome this by pinging their Lambda once every 5 or 10 minutes to keep the runtime container for a function alive and also preventing it from going into a cold state.

Is cold start an issue of concern? Whether your function will have a problem like this, or not, is something that you need to test with production, such as with load, and understand the overhead that cold start adds to your FaaS application.

API gateway

One of the things that I mentioned about FaaS earlier is the API Gateway. An API Gateway is a layer that stands in front of backend HTTP services or other resources, such as FaaS, and decides where to route the HTTP request based on the route configuration defined in the API gateway solution. In the context of FaaS, the API Gateway maps the incoming HTTP request parameters to the inputs to the FaaS function. The API gateway then transforms the response that it receives from the function and converts it into an HTTP response and returns that HTTP response back to the caller of the API gateway.

Each cloud provider has an offering in this space:

- AWS has an offering called API gateway
- Microsoft Azure has an offering called Azure API management
- GCP has an offering called Cloud Endpoints

The working of the Amazon API gateway is as shown in the following figure:

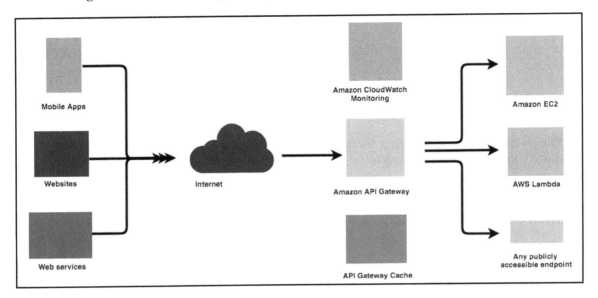

How the Amazon API Gateway works

API gateways provide additional capabilities along with routing the requests, including:

- Authentication
- Throttling
- Caching
- Input validation
- Response code mapping
- Metrics and logging

The best use case for FaaS + API gateway is the creation of a feature-rich HTTP-based microservice with scaling, monitoring, provision, and management all taken care of by the provider in a true serverless computing environment.

The benefits of serverless computing

So far I have covered the definitions of serverless computing and FaaS. Let's now look at the benefits of serverless applications. Let's look at the benefits that serverless applications provide:

- Reduced operational cost
- Rapid development
- Scaling costs
- Easier operational management

Reduced operational cost

As we covered earlier in the book, serverless or FaaS applications run on the cloud provider in a fully managed environment. As there are only certain pre-defined runtimes where you can run your functions and the same runtimes are used by many other people within the cloud provider environment, the cloud provider is able to utilize the economy of scale effect and reduce the operational cost required to run your functions. The gains in cost that the cloud provider gets are also due to the fact that everyone shares the same infrastructure, including networking, and everyone will be using it only for a certain period of time rather than using it all the time, like in a traditional application.

These reduced costs of running the functions are passed down to the people consuming these FaaS offerings. They are charged very little for the execution of the functions and are charged in *ms* intervals. You will see similar benefits in using IaaS and PaaS solutions; however, FaaS takes it to the next level.

Rapid development

As FaaS applications run in an infrastructure that is fully managed by the cloud provider, automatically provisioned and automatically scaled based on the load by the cloud provider, you as a developer can just focus on writing the code that is required to solve your business problem rather than spend time figuring out how to spin up the server, making sure that it is highly available and scales based on the load.

AWS, Microsoft Azure, and GCP all provide various tools to develop and deploy your functions to their environment easily. We will talk about these in later chapters when we talk about setting your development environment and when we are ready to deploy our serverless applications.

Scaling costs

With FaaS offerings, horizontal scaling is something that is automatically managed by the cloud provider. They also take care of scaling up and scaling down the infrastructure that is required to process your functions. What this means is that you don't have to spend any time in developing the solutions yourself, everything is automatically taken care of for you. The cloud provider also takes care of ensuring that your functions are run in an environment that is highly available and that it runs across multiple **availability zones** (**AZs**) within a region. The other big benefit that you get is that the cloud provider takes care of patching the infrastructure automatically for you and you don't have to worry about it when there are security vulnerabilities to patch for the operating system or runtimes.

The big benefit with FaaS offerings is that for the compute infrastructure you *only pay for what you need* down to 100 ms execution time (AWS Lambda). Based on what your application traffic patterns are, this could result in huge cost savings for you:

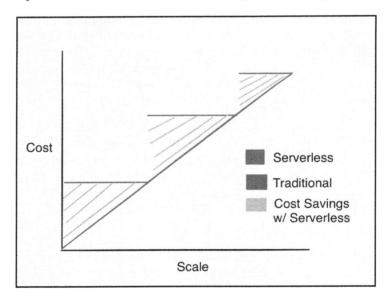

Cost savings with serverless compared to traditional infrastructure

If you look at the preceding diagram, you will see that in a traditional infrastructure environment, you will always scale up in step functions to ensure that you are able to handle the load without effecting your application, but in a serverless/FaaS infrastructure environment, you scale up for what you need and don't have to scale up in step functions to handle your peak load. This gives you tremendous cost savings.

Another example would be, let's say, your application with traditional infrastructure processes only one request every minute and takes 100 ms to process each request, which will result in CPU usage of about 0.2 percent for the entire hour. If you look at the utilization of this infrastructure, it is very inefficient and you could have a lot of other applications running on the same infrastructure without impacting your application. With FaaS offerings, you will only pay for the 100 ms or 200 ms of computer time per minute, as that is what is used by your application and that would result in an overall time of 0.3% for the entire hour, which will result in huge savings for running your application in serverless architecture.

Easier operational management

So far we have talked about the benefits that serverless computing provides in areas such as scaling, rapid development, and reduced operational costs. Let's look at how FaaS offerings help us in reduced operation management of the application.

Easier packaging and deployment

The packaging and deployment of your application in a FaaS environment is really simple compared to deploying your application to a container or even an entire server. With FaaS, all you will be doing is creating your artifact (JAR (JVM)/ZIP (Node.js or Python)) and then uploading them directly to the FaaS offerings. You don't need any additional deployment or configuration management tools to deploy your applications to a FaaS environment. Some of the cloud providers do provide access to write the application directly in the console itself.

As there is no need to have additional configuration or deployment tools, system administration is significantly reduced.

Time to market

As the operational management in a FaaS environment is significantly reduced, the time it takes to make a business idea a reality is significantly less than what it takes in a traditional infrastructure environment, which means there is more time to try out more business ideas, which in turn is a win for your business. As less time is spent on operations, you have more people to work on solving business problems, which in turn can help you bring your idea to market faster.

What serverless computing is not

So far, I have talked about serverless computing and the benefits that it provides over traditional infrastructure architectures. Let's spend some time understanding what's not serverless as well before we look at the drawbacks of serverless computing.

Comparison with PaaS

Given that serverless applications or FaaS applications do tend to be similar to *The Twelve-Factor* applications, people often compare them to PaaS offerings. However, if you look closely, PaaS offerings are not built to bring your entire application up and down for every request, but FaaS or serverless applications are built to do that. For example, if you look at a popular PaaS offering from AWS, AWS Elastic Beanstalk, it is not designed to bring up the entire infrastructure every time a request is processed. However, it does provide lots of capabilities to the developers, where it makes the deployment and management of web applications very easy.

The other key difference between PaaS and FaaS is scaling. With PaaS offerings, you still need a solution to handle the scaling of your application to the load. But with FaaS offerings, this is completely transparent. Lots of PaaS solutions, such as AWS Elastic Beanstalk, do offer autoscaling based on different parameters, such as CPU, memory, or network. However, this is still not tailored towards individual requests, which makes FaaS offerings much more efficient in scaling and provides best bang for buck in terms of cost.

Comparison with containers

Another comparison that is quite popular for FaaS offerings is with containers.

Let's look at what containers are, as we haven't discussed them so far. Containerization of the infrastructure has been around for a long time, but it was made popular in 2013 by Docker when they combined operation system level virtualization with filesystem images on Linux. With this, it became easy to build and deploy containerized applications. The biggest benefit that Docker-containers provides is that, unlike **Virtual Machines** (**VMs**), they share the same operating system as the host, which tremendously reduces the size of the image that is required to run a containerized application. As the footprint of Docker containers is less, you can run multiple Docker containers on the same host without significant impact on the host system.

As container runtimes gained popularity, container platforms started to evolve. Some of the notable ones are:

- CloudFoundry
- Apache Mesos

The next step in the evolution of containerization was providing an API that let developers deploy Docker images across a fleet of compute infrastructures. The most popular container orchestration and scheduling platform that is out there right now is **Kubernetes.** It started as an internal project within Google in 2004, called **Borg.** Later, Google open sourced the solution as **Kubernetes** and it is right now the most commonly used container platform out there. There are other solutions as well, such as **Mesosphere.**

And even further advancement in container solutions was cloud-hosted container platforms, such as Amazon **EC2 Container Service** (**ECS**) and **Google Container Engine** (**GKE**), which, like serverless offerings, eliminates the need to provision and manage the master nodes in the cluster. However, you still have to provision and manage the nodes on which the containers will be scheduled to run. There are a lot of solutions that are out there that help in the maintenance of nodes within the cluster. AWS introduced their new container offering called **Fargate**, which is completely serverless, where you don't have to provision the nodes within the cluster ahead of time. It is still early days for **Fargate,** but if it offers what it promises, it will certainly help a lot of developers who don't have to spend time provisioning and managing nodes within the cluster.

Fundamentally, the same argument that I made for PaaS still holds true with containers as well. For serverless offerings or FaaS offerings, scaling is automatically managed and is transparent. The scaling also has fine grain control. Container platforms do not yet offer such a solution. There are scaling solutions within container platforms, such as Kubernetes Horizontal Pod Autoscaling, which do scale based on the load on the system. However, at the moment, they don't offer the same level of control that FaaS offerings provide.

As the gap of scaling and management between FaaS offerings and hosted container solutions narrow, the choice between the two may come down to the type of the application. For example, you would choose FaaS for applications that are event driven and containers for request-driven components with a lot of entry points. I expect FaaS offerings and container offerings to merge in the coming years.

#NoOps

Serverless computing or FaaS doesn't mean *No Ops* completely. Definitely, there is no system administration required to provision and manage infrastructure to run your applications. However, there are still some aspects of **operations (Ops)** involved in making sure your application is running the way it is supposed to run. You need to monitor your application using the monitoring data that FaaS offerings provide and ensure that they are running optimally.

Ops doesn't just mean system administration. It also includes monitoring, deploying, securing, and production debugging. With serverless apps, you still have to do all these and, in some cases, it may be harder to do Ops for serverless applications as the tool set is relatively new.

Limits to serverless computing

So far, I have talked about many things regarding serverless computing. Let's look at the drawbacks of serverless computing as well.

Serverless architecture has its limits as well and it is very important to realize the drawbacks to implementing serverless applications along with recognizing when to use serverless computing and how to implement it so that you will be able to address these concerns ahead of time. Some of these limits include:

- Infrastructure control
- Long running application
- Vendor lock-in

- Cold start
- Shared infrastructure
- Server optimizations is a thing of past
- Limited number of testing tools

We will look at the options for addressing some of these issues in the following sections.

Infrastructure control

As I mentioned previously, with a serverless architecture you will not have access to control the underlying infrastructure as that is controlled by the cloud provider. However, developers are still able to choose which runtime that they want to run their function on, such as Node.js, Java, Python, C#, and Go. They still have control over the choice of the memory requirements for their function and the timeout duration for their function execution.

Long running application

One of the benefits of serverless architectures is that they are built to be fast, scalable, event-driven functions. Therefore, long-running batch operations are not well suited for this architecture. Most cloud providers have a timeout period of five minutes, so any process that takes longer than this allocated time is terminated. The idea is to move away from batch processing and into real-time, quick, responsive functionality.

Vendor lock-in

One of the biggest fears with serverless applications concerns vendor lock-in. This is a common fear with any move to cloud technology. For example, if you start committing to using Lambda, then you are committing to using AWS and either you will not be able to move to another cloud provider or you will not be able to afford transition to a cloud provider.

While this is understandable, there are many ways to develop applications to make a vendor switch using functions easier. A popular and preferred strategy is to pull the cloud provider logic out of the handler files so it can easily be switched to another provider. The following code illustrates a poor example of abstracting cloud provider logic.

The following code shows the handler file for a function that includes all of the database logic bound to the FaaS provider (AWS, in this case):

```
const database = require('database').connect();
const mail = require('mail');
module.exports.saveCustomer = (event, context, callback) => {
 const customer = {
 emailAddress: event.email,
 createdAt: Date.now(),
 };
 database.saveCustomer(customer, (err) => {
 if (err) {
 callback(err);
 } else {
 mail.sendEmail(event.email);
 callback();
 }
 });
};
```

The following code illustrates a better example of abstracting the cloud provider logic.

The following code shows a handler file that is abstracted away from the FaaS provider logic by creating a separate `Users` class:

```
class Customers {
 constructor(database, mail) {
 this.database = database;
 this.mail = mail;
 }
 save(emailAddress, callback) {
 const customer = {
 emailAddress: emailAddress,
 createdAt: Date.now(),
 };
 this.database.saveCustomer(customer, (err) => {
 if (err) {
 callback(err);
 } else {
 this.mail.sendEmail(emailAddress);
 callback();
 }
 });
 }
}
module.exports = Customers;
const database = require('database').connect();
const mail = require('mail');
```

```
const Customers = require('customers');
let customers = new Customers(database, mail);
module.exports.saveCustomer = (event, context, callback) => {
  customers.save(event.email, callback);
};
```

The second method is preferable both for avoiding vendor lock-in and for testing. Removing the cloud provider logic from the event handler makes the application more flexible and applicable to many providers. It makes testing easier by allowing you to write unit tests to ensure it is working properly in a traditional way. You can also write integration tests to verify that integrations with external services are working properly.

Most of the serverless offerings by cloud providers are implemented in a similar way. However, if you had to switch vendors, you would definitely need to update your operational toolsets that you use for monitoring, deployments, and so on. You might have to change your code's interface to be compatible with the new cloud provider.

If you are using other solutions provided by the cloud vendor that are very much specific to the cloud provider, then moving between vendors becomes extremely difficult, as you would have to re-architect your application with the solutions that the new cloud provider provides.

Cold start

I have already discussed cold start earlier in the chapter. Let's recap about the concern we have regarding cold start. The concern about cold start is that a function takes slightly longer to respond to an event after a period of inactivity. The time it takes varies between the run times that your application chooses.

This does tend to happen, but there are ways around the cold start if you need an immediately responsive function. If you know your function will only be triggered periodically, an approach to overcoming the cold start is to establish a scheduler that calls your function to wake it up every so often. Within AWS, you can use CloudWatch Event Scheduler to have your Lambda function invoked every 5 to 10 minutes so that AWS Lambda will not mark your function as inactive or cold. Azure Functions and Google Functions also have similar capability to have functions invoked on a schedule.

Shared infrastructure

A multi-tenant infrastructure or shared infrastructure refers to an infrastructure where multiple applications of different customers (or tenants) are being run on the same machine. It is a very well-known strategy to achieve the economy of scale benefits that I mentioned earlier as well. This could be a concern from a business perspective since serverless applications can run alongside one another regardless of business ownership. Although this doesn't affect the code, it does mean the same availability and scalability will be provided across competitors. There could be situations where your code might be affected as well due to noisy neighbors (high load generating function). A multi-tenant infrastructure also has problems related to security and robustness, where one customer's function can take down another customer's function.

This problem is not unique to serverless offerings—they exist in many other service offerings that use multi-tenancy, such as Amazon EC2 and container platforms.

Server optimization is a thing of the past

As I mentioned earlier, you will not have access to control any aspects of the underlying infrastructure where your functions are executed by the cloud provider. As there is no access to the underlying infrastructure, you will lose access to optimizing the server for your application to improve performance for your clients. If you need to perform server optimizations so that your application can run optimally, then use an IaaS offerings, such as AWS EC2 or Microsoft Azure Virtual Machines.

Security concerns

Serverless computing also has security issues. However, the types of security issues that I have to deal with are significantly better than what I have to deal with when running applications on a traditional infrastructure. The same set of security issues related to your application remain the same in serverless computing. Different serverless offerings use different security implementations so as you start to use different serverless offerings for your applications it increases the surface area that is required for malicious intent and also increases the chances of a security attack.

Deployment of multiple functions

The tooling for deploying a single FaaS function is very robust at the moment. However, the tooling required to deploy multiple functions at the same time or co-ordination of deploying multiple functions is lacking.

Consider a case where you have multiple functions that make a serverless application and you need to deploy all of them at once. There are not many tools out there that can do that for you. The tooling to ensure zero downtime for serverless applications is not robust enough yet.

There are open source solutions, such as **Serverless Framework**, that are helping to solve some of these issues, but they can only be done with support from the cloud provider. AWS built the AWS Serverless Application model to address some of these concerns, which I will talk about in later chapters.

Limited number of testing tools

One of the limitations to the growth of serverless architectures is the limited number of testing and deployment tools. This is anticipated to change as the serverless field grows, and there are already some up-and-coming tools that have helped with deployment. I anticipate that cloud providers will start offering ways to test serverless applications locally as services. Azure has already made some moves in this direction, and AWS has been expanding on this as well. NPM has released a couple of testing tools so you can test locally without deploying to your provider. Some of these tools include node-lambda and aws-lambda- local. One of my current favorite deployment tools is the serverless Framework deployment tool (`https://serverless.com/framework/`). It is compatible with AWS, Azure, Google, and IBM. I like it because it makes configuring and deploying your function to your given provider incredibly easy, which also contributes to a more rapid development time.

Integration testing of your serverless applications is hard. As with the FaaS environment, you depend on external resources to maintain state. You need to make sure your integration tests cover these scenarios as well. Typically, as there are not a lot of solutions out there where you can run these external resources locally, people stub these external resources for the purpose of integration testing. The challenge will be in making sure that the stubs that you create are always in sync with the implementation of the external resources and some vendors may not even provide a stubbed implementation for their resources.

To ensure that your functions works, integration tests are usually run on production-like environments with all the necessary external resources in place. As our functions are very small compared to traditional infrastructure, we need to rely more on integration testing to ensure that our functions run optimally.

Summary

In this chapter, you learned about serverless applications and architecture, the benefits and use cases, and the limits to using the serverless approach. It is important to understand the serverless architecture and what it encompasses before designing an application that relies on it. Serverless computing is an event-driven, FaaS technology that utilizes third-party technology and servers to remove the problem of having to build and maintain infrastructure to create an application.

Serverless computing may not be the right approach for every problem that is out there, so be cautious if anyone says that serverless computing will replace all of your existing application architectures. Serverless computing might be the answer for the new architectures that you are building now and it may very well replace your existing architectures but there are drawbacks as well to serverless computing, so keep those in mind when you design your serverless application architecture. As the tooling around serverless computing improves in the coming years, you will see that these drawbacks will become a thing of the past.

The benefits that serverless computing provides are significant. They include reduced operational costs, and rapid development, and deployment of your serverless applications. Other benefits include easier operational management and reduced environmental impact through better utilization of compute infrastructures.

The next chapter will discuss the tools and a programming language that is required to write your Serverless applications. It will introduce the different SDKs that AWS, Microsoft Azure, and Google Cloud offer to write serverless applications.

Development Environment, Tools, and SDKs

2

In this chapter, we will look at how to set up your development environment, which programming language to use, the tools that you can use, and the SDKs that are provided by AWS, Microsoft Azure, and Google Cloud for developing serverless applications.

In this chapter, we will cover the following topics:

- Development environment setup
- Tools
- SDKs from cloud providers

Development environment and tools

Let's look at the development environment and the tools that we will need to create and run the serverless applications that we will create in later chapters. We will be using Visual Studio Code for code editing, Node.js and JavaScript for writing our serverless applications, and we will use tools such as Postman to test our serverless applications. Let's start by looking at what Visual Studio Code is, the benefits it provides, its installation instructions, and the Visual Studio Code user interface.

Visual Studio Code

Microsoft's Visual Studio Code is a free, open source code editor that runs on all operating systems (macOS, Linux, and Windows). It supports development operations such as task running, debugging, and version control. It provides the tools developers will need for a code, build, and debug cycle, leaving more complex workflows to more fully featured IDEs.

Visual Studio Code is a lightning fast code editor, perfect for day-to-day use. With support for hundreds of languages, it aids productivity with auto-indentation, syntax highlighting, box-selection, bracket-matching, snippets, and more. It features intuitive keyboard shortcuts, easy customization of the editor using user-defined settings, and its community-contributed keyboard shortcut mappings will let you navigate your source code with ease. It also has built-in support for code completion—IntelliSense, navigation through UI, rich semantic code understanding, and code refactoring.

Debugging is often the feature that developers miss most in a leaner code editor experience, and with Visual Studio Code not only is it available, but it is very easy to debug your applications. Visual Studio Code has an interactive debugger, so you can inspect variables, step through source code, view call stacks, and execute commands in the console.

Visual Studio Code also integrates with scripting and build tools to perform common tasks, making everyday workflows easier and faster. It has support for Git so you can work with source control without leaving the editor, including committing changes to Git and viewing pending changes with diffs:

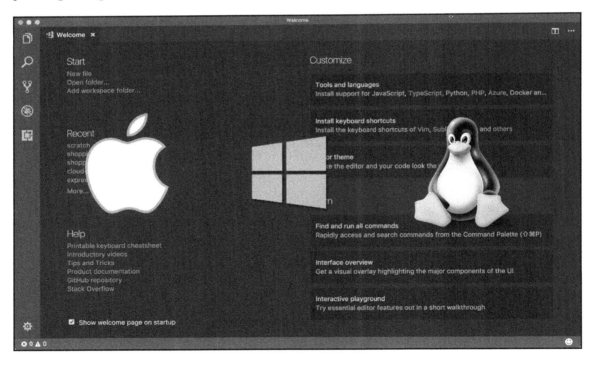

Let's have a look at the features of Visual Studio:

- IntelliSense: Go beyond syntax highlighting and auto-complete with IntelliSense, which provides smart completions based on variable types, function definitions, and imported modules.
- Print statement debugging is a thing of the past: Debug code right from the editor. Either launch it or attach it to your running apps and debug with breakpoints, call stacks, and an interactive console.
- Git commands built-in: Working with Git and other SCM providers has never been easier. Review diffs, stage files, and make commits right from the editor. Push and pull from any hosted SCM service.
- Extensible and customizable: Visual Studio Code has many features out-of-the-box. It also let's you customize and extend Visual Studio Code in the form of plugins and settings configurations. You can find more information about Visual Studio Code and its extensibility at `https://code.visualstudio.com/Docs/editor/whyvscode`.

Visual Studio Code ships monthly releases (`https://code.visualstudio.com/updates`) and supports auto-update when a new release is available. If you're prompted, accept the newest update and it will be installed (you won't need to do anything else to get the latest update).

Setting up Visual Studio Code

Setting up Visual Studio Code is quick and easy. Visual Studio Code is a lightweight editor and can be run on most available hardware and platforms. I have listed the system requirements for Visual Studio Code in the following sections, which you can use to check whether your computer configuration will support running it.

Hardware

Visual Studio Code is a relatively small download, being less than 100 MB, and having a disk footprint of 200 MB. It is a lightweight editor that can be run easily on today's hardware.

Recommended CPU and memory:

- 1.6 GHz or faster processor
- 1 GB of RAM

Platforms

VS Code needs at least the following operating system versions to perform optimally:

- OS X Yosemite and above
- Windows 7, 8.0, 8.1, and 10 (32-bit and 64-bit)
- Linux (Debian): Debian 7, Ubuntu Desktop 14.04
- Linux (Red Hat): CentOS 7, Red Hat Enterprise Linux 7, Fedora 23

Additional Windows requirements

If you are running Windows 7, please make sure .NET Framework 4.5.2 is installed.

Additional Linux requirements

Following are the additional Linux requirements if you are running a Linux systems:

1. GLIBC version 2.15 or later
2. GLIBCXX version 3.4.15 or later

Let's look at how we can get Visual Studio Code running on different platforms.

Installing on macOS

Take a look at the following installation steps:

1. Download the Visual Studio Code installer for Mac from `https://go.microsoft.com/fwlink/?LinkID=534106`
2. Double-click on the downloaded package to expand the contents
3. Move **Visual Studio Code.app** to the Applications folder, which makes it available in the *Launchpad*
4. Add Visual Studio Code to your Dock by right-clicking on the icon, then select **Options**, followed by *Keep in Dock*.

Launching VS Code from the Command Line

Let's take a look at the following steps:

1. You can also run Visual Studio Code from the Terminal by typing `code` after adding it to the PATH environmental variable:
2. Launch Visual Studio Code
3. Open the **Command** palette by pressing Shift+ *cmd + P*
4. Type `shell command` to find the **Shell Command: Install 'code' command in PATH** command
5. Press *Enter* and Visual Studio Code will be added to the PATH

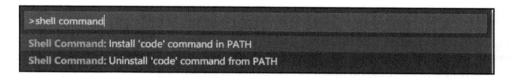

6. Restart the terminal for the new **$PATH** value to take effect
7. You'll be able to type `code` in any folder to start editing files in that folder

> If you had earlier versions of Visual Studio Code and have added Visual Studio Code as an alias in your **.bash_profile** or equivalent for other shells, then remove that reference from the file and replace that by following the above steps to run `Shell Command: Install code command in PATH` command.

Manually adding Visual Studio Code to your path

If you plan to manually add Visual Studio, then refer to the following code:

```
cat << EOF >> ~/.bash_profile
# Add Visual Studio Code (code)
export PATH="$PATH:/Applications/Visual Studio
Code.app/Contents/Resources/app/bin"
EOF
```

Touch Bar support

Out of the box, Visual Studio Code supports Touch Bar and adds actions to navigate in editor history, as well as the full debug tool bar to control debugging through your Touch Bar.

Installing on Linux

As there are multiple Linux distributions and installation is different for each of them, let's look at each one of them.

Debian and Ubuntu-based distributions

The easiest way to install VS Code on Debian/Ubuntu-based distributions is to download and install the 64-bit `.deb` package from `https://go.microsoft.com/fwlink/?LinkID=760868`. If you have the graphical software center available, then install the 64-bit `.deb` package from there, and if it is not available then install it using the command line:

```
sudo dpkg -i <file>.deb
sudo apt-get install -f # Install dependencies
```

The `.deb` package installation will automatically install the `apt` repository and it will also install the signing key which enables auto-updating using the regular system mechanism. You can download the 32-bit .deb package and `.tar.gz` binaries from `https://code.visualstudio.com/Download`

The repository and key can also be installed manually using the following script:

```
curl https://packages.microsoft.com/keys/microsoft.asc | gpg --dearmor >
microsoft.gpg
sudo mv microsoft.gpg /etc/apt/trusted.gpg.d/microsoft.gpg
sudo sh -c 'echo "deb [arch=amd64]
https://packages.microsoft.com/repos/vscode stable main" >
/etc/apt/sources.list.d/vscode.list'
```

Then run the following commands to update the package cache and install the package:

```
sudo apt-get update
sudo apt-get install code # or code-insiders
```

RHEL, Fedora, and CentOS-based distributions

Stable versions of 64-bit Visual Studio Code are shipped through a yum repository for RHEL, CentOS, and Fedora distributions. Once you run the following script, it will install the key and repository:

```
sudo rpm --import https://packages.microsoft.com/keys/microsoft.asc
sudo sh -c 'echo -e "[code]\nname=Visual Studio
Code\nbaseurl=https://packages.microsoft.com/yumrepos/vscode\nenabled=1\ngp
gcheck=1\ngpgkey=https://packages.microsoft.com/keys/microsoft.asc" >
/etc/yum.repos.d/vscode.repo'
```

Then run the following commands to update the package cache and install the package using dnf (Fedora 22 and above):

```
dnf check-update
sudo dnf install code
```

Or, if you are on an older version of Fedora, use yum:

```
yum check-update
sudo yum install code
```

openSUSE and SLE-based distributions

The yum repository mentioned above for RHEL, CentOS, and Fedora distributions also works for openSUSE and SLE-based systems. The following script will install the signing key and repository:

```
sudo rpm --import https://packages.microsoft.com/keys/microsoft.asc
sudo sh -c 'echo -e "[code]\nname=Visual Studio
Code\nbaseurl=https://packages.microsoft.com/yumrepos/vscode\nenabled=1\nty
pe=rpm-
md\ngpgcheck=1\ngpgkey=https://packages.microsoft.com/keys/microsoft.asc" >
/etc/zypp/repos.d/vscode.repo'
```

Then run the following commands to update the package cache and install the package:

```
sudo zypper refresh
sudo zypper install code
```

AUR package for Arch Linux

The **Arch User Repository (AUR)** package for Visual Studio Code is community maintained at https://aur.archlinux.org/packages/visual-studio-code-bin.

Nix package for NixOS (or any Linux distribution using Nix package manager)

If you have a Linux distribution that doesn't fit into any one of the ones listed above, then you can follow the following instructions to get Visual Studio Code running for your Linux distribution.

The community-maintained Nix package is available at: https://github.com/NixOS/nixpkgs/blob/master/pkgs/applications/editors/vscode/default.nix in the nixpkgs repository. In order for you to install it using Nix, set the allowUnfree option to true in your config.nix and run the following command:

```
nix-env -i vscode
```

Installing the .rpm package manually

The 64-bit .rpm package can also be manually downloaded from https://go.microsoft.com/fwlink/?LinkID=760867 and installed. However, auto-updating of Visual Studio Code won't work unless the preceding repository is installed. Once you have downloaded it, you install it using your package manager, for example with dnf:

```
sudo dnf install <file>.rpm
```

 Visual Studio Code 32-bit and .tar.gz binaries are also available on the download page at https://code.visualstudio.com/Download.

Installing on Windows

The following instructions demonstrate how to install Visual Studio Code on Windows:

1. Download the Visual Studio Code installer for Windows at `https://go.microsoft.com/fwlink/?LinkID=534107`.

2. Once it is downloaded on your computer, run the installer `VSCodeSetup-version.exe` to get Visual Studio Code installed. It will only take a minute for the installer to complete the installation.

3. By default, Visual Studio Code will be installed to the `C:\Program Files\Microsoft VS Code` directory on a 64-bit machine.

   If you prefer to install it using a `.zip` archive, then that is available at `https://code.visualstudio.com/docs/?dv=winzip`.

 If your Windows operating system is Windows 7, then .NET Framework 4.5.2 or higher is required for Visual Studio Code. You can download .NET Framework 4.5.2 from `https://www.microsoft.com/en-us/download/details.aspx?id=42643`. Make sure it is installed so that Visual Studio Code works properly.

 Setup will optionally add Visual Studio Code to your `%PATH%`, so from the command prompt you can type `code` to open Visual Studio Code on that folder. You will have to restart your command prompt after the installation for the change to the `%PATH%` environmental variable to take effect.

4. To install a 32-bit version of Visual Studio Code, a 32-bit installer is available at `https://go.microsoft.com/fwlink/?LinkId=723965` and a Zip archive is available at `https://go.microsoft.com/fwlink/?LinkID=733265`.

Icons are missing

If you installed Visual Studio Code on a Windows 7 or 8 machine and some of the icons do not appear in the workbench and editor, the following instructions show you how to resolve this.

Why are some icons not appearing in the workbench and editor?

Visual Studio Code uses SVG icons and there have been instances where the `.SVG` file extension is associated with something other than image/svg+xml. Microsoft is looking at options to fix it, but for now here's a workaround:

Using the Command Prompt:

1. Open an Administrator Command Prompt.
2. Type `REG ADD HKCR\.svg /f /v "Content Type" /t REG_SZ /d image/svg+xml`.

Using the Registry Editor (`regedit`):

1. Start `regedit`
2. Open the `HKEY_CLASSES_ROOT` key
3. Find the `.svg` key
4. Set its `Content Type` Data value to `image/svg+xml`
5. Exit `regedit`

Visual Studio Code User Interface

Like the vast majority of other code editors, Visual Studio Code also adopts a common user interface and layout of an explorer/side bar on the left, showing all of the folders and files you have access to, and an editor/editor groups on the right, showing the content of the files you are editing and have opened.

Basic layout

Visual Studio Code comes with an intuitive and simple layout that provides ample room to browse, while maximizes the space provided for the editor and for access to the full contents of your folder or project.

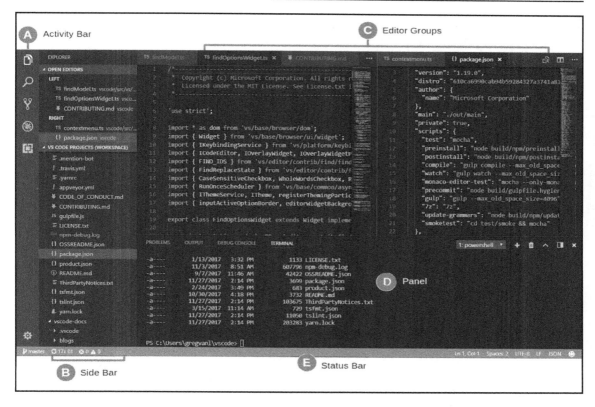

Visual Studio Code User Interface

The user interface is divided into five areas:

- **Editor**: This is the main area where you will edit your files. You can have up to three editors opened side by side.
- **Side Bar**: This is where different views like Explorer/Source Control are, which will assist you while working on your code.
- **Status Bar**: This is where you will see information about the files you are editing and the files that you have already opened.
- **Activity Bar**: This bar is located on the far left hand side and this will let you switch between different views and gives you context specific indicators like the number of outgoing changes when source control, such as Git, is enabled.
- **Panels**: This has the capability of displaying different panels below the editor space for debug information or for output, errors, and warnings, or an integrated terminal. You can move the panel to the right for more vertical space.

Each time you open Visual Studio Code, it will open up in the same state as it was in when it was last closed. The folder, layout, and opened files will be preserved and they will be reopened.

All the opened files in each editor are displayed with tabbed headers in **Tabs** at the top of the editor region.

Side-by-side editing

In Visual Studio Code, you can have up to three editors open side by side for editing. There are multiple ways to open the editors side by side when you already have one editor open. The following instructions show you how:

- *cmd* + \ (macOS) or *Ctrl* + \ to split the active editor into two
- *cmd* (macOS) or *Ctrl* click on a file in the Explorer
- From the Explorer context menu on a file—**Open to the Side**
- On the upper-right of an editor, click the **Split Editor**
- Drag and drop a file to the other side of the editor region
- *cmd* + *Enter* (macOS) or *Ctrl+Enter* in the **Quick Open** (*cmd* + *P*) file list

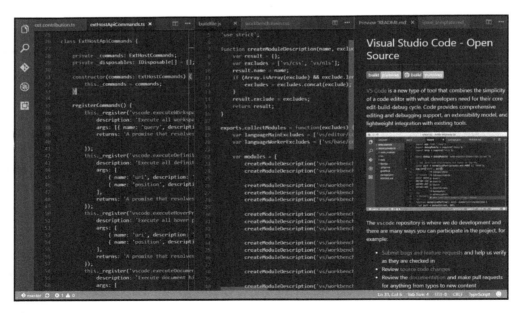

Visual Studio Code side- by-side editing

When you have more than one editor open, you can switch between them quickly by holding the *cmd* (macOS) or *Ctrl* key and pressing *1*, *2*, or *3*.

 You can resize editors and reorder them. Drag and drop the editor title area to reposition or resize the editor.

Explorer window

The Explorer window is used to open, browse, and manage all of the files and folders in your project.

After opening a folder in Visual Studio Code, the contents of the folder are shown in the Explorer window. With the contents available in the Explorer window, you can do many things:

- Create, rename, and delete files and folders
- Move files and folders with drag and drop
- Use the context menu to explore all options

 You can drag and drop files into the Explorer from outside Visual Studio Code to copy them.

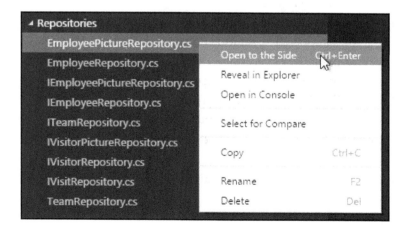

Visual Studio Code works very well with other command-line tools that you might already be using. If you want to run a command-line tool in the context of the folder you currently have open in Visual Studio Code, right-click the folder and select **Open in Terminal** (macOS or Linux) (or **Open in Command Prompt** on Windows).

You can also navigate to the location of a file or folder in the Windows File Explorer Window by right-clicking on a file or folder and selecting **Reveal in Explorer** (or **Reveal in Finder** on macOS, or **Open Containing Folder** on Linux).

 Type *cmd + P* (**Quick Open**) to quickly search and open a file by its name.

Keyboard shortcuts

Visual Studio Code has a lot of handy keyboard shortcuts that help you to quickly navigate between editors and editor groups (`https://code.visualstudio.com/docs/getstarted/userinterface#_editor-groups`)

You can change the default keyboard shortcuts. The instructions to change the default Key Bindings can be found at `https://code.visualstudio.com/docs/getstarted/keybindings`. Substitute *Ctrl* with *cmd* on macOS:

- *Alt + Ctrl + →* Move right editor
- *Alt + Ctrl + ←* Move left editor
- *Tab* open the next editor in the editor group MRU list
- *Tab + Shift + Tab* open the previous editor in the editor group MRU list
- *Ctrl + 1* go to the leftmost editor group
- *Ctrl + 2* go to the center editor group
- *Ctrl + 3* go to the rightmost editor group
- *Ctrl + K* or *Ctrl + ←* go to the previous editor group
- *Ctrl + K* or *Ctrl + →* go to the next editor group
- *Ctrl + W* close the active editor
- *Ctrl + K W* close all editors in the editor group
- *Ctrl + K, Ctrl + W* close all editors

Node.js

Node.js® is a JavaScript runtime built on Chrome's V8 JavaScript engine. Node.js uses an event-driven, non-blocking I/O model that makes it lightweight and efficient. The Node.js package ecosystem, npm (https://www.npmjs.com/), is the largest ecosystem of open source libraries in the world. Node.js is a platform for building fast and scalable server applications using JavaScript. We will be using Node.js when we write serverless applications in later chapters, which we will use to deploy to AWS, Microsoft Azure, and Google Cloud Platform.

As an asynchronous event-driven JavaScript runtime, Node is designed to build scalable network applications. In the following, *hello readers* example, many connections can be handled concurrently. Upon each connection, the callback is fired, but if there is no work to be done, Node will sleep:

```
const http = require('http');

const hostname = '127.0.0.1';
const port = 3001;

const server = http.createServer((request, response) => {
  response.statusCode = 200;
  response.setHeader('Content-Type', 'text/plain');
  response.end('Hello readers\n');
});

server.listen(port, hostname, () => {
  console.log(`Node.js Server running at http://${hostname}:${port}/`);
});
```

This is in contrast to today's more common concurrency model, where OS threads are employed. Thread-based networking is relatively inefficient and very difficult to use. Furthermore, users of Node are free from the worries of dead-locking the process, since there are no locks. Almost no function in Node directly performs I/O, so the process never blocks. Because nothing blocks, scalable systems are very reasonable to develop in Node.

Node.js is influenced by, and is similar in design to, systems such as Ruby's Event Machine (`http://rubyeventmachine.com/`) and Python's Twisted Engine (`http://twistedmatrix.com/`). Node.js takes the event model a bit further, presenting an event loop (`https://nodejs.org/en/docs/guides/event-loop-timers-and-nexttick/`) as a runtime construct instead of a library. In other systems, there is always a blocking call to start the event loop, but that is not the case with Node.js. Typically, behavior in other systems is defined through callbacks at the beginning of a script and at the end, the script starts a server through a blocking call such as `EventMachine::run()`. In Node, there is no such start the event loop call. Node simply enters the event loop after executing the input script. Node exits the event loop when there are no more callbacks to perform. This behavior is like browser JavaScript—the event loop is hidden from the user.

Node.js is designed with streaming and low latency in mind, which made HTTP a first-class citizen. This makes Node.js well suited to the foundation of a web framework or library.

Node.js is designed to run without threads, which doesn't mean you cannot take advantage of the multiple cores that are available in modern computers. You can create child processes by calling the `child_process.fork()` API, which will spawn multiple processes based on the CPU cores available on the machine and these child processes are designed to be easy to communicate with one another. The `cluster` module is built upon the same interface, which allows you to share sockets between processes to enable load balancing between your cores.

Node Package Manager

Node Package Manager (**npm**) is a package manager for the JavaScript language. It is the default package manager for the Node.js JavaScript runtime environment. It consists of a command-line client, called `npm`, and an online database of public and paid-for private packages, called the `npm` registry. The registry is accessed via the client, and the available packages can be searched and browsed via the npm website at `https://www.npmjs.com/`. npm is automatically installed when you install Node.js and you should be able to access it by running `npm` in your Terminal (macOS/Linux) / Command Prompt (Windows).

Node.js installation

Node.js® and npm installation is straightforward using the installer package available from the Node.js® web site. The Node.js downloads page at `https://nodejs.org/en/download/` hosts all the binaries/installers for various operating systems. Node.js has two types of release, **Long Term Support** (**LTS**) and current. The LTS release is recommended for most users, and if you want to use the latest and greatest of Node.js, then install the current release. I recommend installing the LTS release for the serverless applications that we will be creating in later chapters.

Installation steps

Follow the steps for Node.js installation:

1. Download the installer from the Nodes.js® downloads page (`https://nodejs.org/en/download/`).
2. Run the installer (the `.pkg` (macOS) / `.msi` (Windows) file you downloaded in the previous step).
3. Follow the prompts in the installer (accept the license agreement, click the NEXT button a bunch of times, and accept the default installation settings):

You can find instructions on how to install Node.js via package managers such as `brew`, `nvm`, `pacman`, and many more at `https://nodejs.org/en/download/package-manager/`.

Node.js tutorial in VS Code

In this section, we will look into how we can write Node.js code in Visual Studio Code. We will also be looking at how to run Node.js code. Visual Studio Code has out-of- the-box support for the Node.js JavaScript language and also has support for Node.js debugging. To demonstrate this, we will create a file, Node.js, which will print `Hello Reader!`:

```
Hello Reader!
```

Let's get started by creating a Node.js file to print `Hello Reader!`.

Create an empty folder called `scratch`, navigate into it, and open it with Visual Studio Code:

```
mkdir scratch
cd scratch
code .
```

You can open files or folders directly from the command line. The period . refers to the current folder, therefore Visual Studio Code will start and open the `Hello` folder.

From the **File Explorer** toolbar, press the **New File** button:

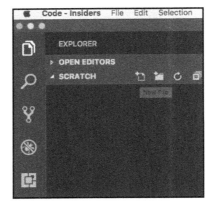

Name the file `hello-readers.js`:

Set the extension of the file to `.js` and, by using the `.js` file extension, Visual Studio Code will interpret this file as JavaScript and will evaluate the contents with the JavaScript language service.

Create a simple string variable in `hello-readers.js` and print the contents of the string to the console:

```
const message = 'Hello Readers!';
console.log(message);
```

If you take a close look, when you typed `console.` in Visual Studio Code IntelliSense, (`https://code.visualstudio.com/docs/editor/intellisense`), the console object was automatically presented to you with one of the options being `.log`. When editing JavaScript files, Visual Studio Code will automatically provide you with IntelliSense for the DOM:

```
JS hello-readers.js ●
  1   const message = 'Hello Readers!';
  2   console.
           ⊕ assert           (method) Console.assert(test?: boolean, m ×
           ⊕ clear            essage?: string, ...optionalParams: any
           ⊕ count            []): void
           ⊕ debug
           ⊕ dir
           ⊕ dirxml
           ⊕ error
           ⊕ exception
           ⊕ group
           ⊕ groupCollapsed
           ⊕ groupEnd
           ⊕ info
```

Also notice that Visual Studio Code knows that `message` is a string based on the initialization to `'Hello Readers!'`. If you type message, you'll see IntelliSense showing all of the string functions available on message:

After experimenting with IntelliSense, revert any extra changes from the source code example above and save the file (*cmd + S*).

Running Hello Readers

It's simple to run `hello-readers.js` with Node.js. From a Terminal on a macOS/Linux or Command Prompt on Windows, just type:

```
node hello-readers.js
```

You should see `Hello Readers!` output to the Terminal and then Node.js returns.

Integrated Terminal

Visual Studio Code has an integrated terminal in which you can run shell commands. You can learn about it more at `https://code.visualstudio.com/docs/editor/integrated-terminal`. With the help of the Integrated Terminal, you can run Node.js directly in it and avoid having to switch out of Visual Studio Code while running command-line tools.

You can access the Integrated Terminal within Visual Studio Code by navigating to **View | Integrated Terminal.** You can also access it by pressing *control* + backtick key on your keyboard and it will open the Integrated Terminal. You can then run node app.js there:

Postman

Postman makes developing APIs easy and it is the most complete toolset for API development. Postman has been designed with developers in mind and it is packed with lots of options and features:

- It is the most widely used REST client around the world
- It has been designed to support API developers from the ground up
- It has an intuitive user interface to create workflows, add tests, send requests to endpoints, and save the responses for the API calls

Postman's options and features are:

- It stores all the requests made
- It supports variable substitutions
- It has support for creating environments
- It has support for tests & pre-request scripts
- It has support for collections
- It supports request descriptions

Installation

Let's look at how to install Postman on macOS, Linux, and Windows. You can install Postman on macOS, Windows, and Linux operating systems as a native app. To install Postman, navigate to the apps download page at `https://www.getpostman.com/apps` and select the installer for macOS / Windows / Linux, depending on your operating system:

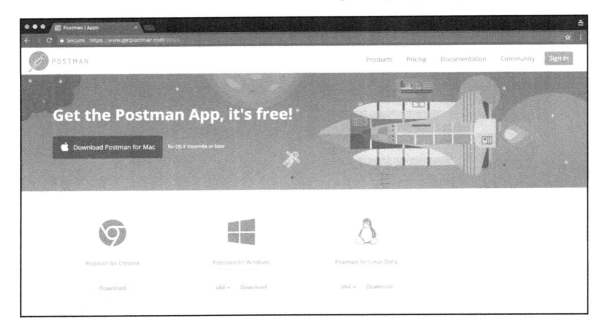

Installing on macOS

On macOS, once you've downloaded the Postman app, you can drag the app file to the `Applications` folder. To open the Postman app, double-click on it, as you would do with any other macOS app.

Installing on Windows

To install Postman on Windows follow the following steps:

1. Download the setup file for Postman on Windows (either 64-bit or 32-bit, based on your operating system)

2. Once you have downloaded the setup file, run the installer to get Postman installed on your machine

Linux installation

As there are many Linux distributions and installation of them can vary, BlueMatador has a blog on how you can install on different Linux distributions. You can find the instructions at `https://blog.bluematador.com/posts/postman-how-to-install-on-ubuntu-1604/?utm_source=hootsuite&utm_medium=twitter&utm_campaign=`.

Updating Postman – native app (macOS, Windows, and Linux)

Postman's apps are designed to check for updates when the app is launched or when the app reloads. If there is an update available, then it will display the change log, along with a prompt asking whether you want to update it:

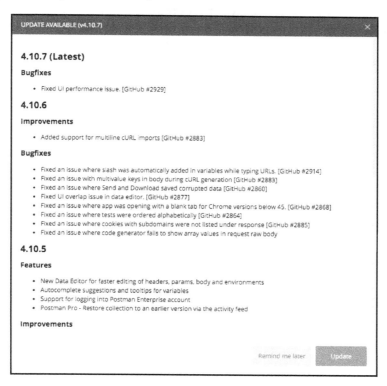

Postman Echo

We will be using `postman-echo.com` in the next section to send a test request using Postman. The `Postman-echo.com` (`https://docs.postman-echo.com/`) is a sample API implementation that Postman hosts so that you can experiment with different types of HTTP requests. It receives the request that you send to it and responds with a response.

Sending the first request using Postman

Let's send our first request for an API using Postman. For this test, we will be using the `postman-echo.com` site, which Postman hosts to test the APIs, as mentioned in the preceding section. Instead of using `postman-echo.com`, you can use other sites that you are familiar with, that will respond to HTTP GET/PUT/POST requests:

- Open Postman on your operating system
- In the URL field, enter `postman-echo.com/get`
- Make sure to have **GET** selected in the HTTP request type field
- Hit the **Send** button to send your API request, and at the bottom you will see the response from the API with JSON data. As we have tested the request/response for `postman-echo.com`, the request that we made is added to the history, as you can see in the following screenshot. You can see `postman-echo.com/get` under the **History** tab of the sidebar:

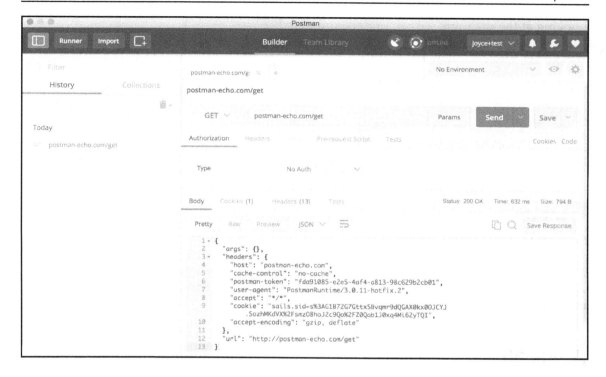

How does this work in Postman?

Let's map the request process with a simple diagram:

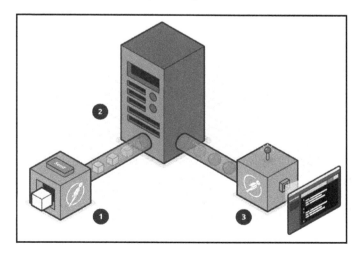

Looking at the diagram, we can understand that:

1. After you enter the request URL (`postman-echo.com/get`) in Postman hit the **Send** button
2. When the API server `postman-echo.com` receives the request, it returns a response
3. Postman receives the response and then it is made available in Postman to visualize the interface

SDKs

Software Development Kits (**SDKs**) are tools that will help you to write serverless applications on the three cloud providers. AWS, Microsoft Azure, and GCP all provide different SDKs for different languages, so that you can integrate their services into your applications. Let's look at the SDKs that each cloud provider has that we would need to integrate into our serverless applications.

AWS Node.js SDK

AWS offers SDKs for many different languages, including Node.js. Some of the languages for which it offers SDKs are:

- Node.js
- Java
- .NET
- Go
- C++
- Python
- Ruby
- iOS
- Android
- Browsers (Internet Explorer, Chrome, Safari etc.,)
- AWS IOT

However, there are many more languages and platforms that could be included in this list. I will be using the AWS Node.js SDK to create serverless applications later in the book. Let's get an overview of the AWS Node.js SDK.

In your Command Prompt or Terminal, run the following command to get the AWS Node.js SDK installed. A prerequisite for this is to have Node.js installed. You can follow the instructions that we provided earlier in the chapter.

Installation

Use the following command for installing AWS SDK:

```
npm install aws-sdk
```

Configuration

On macOS or Linux, create a credentials file at `~/.aws/credentials`, or on Windows create a file at `C:\Users\USERNAME\.aws\credentials`:

```
[default]
aws_access_key_id = your_access_key
aws_secret_access_key = your_secret_key
```

You can find more instructions at `http://docs.aws.amazon.com/AWSJavaScriptSDK/guide/node-intro.html` on how to configure AWS access keys.

After you have installed the `aws-sdk` Node.js SDK, adding the following line will load the AWS Node.js JavaScript files into your application:

```
const AWS = require('aws-sdk');
```

The following code sample shows how to create an S3 bucket and write an object to that bucket. For this example to work, the preceding credentials that you added to the credentials file should have access to creating a new S3 bucket and be able to write an object to that bucket.

Create a file called `createS3Bucket.js` in your working directory with the following code:

```
const AWS = require('aws-sdk');
const s3 = new AWS.S3();
// Bucket names must be unique across all AWS users
const bucket = process.argv[2];
```

```
const bucketKey = 'myBucketKey';
s3.createBucket({
Bucket: bucket
}, (err, data) => {
 if (err) {
 console.log(err);
 } else {
 params = {
 Bucket: bucket,
 Key: bucketKey,
 Body: 'Hello readers!'
 };
 s3.putObject(params, (err, data) => {
 if (err) {
 console.log(err)
 } else {
 console.log(`Successfully uploaded data to ${bucket}/${bucketKey}`);
 }
 });
 }
});
```

Now execute the following command to create the S3 bucket and have an object written to that bucket. S3 bucket names are unique across different AWS accounts, so you will need to use an unique name for the S3 bucket for the preceding code to execute successfully. Note that the name for the S3 bucket that we are going to create is taken as a command-line option to the Node.js script execution, as the following shows, and you should see a message like **Successfully uploaded data to mys3bucketforthebook/myBucketKey**

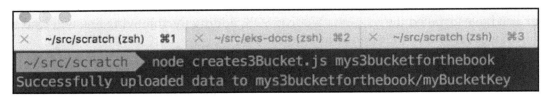

mys3bucketforthebook is the name of the S3 bucket in this case.

In a later section of this book, we will dig deep into the AWS Node.js SDK as we start writing serverless applications for that cloud provider. The API documentation for the AWS Node.js SDK is provided at https://docs.aws.amazon.com/AWSJavaScriptSDK/latest/index.html and it would be good to have familiarity with the SDK before we start writing serverless applications to be run on the AWS cloud.

Microsoft Azure Node.js SDK

Microsoft Azure offers SDKs for many different languages and platforms, including Node.js. Some of the languages for which it offers SDKs are:

- Node.js
- Java
- .NET
- Go
- C++
- Python
- Ruby
- Swift
- iOS
- Android

Many other languages and platforms could be added to this list. I will be using the Azure Node.js SDK to create serverless applications later in the book. Let's get an overview of the Azure Node.js SDK.

In your Command Prompt or Terminal, run the following command to get the Azure Node.js SDK installed. A prerequisite for this is to have Node.js installed. You can follow the instructions that I provided earlier in this chapter.

Installation

Use the following command:

```
npm install azure
```

Azure also has packages for individual APIs as well, such as azure-storage and azure-graph. You can find additional information about the packages available for individual APIs at https://azure.github.io/azure-sdk-for-node/.

Configuration/Authentication

Azure offers different ways of authenticating to its services. You can find the different ways to authenticate at https://github.com/Azure/azure-sdk-for-node/blob/master/Documentation/Authentication.md.

After you have installed the azure-storage Node.js SDK, adding the following line will load the azure-storage Node.js Javascript files into your application:

```
const azureStorage = require('azure-storage');
```

The following code sample shows how to create a storage container in Azure and then uploads a local file `data.txt` to the storage container that we just created. For this code sample to work, the authentication method that you use to connect to Azure services should have access to creating the storage container and be able to upload a file to it.

Ensure that there is a local file called `data.txt` already created in the working directory. Run the following commands to create the file and also make sure that it is not empty:

```
echo "Hello readers" > data.txt
cat data.txt
```

Create a file called **createAzureStorageContainer.js** in your working directory with the following code:

```
const azureStorage = require('azure-storage');
const blobService =
azureStorage.createBlobService(storageConnectionString);
const container = 'storageContainer';
const task = 'storageTask';
const dataFileName = 'data.txt';
blobService.createContainerIfNotExists(container, error => {
 if (error) {
 return console.log(error);
 }
 blobService.createBlockBlobFromLocalFile(
 container,
 task,
 dataFileName,
 (err, res) => {
 if (err) {
 return console.log(err);
 }
 console.dir(res, {
```

```
depth: null,
colors: true
});
}
);
});
```

The code sample already has the name of the **storageContainer** to be created in Azure. Just execute the script using the following command and the local file `data.txt` will get uploaded to the newly created storage container:

```
node createAzureStorageContainer.js
```

In a later section of this book, we will dig deep into the Azure Node.js SDK as we start writing serverless applications for that cloud provider. The API documentation for Azure Node.js SDK is provided at `https://azure.github.io/azure-sdk-for-node/` and it would be good to have familiarity with the SDK before we start writing serverless applications to be run on Microsoft Azure.

Google Cloud Node.js SDK

Google Cloud Platform offers SDKs for many different languages and platforms, including Node.js. Some of the languages for which it offers SDKs are:

- Node.js
- Java
- .NET
- Go
- C++
- Python
- Ruby
- PHP

Many other languages and platforms could be added to this list. I will be using the Google Cloud Node.js SDK to create serverless applications later in the book. Let's get's an overview of the Google Cloud Node.js SDK.

In your Command Prompt or Terminal, run the following command to get the Google Cloud Node.js SDK installed. A prerequisite for this is to have Node.js installed. You can follow the instructions that we provided earlier in the chapter.

Installation

Use the following command for installing Google Cloud Node.js SDK:

```
npm install google-cloud
```

If you want to just install the Google Cloud Storage related libraries, then you can do that by running the following command:

```
npm install @google-cloud/storage
```

Google Cloud platform also has packages for individual APIs, such as `@google-cloud/datastore` and `@google-cloud/storage`. You can find additional information about the packages available for individual APIs that have general availability and Betas at `https://www.npmjs.com/package/google-cloud`.

Configuration/authentication

Once you have a Google Cloud project created, then follow these steps to download the credentials file that is required to execute the code sample:

1. Enable the Cloud Storage API for that project
2. Create a service account
3. Download a private key as JSON

On Linux or macOS, set the environmental variable `GOOGLE_APPLICATION_CREDENTIALS` to the path to which you downloaded the preceding private key JSON file:

```
export GOOGLE_APPLICATION_CREDENTIALS="[PATH]"
```

For example:

```
export GOOGLE_APPLICATION_CREDENTIALS="~/scratch/service-account-file.json"
```

On Windows, set the environmental variable `GOOGLE_APPLICATION_CREDENTIALS` to the path to which you downloaded the preceding private key JSON file using a PowerShell command prompt:

```
$env:GOOGLE_APPLICATION_CREDENTIALS="[PATH]"
```

For example:

```
$env:GOOGLE_APPLICATION_CREDENTIALS="C:\Scratch\service-account-file.json"
```

After you have installed the `@google-cloud/storage` Node.js SDK, adding the following line will load the azure-storage Node.js JavaScript files into your application:

```
const azureStorage = require('azure-storage');
```

The following code sample shows how to upload a local file `data.txt` to Google Cloud Storage. For this code sample to work, the service account that you created earlier in the Google Cloud console should have access so that it can upload a file to Google Storage.

Ensure that there is a local file called `data.txt` already created in the working directory. Run the following commands to create the file and also make sure that it is not empty:

```
echo "Hello readers" > data.txt
cat data.txt
```

Create a file called `uploadFiletoGoogleStorage.js` in your working directory with the following code:

```
const Storage = require('@google-cloud/storage');
const storage = new Storage();
const bucketName = 'myBucket';
const filename = 'data.txt';
storage
  .bucket(bucketName)
  .upload(filename)
  .then(() => {
  console.log(`${filename} successfully uploaded to ${bucketName}.`);
  })
  .catch(err => {
  console.error('ERROR:', err);
  });
```

The code sample already has the name of the storage bucket to upload the local file `data.txt`. Just execute the script using the following command and the local file, `data.txt`, will be uploaded to the Google Cloud Storage bucket.

```
node uploadFiletoGoogleStorage.js
```

In a later section of this book, we will dig deep into the Google Cloud Node.js SDK as we start writing serverless applications for that cloud provider. The API documentation for the Google Cloud Node.js SDK is provided at `https://www.npmjs.com/package/google-cloud` and it would be good to get familiar with the SDK before we start writing serverless applications to be run on Google cloud.

Summary

In this chapter, you learned about setting up a development environment for writing serverless applications by installing Visual Studio Code, and gained an understanding of the Node.js programming language, and installed it. You also learned about Postman and how it can help you to API test serverless applications. You also learned about the different Node.js SDKs that AWS, Microsoft Azure, and GCP provide, which we will be using in later chapters to write our serverless applications.

In the next chapter, we will dig deep into what AWS Lambda is and other serverless offerings from AWS.

Getting Started with AWS Lambda

3

In this chapter, I will introduce you to AWS Lambda, the benefits it brings, use cases of AWS Lambda, and the configuration options that are available for AWS Lambda functions, as well as talking about different deployment options such as versioning and aliases. I will also provide a brief overview of how security around AWS Lambda works.

In this chapter, we will learn the following topics:

- Introduction to AWS Lambda
- Going into depth on how AWS Lambda works
- Use cases of AWS Lambda
- Configuration options for AWS Lambda functions
- AWS Lambda (FaaS) Function versioning, aliases, and environment variables
- Securing AWS Lambda using AWS **Identity and Access Management** (**IAM**)

What is AWS Lambda?

AWS Lambda is a compute service through which you can run your functions. It will run your functions without the need for you to provision or manage any compute infrastructure. AWS Lambda can not only execute your functions, but can also easily scale to thousands of executions per second. As the server management is abstracted away from the developer, they can just focus on solving the business problem rather than having to also focus on server management and scaling the solution. The other big benefit in terms of cost is that you only pay the compute cost for the time AWS Lambda is executed, which provides you with higher utilization of resources at a significantly lower price than what you would be typically paying if you were to run the compute infrastructure all the time. With AWS Lambda, you are charged for every 100 ms your function executes and the number of times your function is executed. AWS Lambda can run any type of code with zero administration by the developer. AWS Lambda also takes care of server maintenance and operating system patching for developers, along with code monitoring and logging. AWS Lambda currently supports these languages:

- Node.js
- C#
- Java
- Python
- Go

As a developer, you have to only provide your code in one of these languages. You can have your AWS Lambda executed in response to events such as changes in the Amazon DynamoDB table or changes to object data in an Amazon S3 bucket, or respond to HTTP requests through Amazon API Gateway. We will deep dive into events and triggers for AWS Lambda in the next chapter.

When you are using AWS Lambda, AWS manages the compute fleet and balances the memory, CPU, and network resources automatically to run your functions. The drawback of this is that you cannot log in to the compute infrastructure or customize the operating system and runtime. These are required for AWS to perform all the administrative activities optimally, such as provisioning capacity, monitoring the compute fleet health, deploying your functions, monitoring AWS Lambda, and applying security patches to the compute fleet. Before we look at the AWS Lambda execution environment and configuration options that are available for developers to customize, let's look at how AWS Lambda works and different use cases where AWS Lambda is being used and how it can help solve your business problem.

How does AWS Lambda work?

A typical life cycle of how AWS Lambda works is shown in this list and the following diagram:

1. Upload your function to either S3 or directly to AWS Lambda.
2. Configure the events/triggers for the AWS Lambda.
3. Based on the events/triggers that you have configured, AWS Lambda will execute the function.
4. Pay for the compute resources only for the time that you have used them:

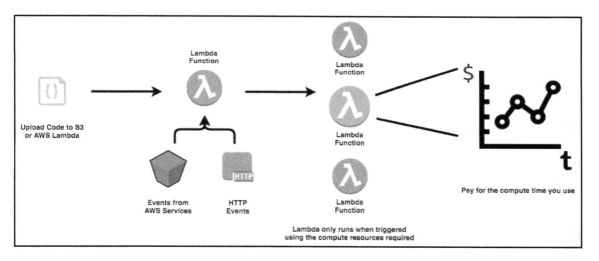

How AWS Lambda works

Use cases

Let's look into different use cases where AWS Lambda helps.

Web apps

By combining AWS Lambda functions with API Gateway and other AWS services such as DynamoDB, S3, and many more, developers are to build powerful and scalable web applications that are able to automatically scale up and down, run across multiple AZs (availability zones), and provide high availability for their applications. They are able to achieve all this with zero administrative effort:

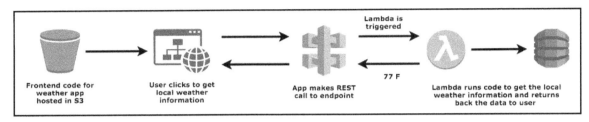

Weather application using Lambda + API Gateway

IOT and mobile backends

With the help of AWS Lambda and API Gateway, you can build backend APIs for mobile that can authenticate, throttle, and process API requests.

Extract, Transform, Load (ETL)

You can use AWS Lambda in ETL processing to perform data validation, sorting, filtering, or any other transformations for your data that you may have in AWS data stores such as S3 or DynamoDB table, and then you can load that transformed data to another data store that is available in AWS.

Data processing

You can have AWS Lambda functions execute code as a response to events and triggers such as those in the data store, changes to system state, or any action performed by users. You can have AWS Lambda directly triggered by different AWS services such as S3, SNS, DynamoDB, CloudWatch, and Kinesis. AWS also has a service called AWS Step Functions (https://aws.amazon.com/step-functions/), through which you can orchestrate multiple AWS Lambda instances and build a workflow.

Real-time processing

With AWS Lambda, you can perform real-time file and stream processing. An example of real-time file processing would be to have AWS Lambda triggered whenever an object is either created or modified in an S3 bucket. Examples of this could be to resize images, create thumbnails for the images, process logs, validate the content, and create aggregations of data stored in an S3 bucket.

By combining AWS Lambda functions and Amazon Kinesis, you can process real-time stream data for applications such as transaction processing, activity tracking on a website, cleansing data, generating metrics, filtering logs, indexing logs, click stream data processing, telemetry of device data, and many more. There are many more use cases with AWS Lambda; I have only covered a few of them here.

Execution environment

Let's look at the execution environment of AWS Lambda. As covered earlier, AWS Lambda doesn't provide the ability to customize/choose the underlying operating system; however, it does let you choose the version of the language framework, such as the Node.js version. Let's look at the operating system and kernel that AWS Lambda uses and to provision the infrastructure to execute your functions:

- Amazon Linux is the operating system that AWS Lambda uses to execute functions. You can find additional details about Amazon Linux **Amazon Machine Image** (**AMI**) at `https://aws.amazon.com/amazon-linux-ami/`.
- AWS Lambda's current Linux kernel version is 4.9.75-25.xx.amzn1.x86_64.

The reason I have provided details about the operating system and kernel is because if you were to include any binaries in your AWS Lambda package, make sure they are compiled in an environment similar to the AWS Lambda execution environment. AWS does change the kernel versions as the latest versions of AMIs are launched, so always refer to the latest kernel version of the AWS Lambda execution environment before targeting that version. Also, note that AWS Lambda only supports 64-bit binaries.

Now, let's look at the language runtime versions that AWS Lambda (FaaS) supports:

- Node.js: v6.10.3 and v4.3.2
- Java: Java 8
- Python: Python 2.7 and 3.6
- .NET Core: .NET Core 2.0 and .NET Core 1.0.1
- Go: Go 1.x

Regardless of which language runtime you choose to run your AWS Lambda in, the following libraries are installed automatically and are available to use in the AWS Lambda execution environment. As they are already installed and available, you don't need to include them in your AWS Lambda package:

- AWS SDK for JavaScript
- AWS SDK for Python 2.7 (Boto 3)
- AWS SDK for Python 3.6 (Boto 3)
- Java 1.8.0 OpenJDK built by Amazon

Environment variables

Let's look at the environment variables that are set and available in the AWS Lambda (FaaS) execution environment. The following list contains the environment variables that are set and made available to AWS Lambda functions. Most of these environment variables are reserved by AWS Lambda and can't be changed by your AWS Lambda function; however, there are a few I have indicated that you can change within your AWS Lambda function. It is good to know and understand that these environment variables exist, as you either use them in your AWS Lambda function or change the ones that you are allowed to change based on your function's needs:

Environment variable name	Reserved	Value
`AWS_EXECUTION_ENV`	Yes	This environment variable value is set to the language runtime the AWS Lambda is going to run
`LAMBDA_TASK_ROOT`	Yes	Path to your Lambda function code
`LAMBDA_RUNTIME_DIR`	Yes	Restricted directory where Lambda runtime related artifacts are stored
`AWS_REGION` `AWS_DEFAULT_REGION`	Yes	This is the AWS region where AWS Lambda is executed

AWS_LAMBDA_LOG_GROUP_NAME AWS_LAMBDA_LOG_STREAM_NAME	Yes	AWS CloudWatch Log Group and Log Streams for your AWS Lambda function
AWS_LAMBDA_FUNCTION_NAME AWS_LAMBDA_FUNCTION_MEMORY_SIZE AWS_LAMBDA_FUNCTION_VERSION	Yes	Your AWS Lambda function's name, the memory size for the function, and the version of your AWS Lambda function
TZ	Yes	Current time; it defaults to UTC
PATH	No	For running executables, this variable contains /usr/local/bin, /usr/bin, or /bin as the values
NODE_PATH	No	This variable contains the path to the Node.js runtime
PYTHONPATH	No	This variable contains the path to the Python runtime

There are additional environment variables that I haven't listed here; you can learn more about them at `https://docs.aws.amazon.com/lambda/latest/dg/current-supported-versions.html`.

Now that we have learned what AWS Lambda is, its use cases, and details about the execution environment of AWS Lambda, let's learn how to create a Lambda using the console and I will talk about the configuration options that are available for AWS Lambda.

Execution context

As I mentioned earlier, whenever AWS Lambda (Faas) executes your functions on your behalf, it will automatically take care of creating, managing, and destroying the resources that are needed to run your Lambda functions. When you create a Lambda function, you specify the amount of memory and timeout that you want for your Lambda function. When a Lambda function is triggered or invoked, AWS Lambda creates an Execution Context based on the configuration settings that you set on your AWS Lambda function. An Execution Context is a temporary runtime environment that AWS Lambda creates, which initializes any external dependencies that are required by your Lambda function, such as connection to a database or HTTP connections to a REST API. As these external dependencies are already created, the subsequent invocations offer better performance as there is no need to initialize them again.

An Execution Context is automatically created and deleted by AWS Lambda; I'm providing this for information only as there is no API for AWS Lambda that lets you manage an Execution Context. It does take some time for the AWS Lambda platform to set up an Execution Context for your Lambda function and do the necessary installations and configurations, which at the end adds latency each time your Lambda function is triggered or invoked. You will see this latency when the Lambda function has been updated or is being invoked for the first time because typically the AWS Lambda FaaS platform tries to reuse the Execution Context for subsequent invocations of your Lambda function.

After your Lambda function has finished execution, AWS Lambda keeps the Execution Context active for some time, anticipating another invocation for your Lambda function to happen. This means that AWS Lambda freezes the Execution Context in time after your Lambda function's execution completes, and unfreezes the Execution context if the AWS Lambda platform chooses to reuse the context when your Lambda function is invoked again.

Execution Context reuse has the following implications:

- If there are any declarations in your AWS Lambda function code outside of the handler method code, then they will remain initialized, which provides additional unintended optimization when your Lambda function is invoked again. For example, within your Lambda function, if you are connecting to DynamoDB, instead of establishing the connection again, the original DynamoDB connection object is used in the subsequent invocations. It is always a good practice to add logic within your Lambda function code to check whether a database connection already exists before creating a new connection.
- Each Execution Context gets 500 MB of disk space in the /tmp directory and this is where the frozen Execution Context resides. This is also the space where it provides a transient cache, which can be used across multiple Lambda invocations. Similar to checking whether the database connection already exists for your Lambda function, you can also add additional code to your AWS Lambda function to check whether the cache has the data that is needed by your Lambda function.

- Callbacks or background processes that are started by your AWS Lambda function and didn't complete execution when your Lambda function ended will resume next time if AWS Lambda chooses to reuse the Execution Context. It is good practice to make sure that they are no background processes or callbacks (Node.js) that are left behind in your code before your Lambda function completes its execution.

AWS Lambda Function–Hello World

Let's look at how to create a *Hello World* AWS Lambda function using AWS Console. I'm assuming you already have an AWS account with admin access and know how to access AWS Console through signing in from `https://aws.amazon.com/`.

Once you have signed in to AWS Console, navigate to Lambda's home page: `https://console.aws.amazon.com/lambda/home?region=us-east-1#/functions`.

1. From Lambda's home page, click **Create Function**, as shown here:

2. Select **Author from scratch** for creating our `Hello World` Lambda function:

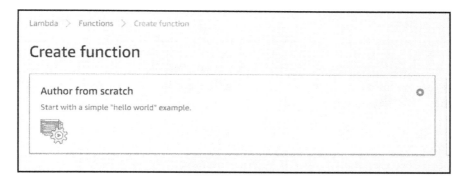

3. In the **Author from scratch** section, enter the following details to create a `Hello World` AWS Lambda (FaaS) function. I'm going to talk in depth about security in a later section of this chapter; with that in mind, I'm going to skip some details around IAM Roles and Policy Templates now:
   - Set **Name** as `myHelloWorldFunction`
   - Set **Runtime** as `Node.js 6.10`
   - For **Role**, select `Create new role from template(s)`
   - Enter `myHelloWorldFunction` as the **Role name**

- From the list of **Policy templates**, select S3 object read-only permissions
- Click on **Create Function** at the bottom:

Now that the myHelloWorldFunction has been created, let's look at the configuration options that are available in the console and I will explain some of them as we look at options available in the console.

The first configuration option that is available in the AWS Lambda console is adding triggers to your function, such as events from S3 buckets, triggering the Lambda based on an SNS notification, and many more triggers. The next chapter is dedicated to talking about Triggers and Events for AWS Lambda, and I will talk about them in detail in the next chapter. For the Hello World example, we don't need an event/trigger as well.

Function code – configuration

AWS provides a great IDE, Cloud9, in the browser to edit Node.js Lambda functions inline with the function code configuration section in the AWS Lambda (FaaS) console itself.

AWS Lambda supports three **Code Entry** types:

- **Edit code inline**
- **Upload a .zip file**
- **Upload a file from Amazon S3**

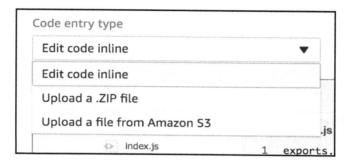

From the AWS Lambda console, you can also change the language runtime associated with your function; you can see the available language runtimes in the AWS Lambda console shown here:

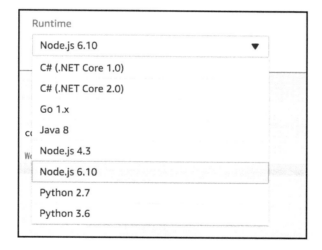

The next thing that you can configure in the Lambda function is the **Handler**. The Handler is the export value in your function, `module-name.export` to be precise. For example, `index.handler` would call `exports.handler` in index.js. For our specific Hello World example, you don't need to change this value:

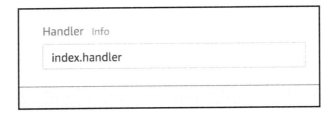

The next configuration option with the Function Code section is modifying the code itself if you have selected **Edit code inline** from the dropdown for Code entry type:

Hello from Lambda callback statement

For our example, let's change the callback statement from `Hello from Lambda` to `Hello World` and click on **Save** on the top:

Click on Save button

Publishing and testing your changes

As we have made changes to the Lambda function through the console, the changes are saved, but they are not live. For the changes made to the Lambda function to be live, you need to publish them. I'm going to cover in detail how you can deploy your AWS serverless application in the following chapters. For now, let's look at how we can do this using the AWS Lambda console:

Once you have saved your changes to your Lambda function, from the **Actions** dropdown, select **Publish new version**:

In the **Publish new version from $LATEST** (I will talk about $LATEST, which is an alias, later in this section) dialog window, enter the **Version description** as `Hello World callback changes` and click on **Publish**:

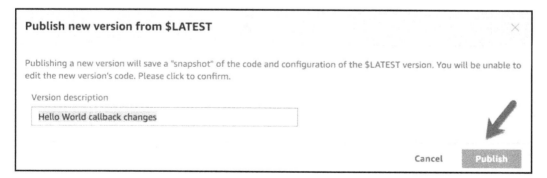

Once the changes to your Lambda function have been published, you will see a message like this in the AWS Lambda console, **Successfully created version 1 for function myHelloWorldFunction.**

Now that we have published the changes to the callback function to log Hello World, let's look at how to test the changes through the AWS Lambda console. Click the **Test** button, which is located in the top-right corner, to invoke your Lambda function with the changes that we made just now:

Once you click on the **Test** button, the **Configure test event** dialog window opens up when you are trying to test your Lambda function the first time using a new Test Event.

In the **Event name** text box, enter `HelloWorldEvent`, leave the rest of the settings as default, and click on **Create**:

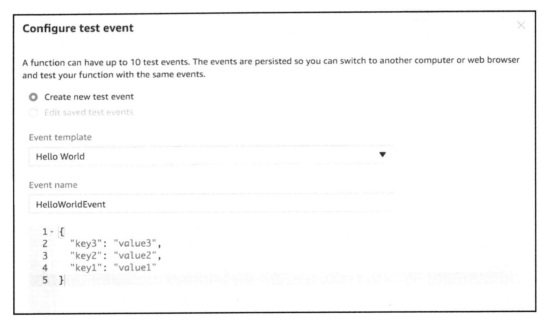

Configure test event

Once you have configured the test event, select or make sure `HelloWorldEvent` is selected in the Test Events dropdown and click on the **Test** button:

You will see the Execution result with a status message of succeeded in the AWS Lambda console. The execution result information box will show the callback message `"Hello World"`, the time it took to execute your Lambda function, the memory consumed by your Lambda function, and the duration that you are billed for that invocation:

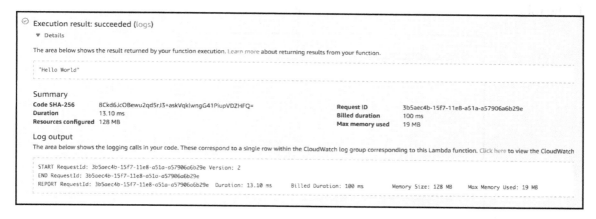

You can also view the logs for your Lambda function in Amazon CloudWatch Logs; I will go into detail about this in later chapters.

Configuring options for AWS Lambda

AWS Lambda provides many configuration options, including customizing how much memory is needed for your Lambda function, maximum execution time, VPC network configuration, creating versions and aliases for your functions for production, and how to set environmental variables and use them in your AWS Lambda functions.

Memory configuration

With AWS Lambda, the only compute resource that you can customize is memory. You can't choose the CPU power that you want for your AWS Lambda function. The AWS Lambda (FaaS) platform allocates CPU resources proportional to the memory that you have chosen for your Lambda function by applying the same ratio as a general-purpose Amazon EC2 instance type, such as the m3 instance type. For example, if you allocated 512 MB of memory to your Lambda function, then your Lambda function will receive four times more CPU power than if you allocate 128 MB to your Lambda function. AWS Lambda lets you choose memory from 128 MB to 3008 MB in increments of 64 MB. With the AWS Lambda console, you can set the amount of memory you need in the **Basic Settings** section.

In the following screenshot, I have changed the memory from 128 MB to 512 MB:

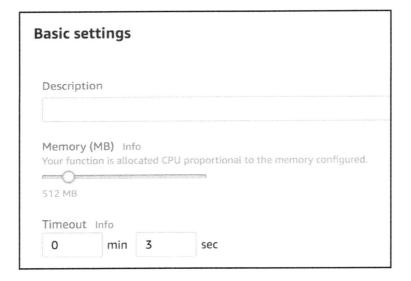

Execution time configuration

As mentioned earlier, you will only pay for AWS resources for the time that they are running. However, to prevent AWS Lambda functions from running indefinitely, you need to specify a timeout. When the timeout is reached, AWS Lambda will terminate Lambda function execution. You can customize the timeout in the **Basic settings** section shown next. The maximum execution time allocated to AWS Lambda functions is 300 seconds.

In the following screenshot, I have customized the timeout to be 1 minute 30 seconds:

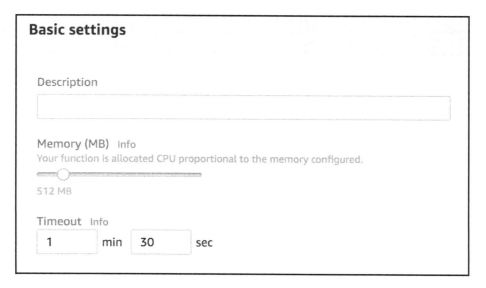

Network configuration

By default, AWS Lambda functions won't be able to access resources that are inside the VPC. If you want to access resources inside a VPC, then you need to select the VPC that you need to connect to from this section. Once you select the VPC, you will have to select the subnets where you want your Lambda function to execute. You also need to select the appropriate security groups so that inbound and outbound rules are set on the Lambda to access resources. You can learn more about VPC at https://aws.amazon.com/vpc/ and you can learn more about VPC support for AWS Lambda at https://docs.aws.amazon.com/lambda/latest/dg/vpc.html.

I have configured the Lambda to be able to access VPC resources using the following configuration. For our example, you don't need to do this configuration:

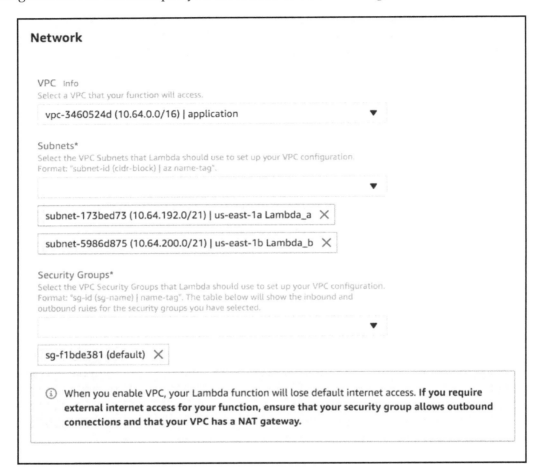

Function versioning and aliases

Now, let's look at how you can manage your Lambda functions for production use with the use of versioning and aliases.

With versioning support for your Lambda function, you have the capability of publishing one or more versions of your AWS Lambda function. As a result, you can have different versions/variations of your AWS Lambda function, such as one version for development, one for production, and one for beta in your development workflow. When you publish a version of your Lambda function, AWS creates an unique **Amazon Resource Name (ARN)** and once the ARN is created, it can't be changed and is immutable.

AWS Lambda also supports creating aliases for each of your Lambda function version. You can think of an alias as a pointer to a particular version of your Lambda function. Aliases also have a unique ARN, like versions. Each alias maintains a specific ARN for the version of your Lambda function to which it points. Aliases can't point to one another; they can only point at function versions. As aliases are pointers to function versions, they are not immutable and can be changed to point to another version of your Lambda function:

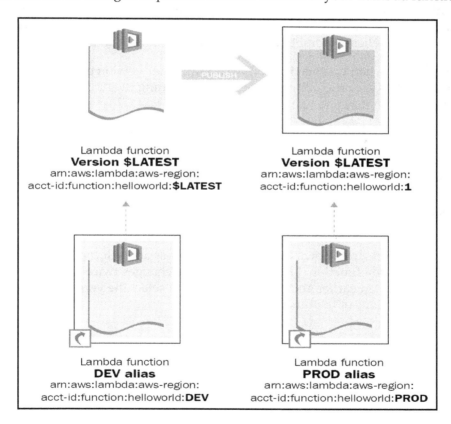

Aliases also help in the process of promoting your AWS Lambda function versions through different environments, such as from the development environment to the production environment, it also abstracts the promotion process from the mapping of your Lambda function version and its event source configuration.

For example, let's assume that Amazon S3 is the event source that triggers your AWS Lambda function when objects are deleted in a bucket. Typically, you will point to a particular version's ARN of your Lambda function in the Amazon S3 event source mapping, in the bucket notification configuration. In this setup, whenever you publish/release a new version of your AWS Lambda function, you have to update the notification configuration of the Amazon S3 bucket properties to point to the right version of your AWS Lambda function. However, if you use aliases for your function, like **PROD**, instead of using the ARN to a particular function version, you don't need to modify the notification configuration of the Amazon S3 bucket and can promote a new version of your Lambda function into production whenever you want. All you would need to do is to just update the PROD alias to point to the correct version of your Lambda function.

This will also apply when you need to roll back to an older version of your Lambda function. Even in this scenario, all you are doing is updating the PROD alias to point to the older function version that you know is working.

With these benefits, I strongly recommend using versioning and aliases for your Lambda function when you have multiple developers and dependencies involved.

There was a walkthrough earlier in this chapter of creating a new version for myHelloWorldFunction; let's now look at how many versions the function has and how to switch between versions.

In the AWS Lambda console, once you have published a new version of your Lambda function, the qualifiers drop-down automatically changes and selects the version that you deployed your Lambda function. I have published the changes twice to the Lambda function that we created earlier and you can see when I select the version drop-down, I can see the different versions of the function:

You can choose between the different versions for your Lambda and continue working on it.

Let's look at how to create an alias for your Lambda function through the AWS Lambda console. From the **Actions** drop-down, select **Create alias**:

In the **Create a new alias** dialog window:

- Enter PROD as the name of the alias
- Enter a **Description** for the alias
- Select a **Version** from the Version drop-down
- Click on the **Create** button:

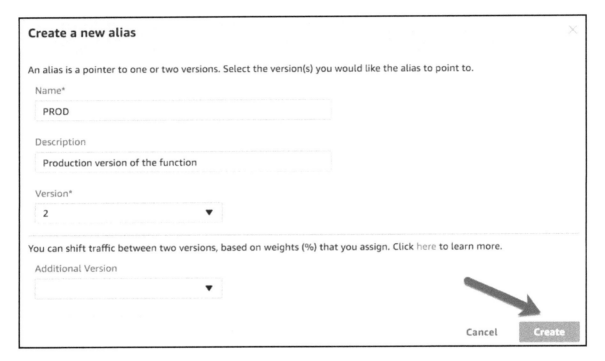

Once you have created the alias, the qualifiers drop-down automatically selects the newly created alias, PROD, and you can switch between using an alias for your function to work on or selecting a specific version.

Traffic Shifting using aliases

During the AWS re:Invent 2017 conference, AWS introduced the concept of Traffic Shifting AWS Lambda functions using aliases. By default, an alias of an AWS Lambda function points to a specific version of your Lambda function. When you update the alias to point to a different version of your Lambda function, then the incoming invocation or traffic turns instantly over to the updated version of your Lambda function. This setup can cause potential instabilities introduced by the updated version. To minimize the impact caused by this sudden change of traffic, you can configure the routing-config parameter on your AWS Lambda function, which allows us to point to two different versions of the same AWS Lambda function, and you can specify through this new feature what percentage of incoming traffic to your AWS Lambda functions is sent to each of those function versions. You can learn more about Traffic Shifting using aliases by following the instructions listed at https://docs.aws.amazon.com/lambda/latest/dg/lambda-traffic-shifting-using-aliases.html.

Environment variables

AWS Lambda supports configuring environment variables for your Lambda function, which enables you to dynamically pass settings to your Lambda function code without having to make changes to your code. Environment variables for your Lambda function are key-value pairs that you can set or modify, as they are configuration settings of your Lambda function. The AWS Lambda platform then makes these Environment variable key-value pairs available to your AWS Lambda function code during execution, and you can access them using the standard APIs to access Environment variables that are supported by the language runtime. For example, to access Environment variables in Node.js, you will use process.env in your Lambda function.

Some examples of how Environment variables help are:

- Connection settings to a database
- Installation directory
- Output directory
- Settings for logging
- Many other uses

By separating these settings from your Lambda function code, you wouldn't need to update your Lambda function code when you have to change the behavior of your function based on different environments or settings.

For example, you have a Lambda function that connects to a different data store as it moves through different development life cycles, ushc as dev, test, and production. The data store information can be different between each stage. In this case, you will create environment variables to reference the right data store name, based on the stage in which it is executing, while at the same time your code remains untouched.

Let's look at how to set Environment variables through the AWS Lambda console.

In the console for the `myHelloWorldFunction` Lambda function, you have the option of setting the environment variables for your Lambda function. Let's create an environment variable called `DATASTORE_NAME` and set its value to `Prod_helloWorld`, as shown here. Make sure to click on the **Save** button after you have made the changes, and you need to publish the changes before you can access the key-value pairs of environment variables in your code. Environment variables are also tied to a particular version of your Lambda function, and are also tied to aliases. You can modify the Environment variable `DATASTORE_NAME` to `test_helloWorld` for the `test` alias of your Lambda function:

Environment variables

You can define Environment Variables as key-value pairs that are accessible from your function code. These are useful to store configuration settings without the need to change function code. Learn more.

DATASTORE_NAME   Prod_helloWorld

Environment variables do have certain rules, and you need to make sure they are followed:

- Total size can't exceed 4 KB
- They need to start with letters [a-zA-Z]
- They can only contain alphanumeric characters and underscores [a-zA-Z0-9_]

Securing AWS Lambda using IAM

In an earlier section, when creating a Lambda function using the console, we talked about creating an IAM role and assigning permissions to the role so that it has access to different AWS resources; let's look at that in detail now.

AWS IAM is a service that helps you securely control access to different AWS services. With IAM, you can control who is authenticated and who is authorized to access the resources. IAM helps controlling access to AWS Services in the following ways.

Authenticating

You can access AWS resources by using these types of identities:

- AWS account root user
- IAM Users
- IAM Roles

For our discussion, I will focus on IAM Roles, as that is what AWS Lambda uses to authenticate against different AWS services. An IAM role is an IAM identity that you can create in an AWS account with specific permissions, but that doesn't need to be associated with any specific person. With an IAM role, you can obtain temporary credentials to access different AWS services and resources. An IAM role with temporary credentials is useful in the following scenarios:

- Federated user access
- AWS service access
- Apps running on EC2 infrastructure

Access control

Even though you have valid credentials to access AWS services, unless you have the necessary permissions to create or access AWS resources, you won't be able to perform operations. To be able to perform all the operations covered earlier, you need to have access to create a Lambda function, create an IAM role, and publish a version of your Lambda function.

When granting permissions, you will decide who is getting the permissions, what AWS resources they get permissions for, and what specific actions you are going to allow on those AWS resources.

There are two ways of managing resources for AWS Lambda using permissions policy, which controls who has access to the resources.

Identity-based policies (IAM policies)

You can attach IAM policies to IAM roles; you can do the following within IAM:

- Attach an IAM permissions policy to an user or a group in your AWS account

- Attach an IAM permissions policy to an IAM role (grant cross-account permissions)

The following is an example IAM policy that grants permission to the ListFunctions action on AWS Lambda resources:

```
{
  "Statement": [
  {
  "Sid": "ListFunctions",
  "Effect": "Allow",
  "Action": [
  "lambda:ListFunctions"
  ],
  "Resource": "*"
  }
  ]
}
```

For additional information on how to use IAM policies on AWS Lambda, you can refer to the documentation at https://docs.aws.amazon.com/lambda/latest/dg/access-control-identity-based.html.

Resource-based policies (Lambda function policies)

Every Lambda function can have resource-based permission policies associated with it. For Lambda, the function itself is the primary resource, and then there are function-level policies called **Lambda function policies**, through which you can grant permissions such as having Amazon S3 invoke your AWS Lambda function as soon as a new object is created in the bucket. You can achieve this by just adding/granting permissions to your AWS Lambda function policy, instead of creating a new IAM role. It is very important to note that Lambda function policies are only used when you are setting up an event source in your Lambda function to grant a service such as Amazon S3 to invoke your Lambda function.

For additional information on resource-based policies for AWS Lambda functions, you can refer to the documentation at `https://docs.aws.amazon.com/lambda/latest/dg/access-control-resource-based.html`.

AWS Lambda permissions model

For an AWS Lambda (FaaS)-based serverless application to work, you need to manage various permissions and access to resources, for example:

- For event sources, you would have to grant the event source such as Amazon S3 permissions so that it can invoke your AWS Lambda function. The exceptions here are for stream-based services such as Amazon DynamoDB streams and Amazon Kinesis Data Streams.

- For stream-based event sources such as Amazon DynamoDB streams and Amazon Kinesis Data Streams, your AWS Lambda function will itself polls and pull the streams on your behalf, and read new records on the stream. Because of this, you have to grant the AWS Lambda function permissions for the relevant actions on the stream.

- When your AWS Lambda function executes, it assumes the role you provided when you created the Lambda function, so you need to grant that IAM role the required permissions so that your AWS Lambda function can access the required AWS resources, such as objects in an Amazon S3 bucket.

I have given an overview of how IAM role policies and resource-based function policies works to secure your AWS Lambda. You can create custom policies based on the needs of your AWS Lambda function.

Summary

In this chapter, you learned what AWS Lambda is, the language runtimes it supports, and how it automatically provisions and manages the infrastructure for your functions so that you can focus on solving business problems rather than spending time on ensuring the infrastructure is highly available and scalable. We also learned about how AWS Lambda works and use cases such as stream-based processing, data processing, web applications, and mobile and IoT backends where AWS Lambda is currently being used. We then learned about the Execution environment of AWS Lambda.

We then learned how to create a Hello World Lambda function using the AWS Lambda console. We learned how to make changes through the AWS Lambda console, publish a new version of the function, and test the changes through the AWS Lambda console. We then learned how to configure different options such as memory settings, maximum execution time, and VPC setup for your Lambda functions. We then learned about different deployment configuration options, such as versioning and aliases, which help simplify production deployment of AWS Lambda functions. We also learned how to create Environment variables and how they help in not having to change your Lambda function code to point to a different data store for each stage as your code progresses through different stages of development life cycles. Towards the end, I gave an overview of how IAM helps secure your Lambda by going over authentication and access control, as well as how IAM-based policies and resource-based function policies further secure your Lambda functions.

In the next chapter, we will discuss the different events and triggers that are available for AWS Lambda functions.

Triggers and Events for AWS Lambda

4

Chapter 1, *What is Serverless Computing?* gave an overview of triggers and events and how they fit into the larger idea of serverless architecture. In this chapter, we will see get overview of the different types of triggers and events that are available within the AWS cloud environment. Different types of triggers, along with screenshots of configurations within the AWS Lambda console, will be covered.

In this chapter, we will cover the following topics:

- A list of triggers that are available for the AWS Lambda environment
- A walk-through of different triggers for the AWS Lambda environment

Triggers for AWS Lambda

Triggers are how AWS Lambda gets invoked. Triggers are custom events that happen across different AWS services. With these triggers in place, AWS Lambda will get invoked, process the custom event, and generate the response to the service that has been defined in AWS Lambda. For AWS Lambda to be invoked, you will need to have at least one event source or trigger. You can have multiple event sources or triggers for your Lambda to get invoked. Let's look at the different triggers or event sources that are available for different AWS services.

API Gateway Trigger

API Gateway + AWS Lambda allows you to invoke Lambda functions over HTTP(s). With API Gateway, you get a custom REST endpoint, and you can configure API Gateway to invoke AWS Lambda on different HTTP methods, such as PUT, GET, DELETE, and other HTTP methods. With this integration in place, when you invoke the custom REST endpoint that has been configured by API Gateway, API Gateway will invoke the configured AWS Lambda function. API Gateway enables proxying the information that it receives on the custom REST endpoint directly over to AWS Lambda functions, without any need for transformations. Within the AWS Lambda function, you can respond back with valid HTTP status codes so that the caller of the custom REST endpoint will see those same HTTP status codes.

Here is a screenshot of a sample API Gateway configuration that shows how to integrate calling an AWS Lambda function and has **Use Lambda Proxy Integration** selected:

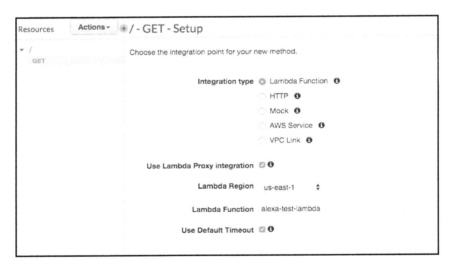

Prior to the Lambda proxy integration feature in API Gateway, the way to integrate AWS Lambda was to use custom mapping templates within API Gateway. This document talks about how you can do that with custom Lambda integration: https://docs.aws.amazon.com/apigateway/latest/developerguide/getting-started-lambda-non-proxy-integration.html. It is highly recommend to use the Lambda Proxy Integration feature in API Gateway.

API Gateway also provides a feature where you can configure it to return a custom Integration Response to the caller of the custom REST endpoint. Here is a screenshot of a custom Integration Response:

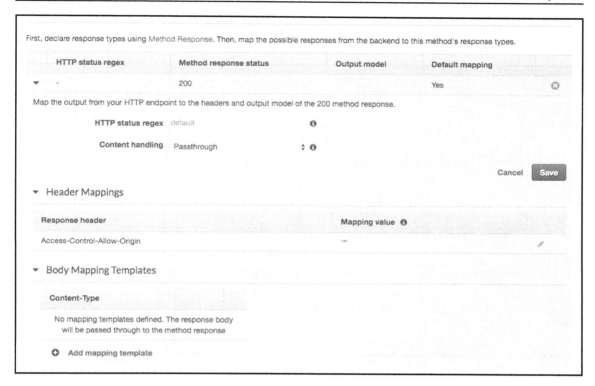

First, declare response types using Method Response. Then, map the possible responses from the backend to this method's response types.

HTTP status regex	Method response status	Output model	Default mapping	
▼ -	200		Yes	⊗

Map the output from your HTTP endpoint to the headers and output model of the 200 method response.

HTTP status regex default ❶

Content handling Passthrough ⬍ ❶

Cancel **Save**

▼ Header Mappings

Response header	Mapping value ❶	
Access-Control-Allow-Origin	'*'	✎

▼ Body Mapping Templates

Content-Type

No mapping templates defined. The response body
will be passed through to the method response

⊕ Add mapping template

AWS IoT Trigger

Internet of Things (IoT) is a network of multiple interrelated computing devices, which
could be your car, your appliances, your thermostats, and many more physical devices that
are embedded with sensors, software, and connectivity to the internet.

IoT Button

You can trigger an AWS Lambda function with a programmable Amazon IoT Dash button.
An IoT Dash button is easy to configure to a Wi-Fi device and is designed for developers to
get started with AWS Lambda functions without the need to write any device-specific code.
You can write code for the IoT button to do various things, such as count the number of
items in an order, order new items, give feedback, and make calls to anyone using third-
party managed services. There are other use cases such as opening garage doors, remotely
starting your car, remotely operating your appliances at home, and many more smart home
use cases.

Here is a screenshot of a sample **IoT Button** configuration on AWS Lambda; you will provide the serial number of the **IoT Button** device:

IoT Button Lambda configuration

IoT rule

You can also configure AWS Lambda to be triggered for a custom IoT action as well, using AWS IoT rules. The prerequisite for this is that you have already configured and registered your IoT device in the AWS IoT console. With this IoT rule configuration, the data that has been passed in an MQTT (machine-to-machine (M2M)/"Internet of Things" connectivity protocol - learn more about MQTT at http://mqtt.org/) message to the IoT device will be passed down to the AWS Lambda function. The benefit of this integration is that you will be able to process the incoming message before you invoke any other AWS service offerings. You can learn more about this at https://docs.aws.amazon.com/iot/latest/developerguide/iot-lambda-rule.html.

Here is a screenshot of how to create a IoT rule to trigger AWS Lambda functions:

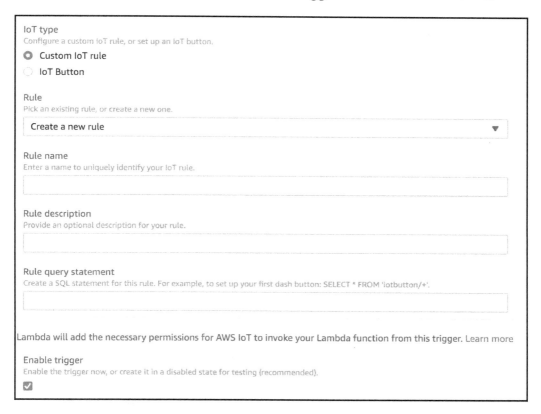

IoT Rule Configuration for AWS Lambda

Alexa trigger

Amazon Alexa is a smart voice assistant for Amazon Echo, Echo Dot, speakers such as Sonos, smart thermostats such as EcoBee, and many other devices from companies that are integrating Alexa.

For this integration to work, you need to create an Alexa application by using the Alexa Skills kit, which provides interaction with your own services for Alexa Skills through AWS Lambda functions. You can find more information about the Alexa Skills kit at `https://developer.amazon.com/docs/ask-overviews/build-skills-with-the-alexa-skills-kit.html`.

Here is a screenshot of configuration with the AWS Lambda console, where you can provide the Alexa application ID:

Configure triggers

Application ID
The Application ID for a skill can be found in the **Alexa section** of the Developer Portal, on the **Skill Information** tab.

Lambda will add the necessary permissions for Amazon Alexa to invoke your Lambda function from this trigger. Learn more

Enable trigger
Enable the trigger now, or create it in a disabled state for testing (recommended).
☑

CloudFront trigger

Amazon CloudFront is global **content delivery network** (**CDN**) service that delivers content to your customers with high transfer speeds and low latency at the edge, as it is distributed across the globe in multiple locations. You can find more information about Amazon CloudFront here: `https://aws.amazon.com/cloudfront/`.

AWS Lambda has a service called **Lambda@Edge**, which lets you run functions at Amazon CloudFront locations and AWS regions in response to events happening at edge locations, without the need for provisioning or managing any infrastructure. With Lambda@Edge, you can use Lambda functions to change and respond to CloudFront events such as:

- Invoking a Lambda function right after the CloudFront service receives a request from the customer
- Invoking a Lambda function right before the CloudFront service forwards the request to the origin (your website)
- Invoking a Lambda function right after the origin has responded to the request
- Invoking a Lambda function right before the response is sent back to the customer

You can find more about AWS Lambda@Edge at `https://docs.aws.amazon.com/lambda/latest/dg/lambda-edge.html`.

Here is a screenshot of the AWS Lambda@Edge and Amazon CloudFront configuration:

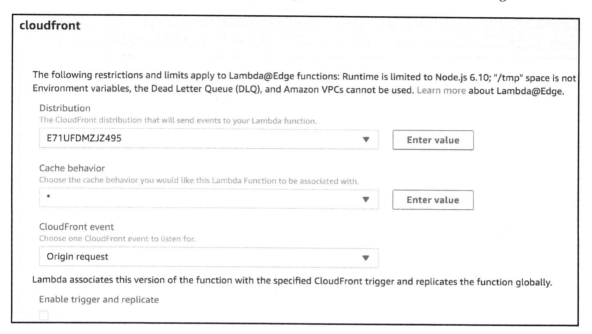

CloudWatch trigger

Amazon CloudWatch is a monitoring service for AWS cloud resources and for the application that you run on AWS. You can use the Amazon CloudWatch service to collect and track metrics, collect and monitor log files, create and monitor alarms, and automatically react to changes in your AWS resources by creating alerts when changes happen. You can learn more about Amazon CloudWatch at `https://aws.amazon.com/cloudwatch/`.

Let's look at what AWS Lambda and Amazon CloudWatch integrations look like.

CloudWatch Events

Amazon CloudWatch Events delivers near-real-time system events for changes that occur in AWS resources. You can learn more about Amazon CloudWatch Events at `https://docs.aws.amazon.com/AmazonCloudWatch/latest/events/WhatIsCloudWatchEvents.html`.

As events are emitted whenever state changes happen to AWS resources, you can create rules to filter the events that you are interested in and then send those events to AWS Lambda functions to process the messages and take action. An example of this is, you can filter for the EC2 RunInstances event and within your AWS Lambda function, you can look for required tags on the EC2 instance. If they are not found on the instance, you can either stop the instance or terminate the instance.

This page has all the Amazon CloudWatch Events Supported Event Types: `https://docs. aws.amazon.com/AmazonCloudWatch/latest/events/EventTypes.html`.

This screenshot is an example configuration of Amazon CloudWatch Events that invokes AWS Lambda whenever there is a `RunInstances` event:

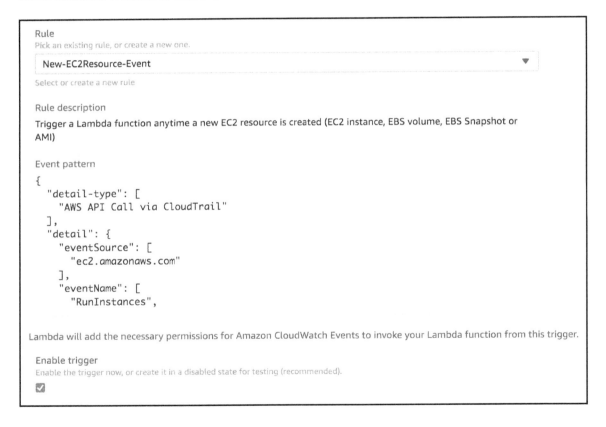

CloudWatch Logs

With the help of AWS Lambda functions, you can perform custom analysis on Amazon CloudWatch logs with Log Subscriptions. Amazon CloudWatch Log Subscriptions provide a near-real-time feed of events and deliver it to your AWS Lambda functions for processing, loading into other systems such as Elasticsearch or Splunk, and analyzing the log data itself. You can find more information about Amazon CloudWatch logs at `https://docs.aws.amazon.com/AmazonCloudWatch/latest/logs/WhatIsCloudWatchLogs.html`.

Here is a screenshot of the AWS Lambda configuration for Amazon CloudWatch logs:

CodeCommit Trigger

AWS CodeCommit is a fully managed source control offering from AWS. It helps customers host highly scalable and secure private Git source control on AWS.

With triggers for the AWS CodeCommit repository, you can create triggers for a repository to invoke AWS Lambda functions and perform certain actions. For example, you can have an AWS Lambda function invoked when a new branch is created outside of your AWS CodeCommit repository. You can find more information about triggers for the AWS CodeCommit repository at `https://docs.aws.amazon.com/codecommit/latest/userguide/how-to-notify.html`.

Here is a screenshot of AWS Lambda configuration to respond to any event on any branch for a given AWS CodeCommit repository:

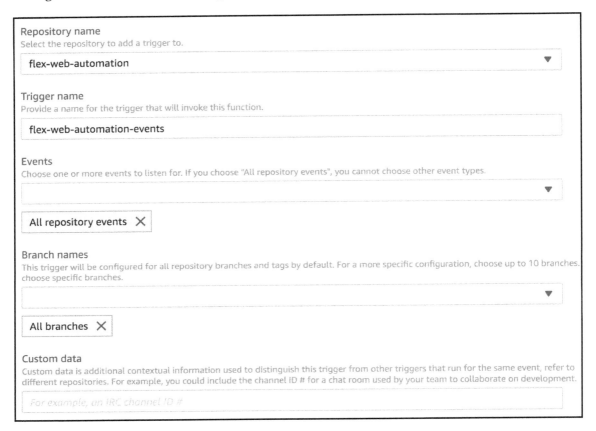

Cognito Trigger

Amazon Cognito is a service that lets you add signup, sign-in, and access control to your mobile apps and websites. Amazon Cognito can provide scalable identity services for millions of users coming to your sites and mobile apps. Amazon Cognito supports enterprise identity providers via SAML 2.0 and social identity providers such as Facebook, Amazon, and Google. You can learn more about Amazon Cognito at `https://aws.amazon.com/cognito/`.

The Amazon Cognito Events functionality provides you with the ability to have your AWS Lambda function invoked in response to Amazon Cognito events. For example, you can invoke your AWS Lambda function for Cognito Sync Trigger events, which are published each time a dataset is synchronized in Cognito. You can learn more about Amazon Cognito Events Sync Triggers at `https://aws.amazon.com/blogs/mobile/introducing-amazon-cognito-events-sync-triggers/`.

Here is a screenshot of configurations in AWS Lambda to be invoked on an Amazon Cognito Sync Trigger on a Cognito identity pool:

Cognito identity pool
Select the Cognito identity pool. The Sync Trigger will be invoked whenever this identity pool dataset is synced.

Mobile_Analytics_shared_pool_do_not_modify

Lambda will add the necessary permissions for Amazon Cognito to invoke your Lambda function from

Enable trigger
Enable the trigger now, or create it in a disabled state for testing (recommended).

Scheduled Events Trigger

With the power of Amazon CloudWatch Events, you can configure your AWS Lambda functions to be invoked on a regular schedule thanks to the schedule event functionality in Amazon CloudWatch Events. You can configure the schedule by hours, days, or weeks, or you can specify a cron expression as well. The following page has more details about Scheduled Event syntax in Amazon CloudWatch Events: `https://docs.aws.amazon.com/AmazonCloudWatch/latest/events/ScheduledEvents.html`

You can find an example use case at `Using AWS Lambda with Scheduled Events`.

An example Scheduled Event would look like this:

```
{
  "account": "55334567897052",
  "region": "us-west-2",
  "detail": {},
  "detail-type": "Scheduled Event for AWS Lambda",
  "source": "aws.events",
  "time": "1972-02-02T00:00:00Z",
```

```
"id": "acc54f9d-aba8-22e4-8b6a-946c825a1d9b",
"resources": [
"arn:aws:events:us-west-2:55334567897052:rule/my-schedule-lambda-event"
]
}
```

Here is a screenshot of an Amazon CloudWatch Scheduled Event rule configured with a cron expression to run every day at 7 am GMT:

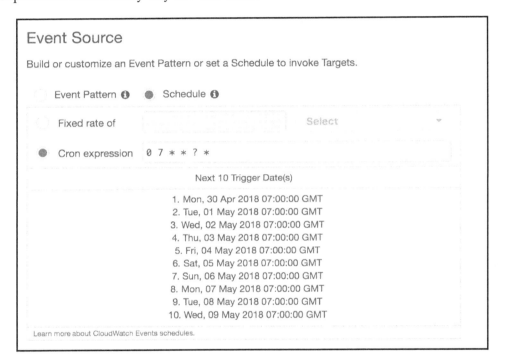

AWS Config Trigger

AWS Config Service provides you with the ability to audit, assess, and evaluate configurations for your AWS resources. AWS Config Service monitors and stores data about your AWS resource configurations and provides you with the ability to automate any deviations from the desired configurations. You can learn more about AWS Config at https://aws.amazon.com/config/.

With AWS Lambda functions, you can evaluate deviations from configurations for your AWS resources using AWS Config Service custom rules. As AWS Config Service sees AWS resources getting created, modified, and deleted, AWS Config custom rules will trigger the AWS Lambda function and send over the information to it.

Here is a screenshot that shows how you can trigger an AWS Lambda function (config-test) whenever AWS Config records the `EC2:EIP` event:

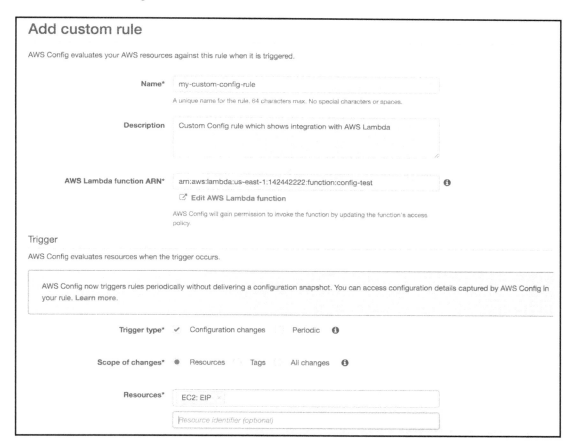

DynamoDB Trigger

Amazon DynamoDB is a fast NoSQL database for all applications that are looking for single-digit-millisecond latency at scale. It is a fully managed cloud database provided by AWS. You can learn more about it at `https://aws.amazon.com/dynamodb/`.

You can invoke your AWS Lambda functions as triggers in response to updates that are made to DynamoDB tables. To be able to leverage this feature, you would first need to enable Amazon DynamoDB streams for your Amazon DynamoDB table. With DynamoDB streams enabled, AWS Lambda polls the stream and invokes your function to process the data from the stream. You can configure AWS Lambda to read data from streams in batches.

Here is a screenshot of an AWS Lambda configuration to poll a records batch size of 100 from an Amazon DynamoDB table:

DynamoDB table
Select a DynamoDB table to listen for updates on.

ChangeRequestLog

Batch size
The largest number of records that will be read from your table's update stream at once.

100

Starting position
The position in the stream to start reading from. For more information, see ShardIteratorType in the Amazon

Latest

In order to read from the DynamoDB trigger, your execution role must have proper permission

Enable trigger
Enable the trigger now, or create it in a disabled state for testing (recommended).
☑

Kinesis Trigger

A Kinesis Trigger can be created for capturing and storing terabytes of data per hour from a large number of sources. Let's look at the types of Kinesis Trigger.

Amazon Kinesis Data Streams

Amazon Kinesis Data Streams enable you to continuously capture data from a wide variety of sources such as clickstreams, your IT logs, social media feeds, financial information, and many more types of data. Amazon Kinesis Data Streams can store terabytes of data per hour. You can learn more about Amazon Kinesis Data Streams at `https://aws.amazon.com/kinesis/data-streams/`.

You can configure your AWS Lambda function to automatically poll Amazon Kinesis Data Streams and process the data available within a stream.

Here is a screenshot of an AWS Lambda configuration to poll a records batch size of 100 from Amazon Kinesis Data Streams:

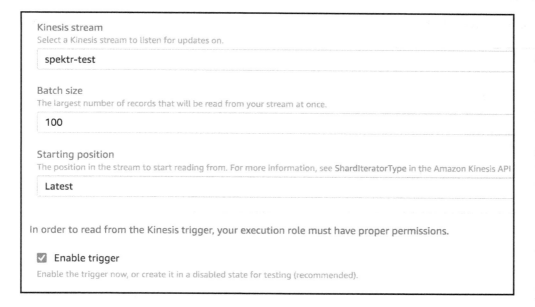

Amazon Kinesis Data Firehose

Amazon Kinesis Data Firehose is a fully managed service from AWS that provides you with the ability to deliver streaming data directly to Amazon S3, Amazon Redshift, and **Amazon Elasticsearch Service (Amazon ES)**. You can learn more about Amazon Kinesis Data Firehose at `https://docs.aws.amazon.com/firehose/latest/dev/what-is-this-service.html`.

With AWS Lambda functions, you process the data sent to Amazon Kinesis Data Firehose before it is sent to a downstream service such as Amazon S3.

S3 Trigger

Amazon S3 is an object storage built to store and retrieve any amount of data from anywhere. You can learn more about Amazon S3 at `https://aws.amazon.com/s3/`.

You can have AWS Lambda functions invoked to process Amazon S3 events, such as object created or object deleted events. You can have the AWS Lambda function invoked whenever a new photo is created in an Amazon S3 bucket, which will automatically create a thumbnail for the photo that was uploaded to the S3 bucket.

Here is a screenshot of AWS Lambda configuration to invoke all Object Created events:

Bucket
Please select the S3 bucket that serves as the event source. The bucket must be in the same region as the function.

    binv2

Event type
Select the events that you want to have trigger the Lambda function. You can optionally set up a prefix or suffix for have multiple configurations with overlapping prefixes or suffixes that could match the same object key.

    Object Created (All)

Prefix
Enter an optional prefix to limit the notifications to objects with keys that start with matching characters.

    e.g. images/

Filter pattern
Enter an optional filter pattern.

    e.g. .jpg

Lambda will add the necessary permissions for Amazon S3 to invoke your Lambda function from this

☑ Enable trigger
Enable the trigger now, or create it in a disabled state for testing (recommended).

SNS Trigger

Amazon **Simple Notification Service** (**SNS**) is a fully managed pub/sub (`https://aws.amazon.com/pub-sub-messaging/`) messaging and mobile notifications service, which coordinates the delivery of messages to subscribers. With SNS, you can send messages to a wide variety of subscribers, including services such as AWS Lambda, along with distributed systems and mobile devices. You can learn more about Amazon SNS at `https://aws.amazon.com/sns/`.

You can invoke AWS Lambda functions to process Amazon SNS notifications. When a message is published to an Amazon SNS topic, the message is sent to the AWS Lambda function as a payload parameter.

With this integration, you can trigger an AWS Lambda function in response to Amazon CloudWatch alarms and many other AWS services that leverage Amazon SNS.

Here is a screenshot of AWS SNS configuration with the AWS Lambda console:

Summary

In this chapter, we learned about different types of triggers that are available for AWS Lambda functions, along with a walkthrough of different triggers for AWS Lambda functions. The most commonly and widely used triggers are the HTTP Event Trigger using Amazon API Gateway, S3 object triggers, DynamoDB streams, and CloudWatch Events (scheduled).

In the next chapter, we will author our first serverless application using AWS Lambda functions.

5
Your First Serverless Application on AWS

In this chapter, we will learn about how to write serverless applications to run on AWS using Node.js, the AWS **Serverless Application Model (SAM)**, how to deploy a serverless application to AWS using the AWS SAM, how to test a serverless application, and how to trigger a serverless application using Amazon API Gateway (HTTP event trigger).

There are multiple ways to create serverless apps on the AWS platform. This chapter covers two of those methods:

- Firstly, we will look into how we can create an AWS Lambda function through the AWS Console, and then test it through the Console.
- Secondly, we will look into how we can create an AWS Lambda function through Visual Studio Code, deploy it using the AWS SAM, integrate it with API Gateway, and test it by making HTTP calls to the Amazon API Gateway endpoint.

Technical requirements

To deploy and test the serverless app that we develop in this chapter, you will need an AWS account. You can create a Free Tier AWS account by visiting this link: `https://aws.amazon.com/free/`. The Free Tier offers 12 months' access to some of the most popular AWS services and indefinite access to some products. The AWS Free Tier includes 1 million AWS Lambda invocations per month for free, and 1 million Amazon API Gateway API calls per month for free, which is more than sufficient for testing the serverless apps that we will build as part of this chapter.

Your first serverless app (using the AWS Console)

In this section, we will learn how to create, test, and update a function. We will also learn how to publish a new version and create an alias for a Lambda function.

Creating a function

Let's look at how can we create an AWS Lambda function through the AWS Lambda Console:

1. Once you have created an AWS Free Tier account, log in to your AWS account through the AWS Management Console at `https://aws.amazon.com/console/`.
2. Once you have logged in to the AWS Console, navigate to the AWS Lambda Console.
3. From the AWS Lambda Console, click the **Create a function** button:

4. Once you have clicked the button, you will be presented with three different options to create an AWS Lambda function:
    - Authoring an AWS Lambda function from scratch
    - Creating an AWS Lambda function from a list of preconfigured blueprints to kickstart your AWS Lambda functions
    - Pick an already published serverless app from the **Serverless Application Repository**, which consists of apps published by developers and companies on AWS

5. In our case, let's select the **Blueprints** option:

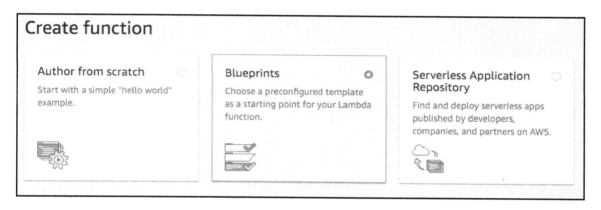

6. In the Blueprints filter box, add a filter called **hello-world** and select the blueprint called **hello-world**.
7. You should see **A starter AWS Lambda function** in Node.js. Click on the **Configure** button at the bottom:

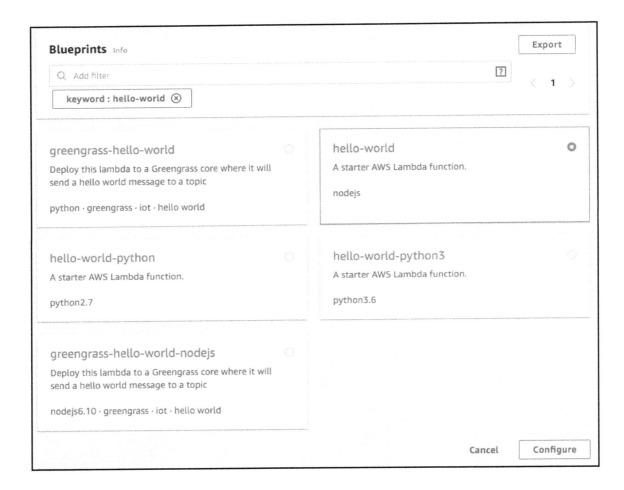

8. Now, you will be presented with options to configure the AWS Lambda function that you are creating:

   1. Name your Lambda function `myFirstHelloWorldFunction`.

   2. Select **Create new roles from template(s)** from the dropdown for the **Role**.

   3. Give your role the same name as the Lambda function to easily identify the IAM role.

   4. From the list of **Policy templates**, select **Basic Edge Lambda permissions**.

   5. Click on the **Create function** button at the bottom:

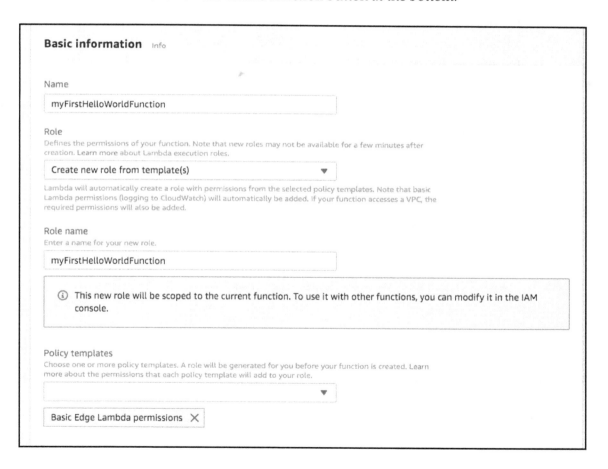

You can learn more about the different policy templates at `https://docs.aws.amazon.com/lambda/latest/dg/policy-templates.html`

At the time of writing this book, Node.js 8.10 is the latest version that AWS Lambda functions support. You will be able to see the version that is configured for your AWS Lambda function, along with the option to change it, in the configuration for your AWS Lambda function.

9. The other configuration setting that is very important is the name of the handler for your AWS Lambda function.
10. For the one that we created, it will be set as `index.handler`, which is the `module-name.export` value of your AWS Lambda function.
11. In this case, the AWS Lambda function will call `exports.handler` in the `index.js` file that was created as part of the blueprint:

12. If you examine the code that the blueprint created, it should be like the following:

```
console.log('Loading function');

exports.handler = async (event, context) => {
    // console.log('Received event:', JSON.stringify(event, null, 2));
    console.log('value1 =', event.key1);
    console.log('value2 =', event.key2);
    console.log('value3 =', event.key3);
    return event.key1; // Echo back the first key value
    // throw new Error('Something went wrong');
};
```

You can find this AWS Lambda function code at `https://github.com/PacktPublishing/Hands-On-Serverless-Computing/blob/master/Your-first-Serverless-application-on-AWS/hello-world-blueprint.js`

The preceding code prints the whole event that triggered the AWS Lambda function (which is commented out), then it prints three different keys from the event, named key1, key2, and key3, and finally, it returns key1. When we test this AWS Lambda function through the console, we need to make sure that the test event has these three keys defined.

Testing the function

Next, let's look at how can we test the newly created AWS Lambda function using the AWS Lambda Console. At this point, as we don't have any triggers defined for our AWS Lambda function, we will just use the AWS Lambda console to configure a test event and invoke our AWS Lambda function.

To test the newly created AWS Lambda function:

1. Click on the Test button, which opens up the **Configure test event** dialog box.
2. In Configure test event, select the Hello World event template.
3. Set a name for the event, for example, myHelloWorldEvent, and click on the Create button.
4. The Hello World event template should look like this JSON snippet:

```
{
  "key3": "value3",
  "key2": "value2",
  "key1": "value1"
}
```

Here is a screenshot of **Configure test event**:

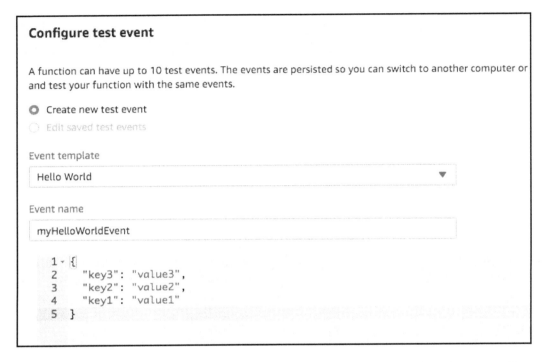

5. Now, ensure that the **myHelloWorldEvent** event is selected in the events list to test your AWS Lambda function in the Console next to the **Test** button:

6. Now, when you click the **Test** button, you will see an execution result saying that it succeeded and will provide a link to CloudWatch Logs to view the log of your AWS Lambda function execution.

7. In the console, you will also see the value of key1 logged, which in our case is value1 as that is what was configured in the test event:

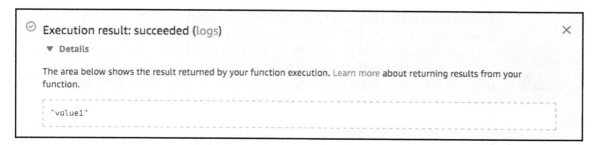

8. The console output also logs the **Summary** of this AWS Lambda function execution, including the time it took to execute, the memory that was configured for the AWS Lambda function, the max memory that was consumed by the AWS Lambda function execution, and the duration for which you are billed for the AWS Lambda execution. The summary section also includes a link to the CloudWatch log group:

Summary

Code SHA-256	UMJK1Wkhd9I8dEwu55A8uafu7MqA/8RpsdstqlDuEcI=	**Request Id**	ad69b14e-6392-11e8-8380-df2574fbd5d5
Duration	13.76 ms	**Billed duration**	100 ms
Resources configured	128 MB	**Max memory used**	46 MB

Log output

The area below shows the logging calls in your code. These correspond to a single row within the CloudWatch log group corresponding to this Lambda function. Click here to view the CloudWatch log group.

```
START RequestId: ad69b14e-6392-11e8-8380-df2574fbd5d5 Version: $LATEST
2018-05-29T22:50:26.510Z        ad69b14e-6392-11e8-8380-df2574fbd5d5    value1 = value1
2018-05-29T22:50:26.510Z        ad69b14e-6392-11e8-8380-df2574fbd5d5    value2 = value2
2018-05-29T22:50:26.510Z        ad69b14e-6392-11e8-8380-df2574fbd5d5    value3 = value3
END RequestId: ad69b14e-6392-11e8-8380-df2574fbd5d5
REPORT RequestId: ad69b14e-6392-11e8-8380-df2574fbd5d5  Duration: 13.76 ms      Billed Duration: 100 ms
Memory Size: 128 MB     Max Memory Used: 46 MB
```

Quick primer on Amazon CloudWatch: Amazon CloudWatch is a monitoring service for AWS Cloud resources and for the application that you run on AWS. You can use the Amazon CloudWatch service to collect and track metrics, collect and monitor log files, create and monitor alarms, and automatically react to changes in your AWS resources by creating alerts when changes happen. You can learn more about Amazon CloudWatch at `https://aws.amazon.com/cloudwatch/`

9. If you navigate to the CloudWatch Log Group link that is available in the *Summary*, you can view the logs that are generated by your AWS Lambda function. In this case, the function outputs the three different values of the keys that are configured in the test event that was used to test the Lambda function:

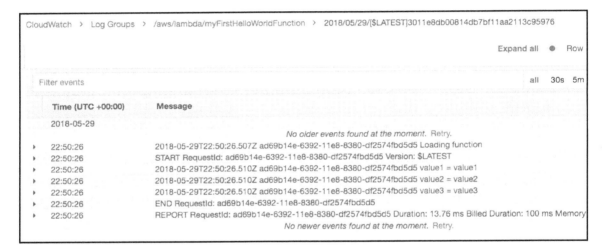

Updating the function

Now that we are able to successfully test our AWS Lambda function through the console, let's look at how to make changes to the Lambda function through the console, deploy those changes through the console, and see if our changes are reflected by testing the AWS Lambda function as in the following steps:

1. In the AWS Lambda console, select the AWS Lambda function `myFirstHelloWorldFunction`, which we created previously, and navigate to the **Function code** section to modify the code.

2. The only change that we will be making is to uncomment the line that prints the entire event that is sent to the AWS Lambda function. Once you make the change, the code will look like this:

```
console.log('Loading function');
exports.handler = async (event, context) => {
  console.log('Received event:', JSON.stringify(event, null, 2));
  console.log('value1 =', event.key1);
  console.log('value2 =', event.key2);
  console.log('value3 =', event.key3);
  return event.key1; // Echo back the first key value
  // throw new Error('Something went wrong');
};
```

3. You can find the preceding AWS Lambda function code at https://github.com/PacktPublishing/Hands-On-Serverless-Computing/blob/master/Your-first-Serverless-application-on-AWS/hello-world-blueprint-modified.js

4. Once the changes have been made, click on the **Save** button in the top right-hand corner, which deploys the changes to the $LATEST version of your AWS Lambda function.

5. With the changes in place, click on the Test button with myHelloWorldEvent selected.

6. In the output of your AWS Lambda function execution, you should now see the whole event printed, along with the values of each key:

Log output

The area below shows the logging calls in your code. These correspond to a single row within the CloudWatch log group Lambda function. Click here to view the CloudWatch log group.

```
START RequestId: 1c2dfc89-6396-11e8-a1f1-2fc280f13342 Version: $LATEST
2018-05-29T23:15:00.591Z       1c2dfc89-6396-11e8-a1f1-2fc280f13342     Received event: {
  "key3": "value3",
  "key2": "value2",
  "key1": "value1"
}
2018-05-29T23:15:00.591Z       1c2dfc89-6396-11e8-a1f1-2fc280f13342     value1 = value1
2018-05-29T23:15:00.591Z       1c2dfc89-6396-11e8-a1f1-2fc280f13342     value2 = value2
2018-05-29T23:15:00.591Z       1c2dfc89-6396-11e8-a1f1-2fc280f13342     value3 = value3
END RequestId: 1c2dfc89-6396-11e8-a1f1-2fc280f13342
```

Publishing a new version

By default, when you update and save the AWS Lambda function, it gets saved to **$LATEST version**. However, if you want to create a snapshot of the AWS Lambda function's **$LATEST** version for future reference, AWS provides a mechanism to do so by publishing the function to a named version. You can do this through the AWS console by taking the following steps:

1. Once you have saved the changes to your AWS Lambda function, in the AWS Lambda Console, click on the **Actions** drop-down and select **Publish new version**:

2. In the dialog window, enter a value for the description of the version, for example, `Snapshot created on June 1st 2018`, and click on the **Publish** button:

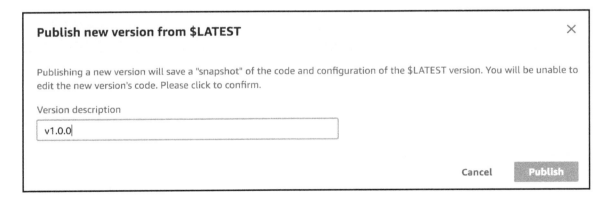

3. Once the **Publish** button is pressed, a new version will be published for your AWS Lambda function, and the version number will be automatically set to **1** by the AWS Lambda platform (assuming this is the first time you are creating a version for your AWS Lambda function).
4. As you publish new versions, they will be auto-incremented by the AWS Lambda platform.
5. You can see the available versions for your AWS Lambda function by selecting the **Version** drop-down:

Creating an alias for a Lambda function

There will be cases where you will need to create slightly different versions of your AWS Lambda function for different environments (test and production), for different environment-specific settings. To handle this use case, the AWS Lambda platform provides you with the capability to create an alias which points to one or more versions of your AWS Lambda function. Let's look at how to create an alias for your AWS Lambda function:

1. In the AWS console, from the **Actions** drop-down, select **Create alias**:

2. In the dialog window that opens up:
   - Enter the name as `prod`
   - Enter the description as `Prod alias for the function`
   - Select the version that you want to create the alias for and press the **Create** button:

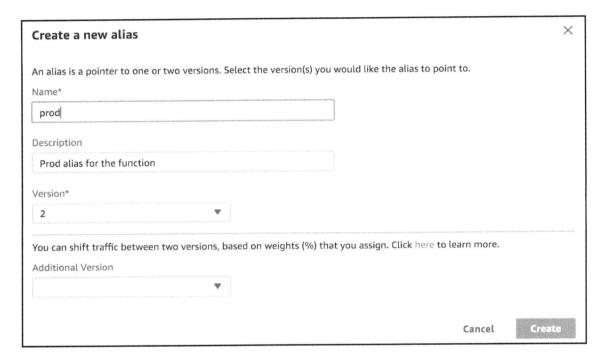

With the alias created, when you invoke your AWS Lambda function from an HTTP event trigger such as the Amazon API Gateway or an S3 event trigger, you can specify the alias of your AWS Lambda function that needs to be invoked.

Your first serverless app (using the AWS SAM)

In the section above Your first Serverless app using AWS console, we looked at how to create, update, deploy, and test AWS Lambda functions through the AWS Console. However, when you are part of a larger team and want to make your AWS Lambda functions production-ready, you will typically be working on your AWS Lambda functions from your local development environment, using certain tools such as the AWS SAM to deploy your AWS Lambda functions to an AWS environment. For this section, we will be using Visual Studio Code (installation instructions are in `Chapter 2`, *Development Environment, Tools, and SDKs*) to write the code for your AWS Lambda function, and the AWS SAM to test and deploy the AWS Lambda function to an AWS environment from your workstation.

Creating a function

Before we start writing code in the Visual Studio Code editor, let's create a working directory on your workstation, where we will be creating the source code files.

If you are using a Windows operating system-based workstation, then open Windows Command Prompt and run the following command to create a directory, where we will be creating the source files:

```
mkdir src
```

If you are using a macOS or Linux operating system, then open a Terminal Window and run the following command to create a directory, where we will be creating the source files:

```
mkdir src
```

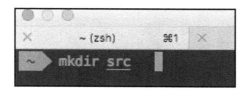

Do the following once the `mkdir src` command is executed:

1. Once you have run the command, navigate to that directory to make sure that the directory has been created.
2. Run the `cd src` command and you shouldn't receive any errors.
3. Now, in the `src` directory, let's create a folder called `hello-world`, where we will be creating our source files using `mkdir hello-world`:

4. With the working folder created, let's open Visual Studio Code and select **Open** from the **File** menu:

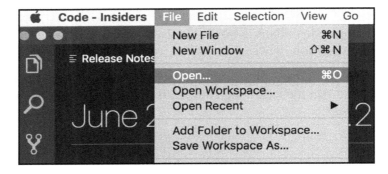

5. In the dialog window that opens up, navigate to the `hello-world` folder that we just created and select the **Open** button:

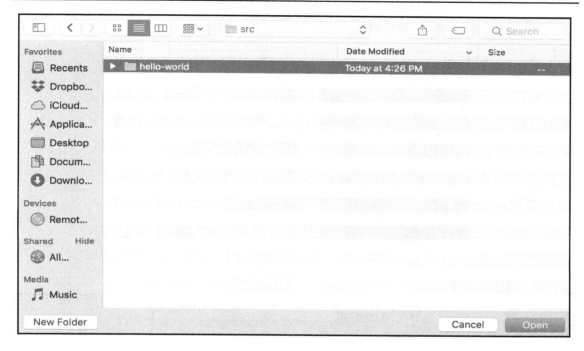

6. Now, the `hello-world` folder is open within Visual Studio Code for us to start writing our AWS Lambda functions. Within Visual Studio Code, from the **File** menu, select **New File**:

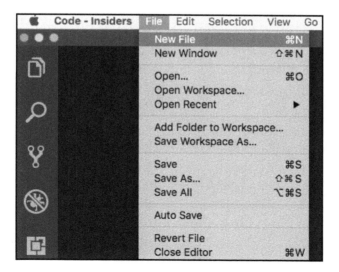

7. Save the file by selecting **Save** from the **File** menu:

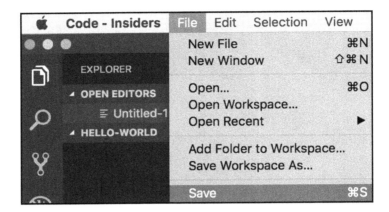

8. Save the file as `index.js`:

9. Let's reuse some of the same code that we used earlier for the AWS Lambda function. In Visual Studio Code editor, enter the following code into the `index.js` file. The following source code will also be used in AWS SAM section when we integrate AWS Lambda functions with Amazon API Gateway:

```
console.log('Loading function');
exports.handler = async (event, context, callback) => {
  console.log('Received event:', JSON.stringify(event, null, 2));
  const name = JSON.parse(event.body).name;
  const helloWorldMsg = `Hello World!, ${name}`;
  const resp = {
  statusCode: 200,
  body: JSON.stringify(helloWorldMsg),
  headers: {
  'Content-Type': 'application/json',
  },
  };
  console.log(helloWorldMsg);
  return resp;
};
```

Make sure to save the file after you have typed the preceding code into `index.js`. You can find the preceding source code at `https://github.com/PacktPublishing/Hands-On-Serverless-Computing/blob/master/Your-first-Serverless-application-on-AWS/hello-world-that-prints-name.js`

Let me take you through what the code is doing here:

- The code is writing everything that it received within the event object to the console output.
- The code is then constructing a `resp` object that will be returned from the AWS Lambda function, and has to be in a particular format for the AWS Lambda function and Amazon API Gateway integration to work. It has to be a HTTP response object. The `resp` object should have a `statusCode` attribute, along with a body that contains a message that you want to return back. In this case, we will be returning `Hello World!, <name attribute from HTTP request body object>`.
- The code then writes `Hello World!` to the console, along with the value of the name attribute that it received as part of the body object.

- The code then returns the same value, `Hello World!`, `<name attribute from HTTP request body object>` as the return value:

With this, our AWS Lambda function, which prints `Hello World`, is complete.

AWS SAM

Let's run through a quick primer on what the AWS SAM is before we start to test and deploy the function to your AWS environment.

In November 2016, AWS introduced the AWS Serverless Application Model, also known as AWS SAM, which used AWS CloudFormation under the hood and extended CloudFormation to provide a simplified mechanism to define and create AWS resources such as Amazon API Gateway, AWS Lambda functions, and Amazon DynamoDB, which are typically the resources that make up an AWS Serverless application. AWS SAM is a model through which you can define your serverless applications through the use of YAML (`http://yaml.org/`) templates. AWS SAM is open sourced and is available for consumption under the Apache 2.0 license.

You can learn more about the AWS SAM at `https://docs.aws.amazon.com/lambda/latest/dg/serverless_app.html`. Using the AWS SAM, you can build and deploy a serverless application from your workstation.

In August 2017, AWS introduced the AWS SAM Local (SAM CLI), with the aim of building and testing serverless applications locally on your workstation. The AWS SAM Local or SAM CLI provides you with a local environment to build, test, and analyze the serverless applications that you build locally before they get deployed to the AWS Lambda platform.

You can find instructions on how to install the AWS SAM Local or SAM CLI at `https://docs.aws.amazon.com/lambda/latest/dg/sam-cli-requirements.html`. As part of the installation, you will be installing Docker for your operating system and the SAM CLI. The easiest way to install SAM on your local workstation is by using `pip` (`https://pypi.org/project/pip/`)—a Python package installer. Type the following code into the command line to see the SAM Installation instructions:

```
pip install aws-sam-cli
```

Once SAM is installed successfully, you should be able to run `sam --version` to see the version of the AWS SAM CLI that is installed locally:

You can even create an AWS serverless application from scratch using `sam init` and by providing the runtime that you want the AWS Lambda function to be created in.

For example, if you want to create an AWS serverless application using Node.js 8.10, then you would run the following command:

```
sam init --runtime nodejs8.10
```

What this does is create a `sam-app` folder with source code for your AWS Lambda function, tests your function, the SAM template to deploy, and the `README.md` file, which has the instructions on how to interact with the serverless application that was initialized. The following is the description of what is generated by `sam init`:

```
├── README.md <-- This instructions file
├── hello_world <-- Source code for a lambda function
│   ├── app.js <-- Lambda function code
│   ├── package.json <-- NodeJS dependencies
│   └── tests <-- Unit tests
│   └── unit
│   └── test_handler.js
└── template.yaml <-- SAM template
```

Please make sure to install SAM CLI so that you will be able to build and test your serverless applications locally, which is what I will be covering in the next section. At the time of writing of this book, AWS SAM CLI only works in the Python 2.7 environment and `pip` should also be in the 2.7 environment.

You can find additional instructions for creating the AWS serverless application using `sam init` at https://docs.aws.amazon.com/lambda/latest/dg/serverless_app.html#serv-app-sam-init

Creating a SAM template for your serverless app

Now that we have installed AWS SAM CLI, let's define a SAM template so that we can test the AWS Lambda function that we created locally earlier, package the serverless application, and deploy it to an AWS environment.

In Visual Studio Code editor, create a new file called `template.yaml` next to where we created the `index.js` file earlier. In the `template.yaml` file, enter the following contents:

```
AWSTemplateFormatVersion: '2010-09-09'
Transform: AWS::Serverless-2016-10-31
Description: >
 hello-world
 SAM Template for hello-world app
Globals:
 Function:
 Timeout: 3
Resources:
 HelloWorldFunction:
 Type: AWS::Serverless::Function
 Properties:
 CodeUri: .
 Handler: index.handler
 Runtime: nodejs8.10
 Events:
 HelloWorld:
 Type: Api
 Properties:
 Path: /hello
 Method: post

Outputs:
 HelloWorldApi:
 Description: "API Gateway endpoint URL for Prod stage for Hello World
function"
 Value: !Sub
```

```
"https://${ServerlessRestApi}.execute-api.${AWS::Region}.amazonaws.com/Prod
/hello/"
  HelloWorldFunction:
  Description: "Hello World Lambda Function ARN"
  Value: !GetAtt HelloWorldFunction.Arn
  HelloWorldFunctionIamRole:
  Description: "Implicit IAM Role created for Hello World function"
  Value: !GetAtt HelloWorldFunctionRole.Arn
```

You can find the preceding AWS SAM template at https://github.com/PacktPublishing/
Hands-On-Serverless-Computing/blob/master/Your-first-Serverless-application-on-
AWS/aws-sam-template.yaml

Let's look at what the SAM template is doing:

```
AWSTemplateFormatVersion: '2010-09-09'
Transform: AWS::Serverless-2016-10-31
```

The first two lines are metadata that defines which version of AWS CloudFormation to use
and what the resulting template would need to transform into, which
is AWS::Serverless-2016-10-31 in this case.

The next part is a description of the AWS serverless application that you are developing:

```
Globals:
  Function:
  Timeout: 3
```

Then, the template has a setting for the timeout of the AWS Lambda function, which in this
case is three seconds.

The next section in the template defines the AWS resources that need to be created for the
serverless application. For the serverless application that we are creating, we will be
creating an AWS Lambda function and Amazon API Gateway, which will act as the HTTP
event trigger for the AWS Lambda function:

```
Resources:
  HelloWorldFunction:
  Type: AWS::Serverless::Function
  Properties:
  CodeUri: .
  Handler: index.handler
  Runtime: nodejs8.10
  Events:
  HelloWorld:
  Type: Api
  Properties:
```

```
Path: /hello
Method: post
```

The preceding code in the SAM template creates an AWS Lambda function with the code that is in the current working directory, defines what the handler for the AWS Lambda function is, defines the runtime, and version of the language to use, which in this case is Node.js 8.10. The template then defines the events that are on the AWS Lambda function and, in this case, it is an API, which is Amazon API Gateway. The template also has the definition of the endpoint and the HTTP method on the Amazon API Gateway, which, when invoked, will trigger your AWS Lambda function, which in this case is /hello and the post HTTP method:

```
Outputs:
  HelloWorldApi:
  Description: "API Gateway endpoint URL for Prod stage for Hello World
function"
  Value: !Sub
"https://${ServerlessRestApi}.execute-api.${AWS::Region}.amazonaws.com/Prod
/hello/"
  HelloWorldFunction:
  Description: "Hello World Lambda Function ARN"
  Value: !GetAtt HelloWorldFunction.Arn
  HelloWorldFunctionIamRole:
  Description: "Implicit IAM Role created for Hello World function"
  Value: !GetAtt HelloWorldFunctionRole.Arn
```

The next section in the template is the output that will be generated when the SAM template runs (the CloudFormation template run) that you can use to get the values for the Amazon API Gateway endpoint that you can hit to invoke the hello world function that we wrote earlier.

Testing a serverless app locally

Now that we have created the SAM template, let's look at how we can test the Amazon API Gateway and AWS Lambda setup locally on your workstation before we package and deploy it to the AWS Lambda platform.

The AWS SAM Local or SAM CLI provides a local environment that simulates the AWS environment locally on your workstation.

Let's start an API endpoint locally through the SAM CLI, through which we will invoke the AWS Lambda function locally on the workstation. The API endpoint that the SAM CLI creates also supports the hot reloading feature, which enables you to test the AWS Lambda functions that need to restart the API endpoint. Running the following command will create the API endpoint locally. It uses the runtime environment defined in the template to spin up a docker container locally on your workstation:

```
sam local start-api
```

```
~/src/hello-world  sam local start-api
2018-06-17 21:37:24 Mounting HelloWorldFunction at http://127.0.0.1:3000/hello [POST]
2018-06-17 21:37:24 You can now browse to the above endpoints to invoke your functions. You do not
eflected instantly/automatically. You only need to restart SAM CLI if you update your AWS SAM temp
2018-06-17 21:37:24  * Running on http://127.0.0.1:3000/ (Press CTRL+C to quit)
```

Once the API endpoint is up and running, you will be able to call the `http://127.0.0.1:3000/hello` endpoint on your local workstation and invoke the AWS Lambda function by invoking the endpoint through the HTTP `post` method with a payload that has name attribute in the JSON payload.

On macOS, Linux, or Powershell on Windows, using the `curl` command let's you post the payload with the name to `http://127.0.0.1:3000/hello` and see if it returns `Hello World!`, `<name from the payload>`. For this test, I'm going to send `kuldeep` as the name in the payload:

```
curl -X POST http://127.0.0.1:3000/hello -H "Content-Type:
application/json" -d '{ "name": "kuldeep" }'
```

The output from the preceding command should be:

```
"Hello World!, kuldeep"
```

This is what it looked like when I ran the command on my local workstation, which matches the output that I was expecting:

You can also use tools such as Postman to test HTTP endpoints, and Postman is available for all operating systems. You can learn more about it at `https://www.getpostman.com/`.

With the help of the SAM CLI, you are able to validate whether your AWS Lambda function works as expected before you deploy to the AWS environment, and you can also test the integration between Amazon API Gateway and your AWS Lambda function. In the next section, let's look at packaging and deploying your AWS serverless application to an AWS environment.

You can find out more information about testing using the SAM at: `https://docs.aws.amazon.com/lambda/latest/dg/test-sam-cli.html`.

Publishing a serverless app

Before we start packaging and deploying the AWS serverless application that we built to AWS, we need to create an S3 bucket where artefacts such as the AWS Lambda function, along with its dependent packages, will be uploaded. You can either create an S3 bucket using the AWS Console or using the AWS CLI. If you already have an S3 bucket that you can use for this, then skip ahead to the *Packaging a serverless app*, subsection.

To be able to use the AWS CLI, you need to first download the AWS CLI and then configure it. The instructions to perform both of these actions are listed at `https://docs.aws.amazon.com/lambda/latest/dg/setup-awscli.html`.

To be able to create an S3 bucket through the console, you can follow the instructions at `https://docs.aws.amazon.com/AmazonS3/latest/gsg/CreatingABucket.html`.

If you prefer creating the bucket using the AWS CLI, you need to run the following command. I have replaced the `<BUCKET_NAME>` in the following command with `kuldeepc`. Keep in mind that S3 bucket names are unique across all AWS accounts:

```
aws s3 mb s3://<BUCKET_NAME>
```

The S3 bucket that I created is visible when I go to the AWS S3 console:

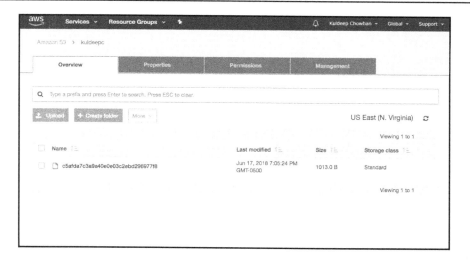

Packaging a serverless app

Now that we have an S3 bucket where we can upload our artifacts, let's run the `sam package` command, which uploads the AWS Lambda function and the corresponding packages, if any, to the S3 bucket that you created. It also generates a `packaged.yaml` file in the current working directory, which has the location of the `CodeUri` pointing to the S3 bucket that we specified on the command line.

Replace the S3 bucket with the S3 bucket that you have created in your account. I have used kuldeepc as the bucket name in the below screenshot. Run the below command to create the package to create Serverless resources on AWS.

```
sam package \
--template-file template.yaml \
--output-template-file packaged.yaml \
--s3-bucket REPLACE_THIS_WITH_YOUR_S3_BUCKET_NAME
```

```
~/src/hello-world  sam package \
   --template-file template.yaml \
   --output-template-file packaged.yaml \
   --s3-bucket kuldeepc
Uploading to c5afda7c3a9a40e0e03c2ebd296977f8  1013 / 1013.0  (100.00%)
Successfully packaged artifacts and wrote output template to file packaged.yaml.
Execute the following command to deploy the packaged template
aws cloudformation deploy --template-file /Users/kuldeepchowhan/src/hello-world/packaged.yaml --stack-name <YOUR STACK NAME>
~/src/hello-world
```

Make sure that the `CodeUri` that is generated in your `packaged.yaml` exists in your S3 bucket. In my case, the `CodeUri` that set was `CodeUri:` `s3://kuldeepc/c5afda7c3a9a40e0e03c2ebd296977f8`.

Deploying a serverless app

Now that we have the artifact uploaded to an S3 bucket and the `packaged.yaml` file generated as well, let's run the `sam deploy` command to deploy the `Hello World` serverless app that we built in this chapter.

Run the below command to deploy the Serverless app on to AWS.

```
sam deploy \
--template-file packaged.yaml \
--stack-name hello-world-app \
--capabilities CAPABILITY_IAM
```

The following is a screenshot of the command:

```
~/src/hello-world  sam deploy \
    --template-file packaged.yaml \
    --stack-name hello-world-app \
    --capabilities CAPABILITY_IAM

Waiting for changeset to be created..
Waiting for stack create/update to complete
Successfully created/updated stack - hello-world-app
~/src/hello-world
```

By running the `sam deploy` command, your serverless application is created using AWS CloudFormation.

You can look at the resources SAM CLI created for you through the AWS Console. In this case, it should have created one AWS Lambda function and one Amazon API Gateway. Let's look at the resources that the SAM CLI created for us.

The Hello World AWS Lambda Function that was created by the SAM CLI is as follows:

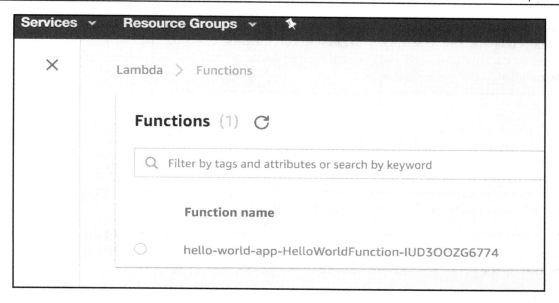

The Hello World Amazon API Gateway that was created by the SAM CLI is as follows. You can access it by navigating to the API Gateway Console within the AWS Console:

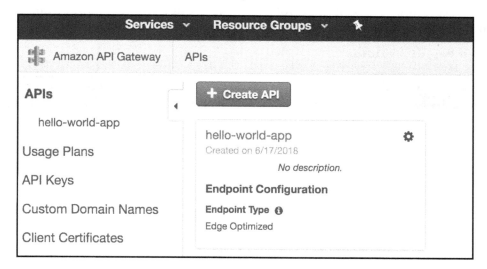

Now that the AWS CloudFormation execution is complete and your AWS serverless app has been created successfully, you need to run the `aws cloudformation describe-stacks` command to find out the URI for the Amazon API Gateway that was created for our Hello World Serverless app:

```
aws cloudformation describe-stacks \
--stack-name hello-world-app \
--query 'Stacks[].Outputs'
```

From the output of the preceding command, grab the `OutputValue` for the `HelloWorldApi` key, which in my case is `https://kxbvgyeshi.execute-api.us-east-1.amazonaws.com/Prod/hello/`, but in your case it will be completely different.

Now, if I hit the preceding endpoint using the same `curl` command that I used earlier to test the serverless app that was running on my local workstation, I should expect the same results as the prior test on my local workstation:

```
curl -X POST
https://kxbvgyeshi.execute-api.us-east-1.amazonaws.com/Prod/hello/ -H
"Content-Type: application/json" -d '{ "name": "kuldeep" }'
```

The test is successful, as shown in the following screenshot, and the output from the command execution was:

```
"Hello World!, kuldeep"
```

As soon as you hit the Amazon API Gateway endpoint, you can navigate to the AWS Lambda Console, select the Hello World Lambda function, and click on the **Monitoring** tab to see whether the AWS Lambda function was also invoked or not, and you can navigate to the AWS Lambda function logs in Amazon CloudWatch for validation:

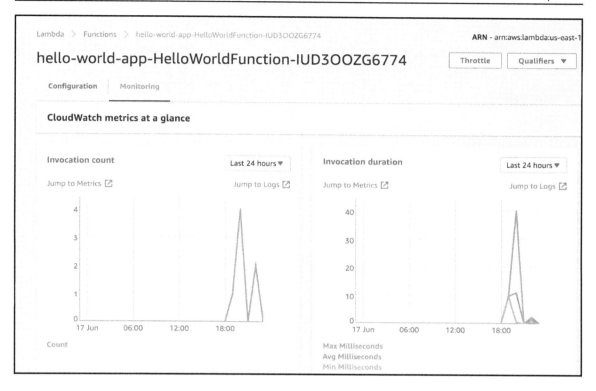

With this, we are now able to successfully deploy our Hello World Serverless application to the AWS environment, and are able to successfully validate that the AWS Lambda function works as expected, and the integration between the Amazon API Gateway and the AWS Lambda function works as expected.

Summary

In this chapter, you learned how to write Hello World serverless applications to run on AWS using Node.js, learned about AWS SAM, learned how to test a serverless application locally on your workstation before deploying it to the AWS environment, learned how to package and deploy a serverless application to AWS using the AWS SAM, and learned how to trigger a serverless application using Amazon API Gateway (HTTP Event Trigger).

6
Serverless Orchestration on AWS

In this chapter, we will learn how to orchestrate serverless apps on AWS using AWS Step Functions. We will first learn what AWS Step Functions is, then look at the benefits it provides. We will then look into how it works, before walking through how to create a basic AWS Step Functions state machine with and without using AWS Lambda functions.

What is AWS Step Functions?

So far, we have learned about writing serverless apps that involve only one AWS Lambda function. However, in reality, you will need multiple distributed apps to perform the complex tasks that you will be developing. AWS Step Functions is a service built by AWS, which helps you to coordinate multiple components (in our case, AWS Lambda functions) of a distributed application using visual workflows. As individual components of distributed applications each perform a discrete function, it helps to change and scale the individual components easily and quickly without having to worry about the other pieces of the distributed applications, as coordination between these discrete components is handled by AWS Step Functions.

AWS Step Functions provides a **graphical user interface (GUI)** through which you can visualize the components of your distributed application as a series of steps, which makes it simple to build and run multiple discrete functions as one. Step Functions will automatically invoke each step and will retry in the event of errors, which in turn helps with building robust distributed applications.

AWS Step Functions is a part of the AWS serverless platform and makes it easy to orchestrate AWS Lambda functions that are part of serverless applications. AWS Step Functions support orchestration across microservices that are built using Amazon ECS (`https://aws.amazon.com/ecs/`) and Amazon EC2 (`https://aws.amazon.com/ec2/`).

The benefits that AWS Steps Functions offers are as follows:

- **Productivity**: AWS Step Functions includes blueprints for commonly used workflows and visual interfaces that you can use to create distributed applications to coordinate between multiple discrete components. You can do all of this in a matter of minutes and then track the execution of each step within Step Functions to make sure that your distributed application is operating as expected. AWS Step Functions also provides you with a mechanism to trigger each step in your Step Functions either in parallel or sequentially.
- **Resilience:** AWS Step Functions automatically triggers each step in your distributed application and retries when there are errors, providing your application with resiliency. AWS Step Functions can handle millions of step executions at the same time to make sure that your distributed application is available as the traffic to your distributed application increases.
- **Agility:** As discrete components of your distributed applications are tied together using AWS Steps Functions, you have the agility to change each component independently without affecting the entire application. AWS Step Functions also supports creating workflows that can span thousands of individual components, which means you can build complex distributed applications using AWS Step Functions.

How does AWS Step Functions work?

With AWS Steps Functions, you can define and operate multiple discrete components as one distributed application quickly with something called a state machine. You can define your application using a visual workflow that AWS Step Functions provides using the AWS Console, the Java API, or AWS CloudFormation templates. The visual console automatically creates the workflow and generates a graph for the individual components, based on the order of execution, which makes designing applications using the visual console very easy. I have illustrated three different diagrams detailing how the AWS Step Functions flow works for a photo processing application.

App using sequential steps

The following diagram illustrates an AWS Step Functions state machine that has steps that execute in a sequential manner. When the state machine starts for this photo processing application, it first executes the steps to upload the RAW file, and once that has been completed, it then runs the step that deletes the RAW file. The step execution, in this case, is sequential:

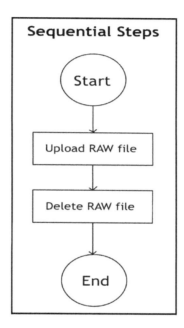

App using branching steps

This diagram illustrates an AWS Step Functions state machine that has steps that execute based on a decision tree or branching:

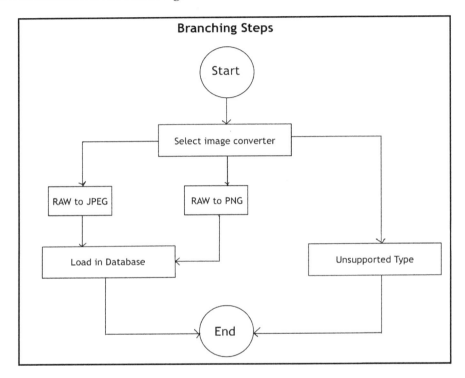

When the state machine starts for this photo processing application, it first runs the step that selects the image converter type **RAW to JPEG** or **RAW to PNG**. Once the image converter type has been determined, it executes that step and then loads the file into a database. If none of the image converter types match, then it executes a step that lets the user know that it is an unsupported type.

App using parallel steps

This diagram illustrates an AWS Step Functions state machine that has steps that execute in parallel:

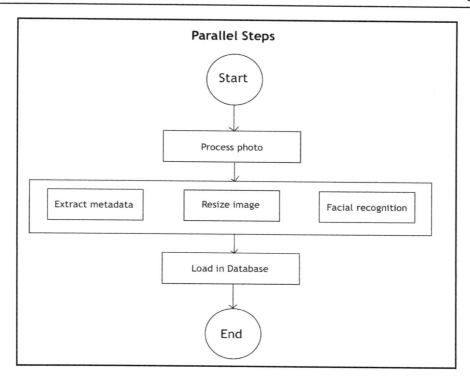

When the state machine starts for this photo processing application, it first runs the step that processes the photo and, once that has been completed, it executes three steps that run in parallel to extract the metadata from the photo, resize the image, and run the facial recognition step. Once the execution of all three parallel steps has been completed, it then loads the photo into a database and ends the execution of the state machine.

Operational visibility

With AWS Step Functions, you can easily monitor whether everything is operating as expected. Once you have created the workflow within AWS Steps Functions, you can navigate to the visual console to see the execution status of your steps and verify that they are executing as expected. It shows the status of the steps that are in executing state, along with the different statuses of the steps, including success, failure, and needs retry.

The following is a screenshot of how the execution status will look when your application is running, and the step that is being executed is shown in blue:

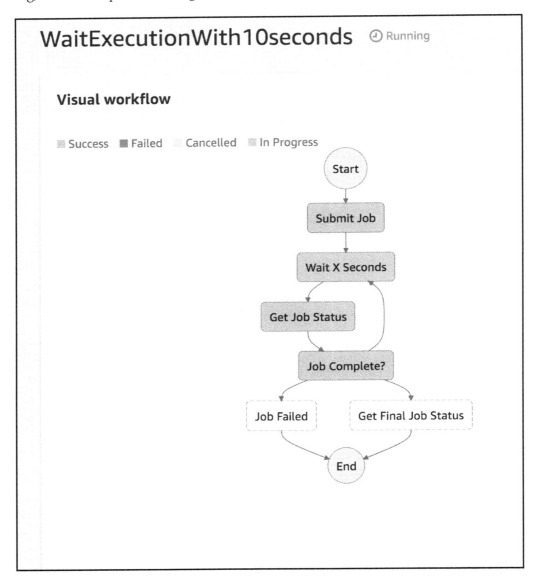

Once the application is complete and is successful, then every step that was executed will be marked in green, as illustrated in the following screenshot:

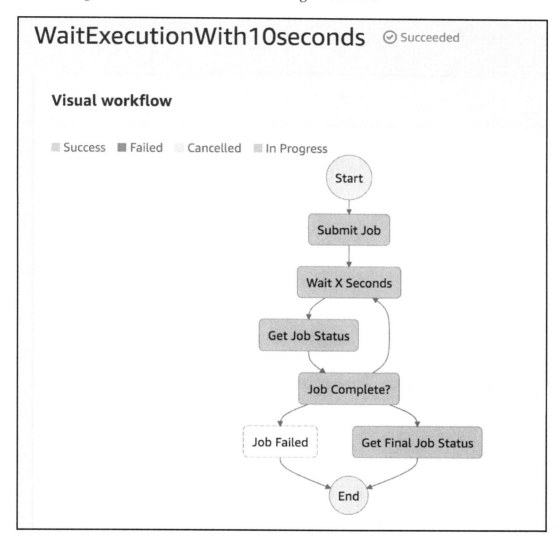

 If any of those steps fail, they will be shown in red.

AWS Step Functions also shows detailed execution history, along with the link to logs for each step that you can look at in Amazon CloudWatch:

Execution event history

ID	Type	Step	Resource	Elapsed Time (ms)	Timestamp
▶ 1	ExecutionStarted		-	0	Jun 18, 2018 07:09:43.396 PM
▶ 2	TaskStateEntered	Submit Job	-	22	Jun 18, 2018 07:09:43.418 PM
▶ 3	LambdaFunctionScheduled	Submit Job	Lambda | CloudWatch logs	22	Jun 18, 2018 07:09:43.418 PM
▶ 4	LambdaFunctionStarted	Submit Job	Lambda | CloudWatch logs	68	Jun 18, 2018 07:09:43.464 PM
▶ 5	LambdaFunctionSucceeded	Submit Job	Lambda | CloudWatch logs	1194	Jun 18, 2018 07:09:44.590 PM
▶ 6	TaskStateExited	Submit Job	-	1194	Jun 18, 2018 07:09:44.590 PM
▶ 7	WaitStateEntered	Wait X Seconds	-	1202	Jun 18, 2018 07:09:44.598 PM

You can create State machines using **Amazon States Language** (**ASL**). You can learn more about ASL at
`https://docs.aws.amazon.com/step-functions/latest/dg/amazon-states-language-sta`
`tes.html`.

Creating your first state machine

Let's create a Hello World state machine that has parallel steps that wait for a certain duration before executing the next step. The main execution components in this state machine are AWS Lambda functions. AWS Step Functions provides multiple starter templates to get started. We will be using one of to them to create a state machine and see how it works.

Once you have signed in to the AWS Console, navigate to the AWS Step Functions landing page and click on **Get Started** within the **Create state machine** section. Clicking on **Get Started** takes us to the page where we can create an AWS Step Functions state machine from scratch, use sample projects, and choose from one of the starter templates. For this exercise, let's select **Templates**, as shown in the following diagram:

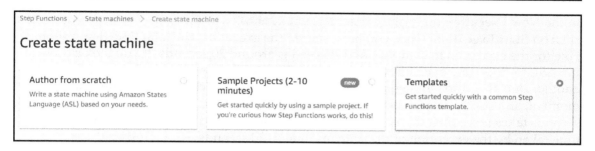

Now, from the list of the starter templates, let's select **Parallel** branches in your state machine template:

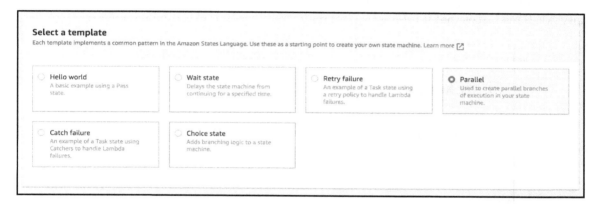

In the **Details** section, make sure to select the checkbox that states **I acknowledge that AWS Step Functions will create an IAM role which allows access to my Lambda functions**.

Leave the rest of the sections in the console as they are and click on **Create State Machine** at the bottom. With that, the state machine should be created for us and we can start an execution of the state machine to see how it works. From the execution of state machine details page of the state machine that we just created, which should have been named **Parallel**, click on **Start Execution**.

In the **New Execution** dialog box, enter FirstExecution as the name of the execution and click on **Start Execution**. Once you have started the execution, the total time that it should take for the execution to complete and succeed is around 20 seconds. If you look closely at the ASL for this state machine, it says wait for 20 seconds, however, at the same time, another step also starts immediately after the Pass step, which doesn't do much at the moment, and starts the next step, which waits for 10 seconds. As the step that waits for 20 seconds takes more time than the combined Pass step and wait for 10s step, the total time taken by the execution of the state machine is 20 seconds.

You can look at the result of the execution on the details page and also view the ASL code of the execution. This is what a successful execution looks like for the FirstExecutionthat we just ran. Please note that this state machine doesn't have any AWS Lambda functions or any AWS resources that it interacts with; that is the reason it executed so quickly:

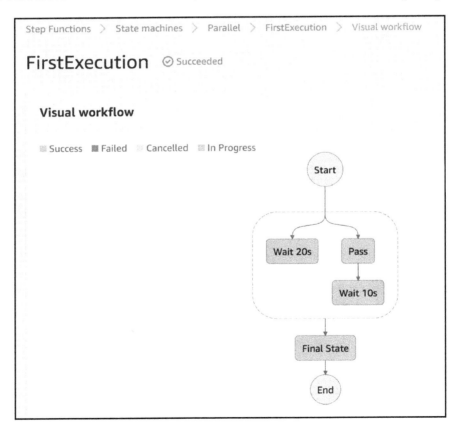

The execution history also shows details about each steps' execution, along with the location of Amazon CloudWatch logs.

The ASL for this state machine will look like the following:

```
{
  "Comment": "An example of the Amazon States Language using a parallel
  state to execute two branches at the same time.",
  "StartAt": "Parallel",
  "States": {
  "Parallel": {
  "Type": "Parallel",
  "Next": "Final State",
  "Branches": [
  {
  "StartAt": "Wait 20s",
  "States": {
  "Wait 20s": {
  "Type": "Wait",
  "Seconds": 20,
  "End": true
  }
  }
  },
  {
  "StartAt": "Pass",
  "States": {
  "Pass": {
  "Type": "Pass",
  "Next": "Wait 10s"
  },
  "Wait 10s": {
  "Type": "Wait",
  "Seconds": 10,
  "End": true
  }
  }
  }
  ]
  },
  "Final State": {
  "Type": "Pass",
  "End": true
  }
  }
}
```

You can also find this ASL for a state machine without any Lambda functions at: `https://github.com/PacktPublishing/Hands-On-Serverless-Computing/blob/master/Serverless-Orchestration-on-AWS/state-machine-without-lambda.json`.

State machine using Lambdas

As mentioned in the previous section, the first state machine that we created doesn't involve any AWS Lambda functions. Let's use the sample projects that Step Functions provides and create a state machine that involves AWS Lambda functions.

Once you have signed in to the AWS Console, navigate to the AWS Step Functions landing page and click on **Get Started** within the **Create state machine** section. Clicking on **Get Started** takes us to the page where we can create an AWS Step Functions state machine from scratch, use sample projects, and choose from one of the starter templates. For this exercise, let's select **Sample Projects (2-10 minutes)**.

From the list of Sample Projects, select **Job Status Poller**:

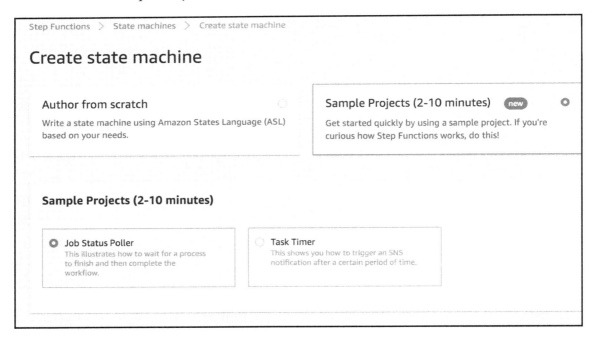

Then, click on **Create Resources**. The **Create Project Resources** dialog box provides the details of the AWS resources that it is creating using AWS CloudFormation. For this sample project, the following resources are being created:

- SubmitJob—AWS Lambda Function

- CheckJob—AWS Lambda Function

- SampleJobQueue—Batch Job Queue

AWS CloudFormation takes anywhere from 2 to 10 minutes, and you need to wait for the machine to be created. Once the creation process is complete, you will be automatically navigated to the **New execution** dialog box of the state machine that has been created.

In the **New execution** box, enter the `FirstExecutionWith10Seconds` delay and modify the JSON in the new execution dialog box by changing `"wait_time"` to 10, as shown here:

```
{
  "jobName": "my-job",
  "jobDefinition": "arn:aws:batch:REGION:ACCOUNT_ID:job-
definition/SampleJobDefinition-9410ea442b828ff:1",
  "jobQueue": "arn:aws:batch:us-east-1:306255272183:job-
queue/SampleJobQueue-39a2373ba12f689",
  "wait_time": 10
}
```

The following is a screenshot of the **New execution** Dialog box with the modified values:

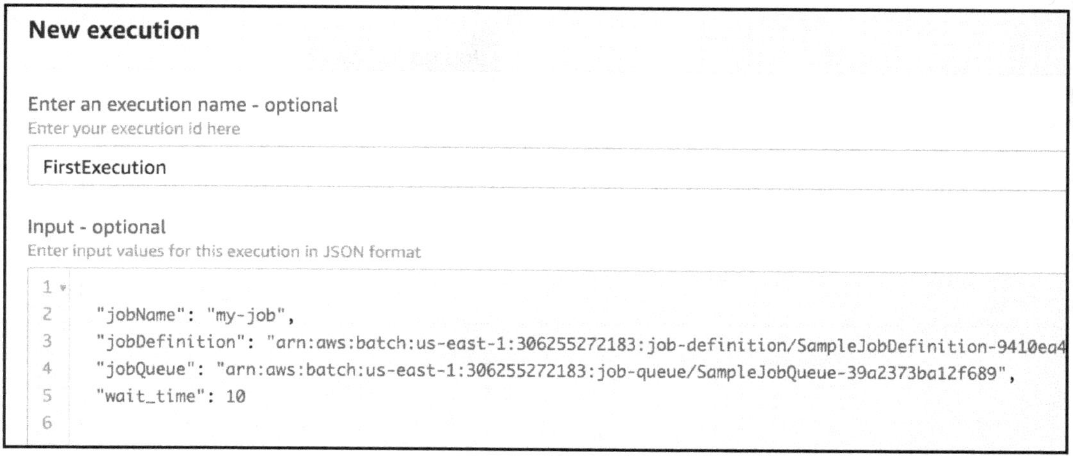

If you look at the visual workflow and ASL that has been created for the state machine, the **Submit Job** and **Job Complete?** steps both involve interacting with AWS Lambda functions:

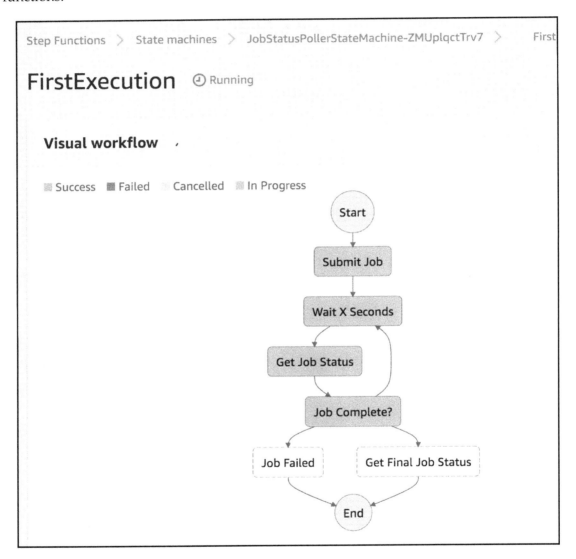

Here is the ASL for the state machine that has been created:

```
{
  "Comment": "A state machine that submits a Job to AWS Batch and monitors
the Job until it completes.",
  "StartAt": "Submit Job",
  "States": {
  "Submit Job": {
  "Type": "Task",
  "Resource": "arn:aws:lambda:us-
east-1:306255272183:function:StepFunctionsSample-JobStatusPol-
SubmitJobFunction-6Z182W8ERLT2",
  "ResultPath": "$.guid",
  "Next": "Wait X Seconds"
  },
  "Wait X Seconds": {
  "Type": "Wait",
  "SecondsPath": "$.wait_time",
  "Next": "Get Job Status"
  },
  "Get Job Status": {
  "Type": "Task",
  "Resource": "arn:aws:lambda:us-
east-1:306255272183:function:StepFunctionsSample-JobStatusPoll-
CheckJobFunction-1IGFUHZPQDVRG",
  "Next": "Job Complete?",
  "InputPath": "$.guid",
  "ResultPath": "$.status"
  },
  "Job Complete?": {
  "Type": "Choice",
  "Choices": [
  {
  "Variable": "$.status",
  "StringEquals": "FAILED",
  "Next": "Job Failed"
  },
  {
  "Variable": "$.status",
  "StringEquals": "SUCCEEDED",
  "Next": "Get Final Job Status"
  }
  ],
  "Default": "Wait X Seconds"
  },
  "Job Failed": {
  "Type": "Fail",
  "Cause": "AWS Batch Job Failed",
```

```
"Error": "DescribeJob returned FAILED"
},
"Get Final Job Status": {
"Type": "Task",
"Resource": "arn:aws:lambda:us-
east-1:306255272183:function:StepFunctionsSample-JobStatusPoll-
CheckJobFunction-1IGFUHZPQDVRG",
"InputPath": "$.guid",
"End": true
}
}
}
```

You can also find this ASL for a state machine with two Lambda functions
at: `https://github.com/PacktPublishing/Hands-On-Serverless-Computing/blob/master/Serverless-Orchestration-on-AWS/state-machine-with-lambda.json`.

Once the execution is complete for each step, you can view the execution of the Lambda function and also view the logs in Amazon CloudWatch. All of these details are available within the Details page of the execution (`FirstExecution`) that we just ran. This will be useful information for troubleshooting any errors you encounter during the execution of your state machine.

Summary

In this chapter, you learned what AWS Step Functions is, how it works, and the benefits it provides. You also learned how to create a basic AWS Step Functions state machine that doesn't have any AWS Lambda functions. Then, you learned how to create a state machine using two AWS Lambda functions.

In the next chapter, we will look at Microsoft Azure Functions.

Getting Started with Azure Functions

7

In this chapter, we are going to learn details about Microsoft Azure Functions, along with configuration options for Azure Functions. In the previous chapters, we learned how to create serverless apps in an AWS environment using both AWS Console and the AWS SAM from your local workstation. We also learned how to test and deploy serverless apps to an AWS environment. In the coming chapters, we will be focusing on Microsoft Azure Functions and we will recreate the same serverless apps that we created and deployed to an AWS environment for a Microsoft Azure environment as well. In the previous chapters, we also looked at invoking AWS Lambda triggers using HTTP triggers; we will also do the same for Microsoft Azure so that you can learn how it works in an Azure environment versus an AWS environment.

We will be learning about the following topics in this chapter:

- An introduction to Azure Functions
- Going into depth with Azure Functions
- Configuration options for Azure Functions
- Azure Functions application settings
- Debugging options for Azure Functions

An introduction to Azure Functions

Azure Functions is a service that Microsoft offers for customers to run *Functions on Azure Platform*. Azure Functions is Microsoft's implementation of **Functions as a Service** (**FaaS**). Its main goal is to enable developers to run small pieces of software code or functions to be run in the Microsoft Azure cloud. If you recall the benefits of FaaS that we learned in `Chapter 1`, *What is Serverless Computing?* one of them is that, the developer is just focused on writing the code to solve the problem at hand, rather than, worrying about infrastructure on where it will run. The developer need not worry about the entire application that is required to run the code and scaling the infrastructure as well when the function receives a lot of traffic. As the developers are focusing on just solving the problem at hand, development can be more productive.

As of June 2018, Microsoft Azure Functions supported the following languages, which means you have the freedom to write functions in any of them:

- C#
- Node.js
- Java
- F#
- PHP

Azure Functions, like AWS Lambda, also charges the user for the duration of the execution of your Azure Functions and automatically scales based on load. Azure Functions are also integrated with many Azure services, which makes developing intelligent apps easy, and you can build seamless connections with Azure services very easily.

Let's break down the features of Microsoft Azure Functions:

- **Language choice**: You can write functions for Azure using C#, Node.js, Java, F#, and PHP
- **Pay per use model**: You will only pay for the time that is spent on the function execution
- **Dependencies**: With npm and NuGet, you can bring the dependencies that are required for your app, and package them up and upload the function to Azure to run it
- **Integration**: Azure Functions integrate seamlessly with other Azure services (which we will explore later in this chapter), which helps in developing intelligent applications

- **Integrated security**: For HTTP triggered (events) Azure Functions, you can protect the functions with OAUTH providers like Azure Active Directory, Microsoft account and many other OAUTH supported providers
- **Development made easy**: With the integration of writing your Function code right in the Azure portal, solving the problem at hand using Azure Functions can be done as quickly as possible

Azure serverless platform

So far, we have been learning about Azure Functions, which is just the FaaS offering from Microsoft Azure. As you are aware by now, just running FaaS typically doesn't make a complete serverless application.

Let's look at the other Azure services that enable you to build serverless apps on Microsoft Azure.

Compute

Azure Functions (https://azure.microsoft.com/en-us/services/functions/) provides an interface to run your code with a choice of programming languages without having to worry about infrastructure. It scales on demand based on the load on your functions.

Database

Azure Cosmos DB (https://azure.microsoft.com/en-us/services/cosmos-db/) is a great addition for any serverless app. It is a multi-region and multi-model database service from Microsoft Azure that automatically scales and replicates data closest to your customers.

Storage

Azure Storage (https://azure.microsoft.com/en-us/services/storage/) is highly available, durable, and scalable storage that is built for developers to build cloud applications in. It is similar to S3 from AWS. You can store structured data, unstructured data, and files in Azure Storage.

Messaging

Azure offers two services in this space for serverless applications.

Event Grid (`https://azure.microsoft.com/en-us/services/event-grid/`) is a managed event routing system from Microsoft Azure that gives us the ability to connect multiple serverless app with events from different Microsoft Azure services.

Service Bus (`https://azure.microsoft.com/en-us/services/service-bus/`) is a managed infrastructure service from Microsoft Azure that provides messaging capabilities to develop distributed cloud solutions across public and private cloud environments.

Security

Azure Active Directory (`https://azure.microsoft.com/en-us/services/active-directory/`) is the identity and access management solution from Microsoft Azure, which provides developers the capability to control access to resources in Azure and also provides authentication to users to access serverless apps that are built on top of Microsoft Azure. This service is similar to IAM from AWS for Identity and Access Management.

Orchestration

Logic Apps (`https://azure.microsoft.com/en-us/services/logic-apps/`) is the offering from Microsoft Azure that provides developers with the ability to build workflows, which enables them to integrate their serverless apps using workflows instead of them having to tie them together using glue code. It is similar to AWS Step Functions from AWS.

API Management

Azure has two offerings in this space for serverless applications.

API Management (`https://azure.microsoft.com/en-us/services/api-management/`) is a solution from Microsoft Azure which helps developers create, monitor, manage, and secure any APIs that they build within Microsoft Azure.

Azure Function Proxies

Azure Function Proxies (https://docs.microsoft.com/en-us/azure/azure-functions/functions-proxies/) from Microsoft Azure provides capability to break your large APIs into multiple Azure Functions while still keeping a single API interface your clients. This is similar to API Gateway and AWS Lambda integration, which we learned about in previous chapters.

Analytics

Azure has two offerings in this space for serverless applications.

Azure Stream Analytics (https://azure.microsoft.com/en-us/services/stream-analytics/) is an offering from Microsoft Azure that provides you with a service for real-time streaming data. It also has an interface where you can write SQL queries and only pay for what is used from the service.

Events Hub (https://azure.microsoft.com/en-us/services/event-hubs/) is a managed service from Microsoft Azure that helps with mass ingestion of small data sets, which typically are generated from sensors and devices. It helps in processing, routing, and storing data generated by these devices.

Azure portal

Before we start looking into the Azure Functions portal, let's look at the process of getting an Azure account. Microsoft Azure offers 12 months of free services (there are limits to how much you can use) and also gives you $200 credit for 30 days to get started. The free account also provides you with 25+ always free services.

You can sign up for a Microsoft Azure Account at https://azure.microsoft.com/en-us/free/.

To be able to create a Microsoft Azure Account, you will need a Microsoft Account. Once you have created the Azure account, a Free Plan subscription is automatically created for you so that you can start building apps to run in the Microsoft Azure Cloud environment.

Dashboards

Let's look at the Azure portal user interface before we look at the Azure Functions interface. As soon as you log in to your Microsoft Azure account, you will see the **Dashboard** page. The page will look similar to this one if you have created a Microsoft Azure account. There won't be a dashboard yet, as you have to create one to customize what you want to see in the dashboard:

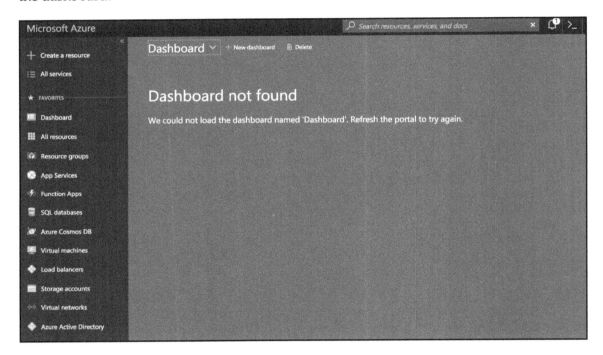

From this page, you can click on **New Dashboard** to create a new dashboard and add the resources you want to see in the dashboard when you log in. On the **New Dashboard** page, give a name to your dashboard and drag and drop the resources from the left-hand side tray over to the dashboard. As this is just a test to see how the dashboard works, feel free to drag and drop random resources:

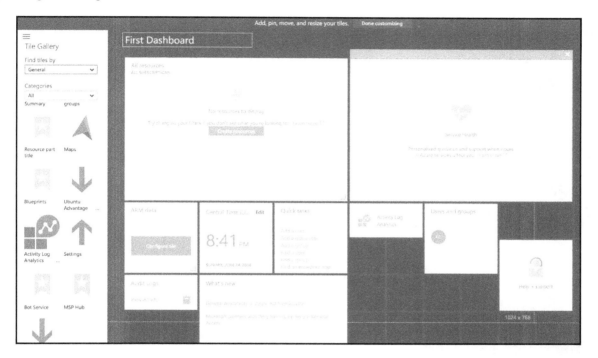

Once you click on the **Done customizing** button, you will be taken back to the screen where the dashboard that you just created will be visible, with the titles and information that you asked for. If you have multiple dashboards, then you will see them as well on that page, with the option to choose the dashboard you want to see. This dashboard feature gives you the option to see the services that you care about, rather than seeing all Azure Cloud services:

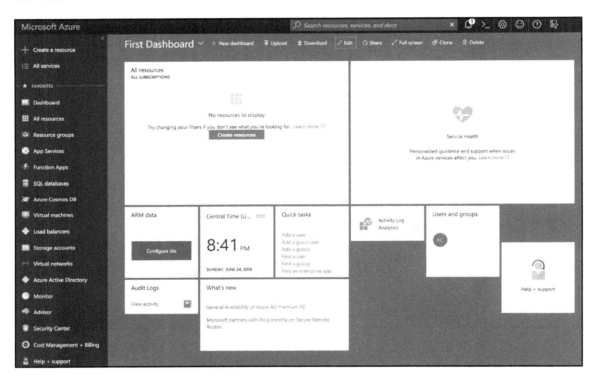

Azure Cloud Shell

Microsoft Azure also provides you with a virtual machine (shell) that runs in Azure, which you can access using your browser to run interactive commands against your Azure environment. It provides you with the ability to administer your Azure account from anywhere using a browser through a shell called Cloud Shell. You can use common tools and programming languages to control your Azure environment. It provides you the ability to choose between a Linux-based Bash Shell or a Windows-based PowerShell.

The Cloud Shell is managed and maintained by Microsoft, which means it gets regularly patched and updated with the latest tools to interact with your Azure environment. The Cloud Shell comes with common Linux shell tools, PowerShell Azure modules, Azure tools, source control tools, a container or Docker toolset, and text editors. The Cloud Shell also has languages that are already installed, such as Node.js, Python, and .NET environments.

You can access Cloud Shell from the top-right side menu. Click on the shell icon and you will see the welcome screen asking you to choose your shell environment, either Bash or PowerShell. You can always change the Azure Cloud shell environment that you want to use, by default when you access Cloud Shell the last accessed shell will be the one that you will get.

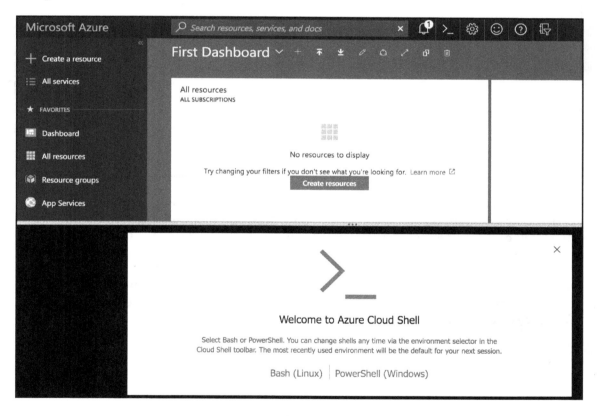

I prefer Bash in the Linux environment, so I will choose Bash as my preferred shell environment in the Cloud Shell's welcome screen. Once you select the shell environment, Cloud Shell will prompt you to create file storage to store the files that you create between your sessions. This is required to persist files across different sessions. For this, Cloud Shell will create a storage account in your Free Trial subscription for a small fee. With the free plan that we have selected for this exercise, the Storage account will be free for 12 months. You will have 5 GB worth of file storage for free for an entire year; if you start using more than 5 GB worth of file storage, then you will be charged for it:

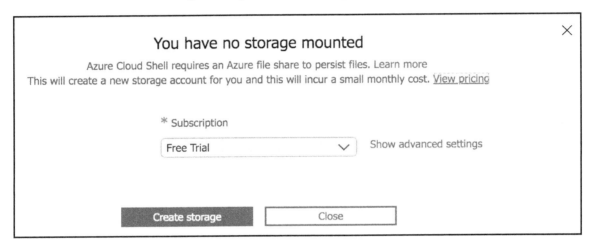

Once you select **Create storage**, it will go ahead and create file storage in the Azure Storage service. Once storage creation is complete, you will be automatically taken to Cloud Shell, where you can start interacting with your Azure environment. From the Cloud Shell environment, you can switch between Bash or PowerShell environments. Azure Cloud Shell times out after 20 minutes of inactivity. Cloud Shell is an temporary host that is created by Microsoft Azure per session and per user. The only way to have the files shared across sessions is to use the file storage that was previously created by the Cloud Shell's Welcome screen wizard:

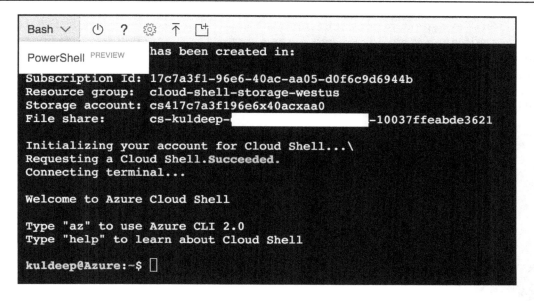

We will be utilizing this Azure Cloud Shell in the subsequent chapters.

Azure Functions console

You can navigate to the Azure Functions console in the Azure Portal by clicking on **All Services** in the left-hand menu, and from the window that pops up, searching for `Function` in the text box and selecting **Function Apps**. Then, you will be taken to the homepage of Azure **Function Apps**:

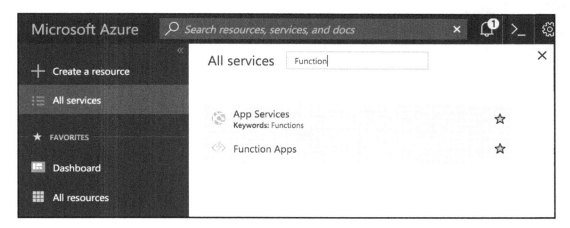

As we don't have any Functions at the moment, you will not see any Functions listed on that screen. If you had already created Azure Functions, then you will see them over in the Function Apps, and you can select the Function that you want to look at details for. We will come back to this again in later sections to look at how this page looks when you have Functions that have been created. Once you have selected Function Apps from the list, it will be automatically added to the Favorites in the left-hand menu:

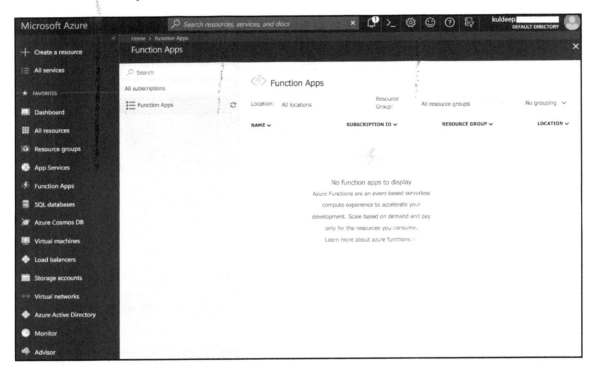

If you already had Azure Function Apps, then the dashboard will look like the following screenshot. It will include:

- List of Function Apps
- Functions that are part of a Function App
- Proxies that are part of a Function App
- Slots that are part of a Function App

We will learn more about all of these in the next chapters:

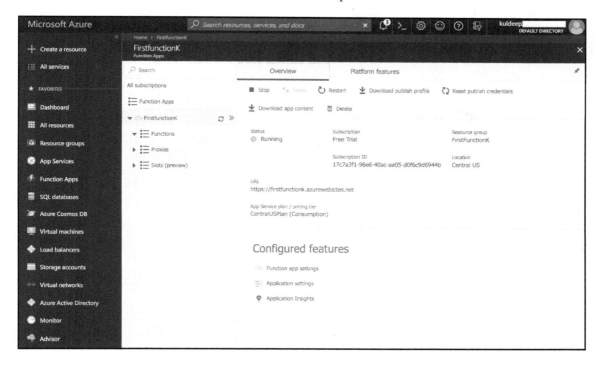

The Function Apps console also shows and lets you manage:

- The HTTP triggers associated with Functions
- Monitoring dashboards for Functions
- Associating state for Functions, along with setting Host and Function Keys

Configuring Azure Functions

So far, we have learned what an Azure Function is, looked at the features that Azure Functions offer, and also looked at the Azure Console along with the Function Apps Console. In this section, we will learn about the different configuration options that are available for Azure Functions. We will be creating Azure Functions in the later chapters; for this section, I will be focusing on the different configuration options that are available for Azure Functions.

Within Azure, there is a higher level construct for Azure Functions called `Function App`. An Azure Function App is one that generates and provides the execution context for Functions that are part of the Azure Function App. The configuration settings applied to an Azure Function App will be applied to all the functions that belong to a given Azure Function App. Let's look at different ways of configuring Azure Function Apps.

Function app settings

For a given Function App, using the **Settings** tab you can configure the different settings. Let's look at some of the settings of a Function App that can be configured.

Runtime

The `runtime` version of the Azure Function App is what is used by the Azure Worker node to run your Azure Function app.

The current Azure Function runtime (version 2.0) supports the following language runtimes:

- Node.js: JavaScript
- C# (both scripting and precompiled)
- F#
- Java

There are additional languages that Azure Functions support as experimental, and you can find the list of experimental languages, along with the supported languages in different Azure Functions runtimes, at this page: `https://docs.microsoft.com/en-us/azure/azure-functions/supported-languages`.

The current Azure Function runtime is also built on .NET Core 2.0 with cross-platform support, which allows the .NET Core to run on macOS, Windows, and Linux:

Overview   Platform features   ⟨⟩   Function app settings ✖

Application settings
Manage application settings

Runtime version
Runtime version: 2.0.11857.0 (beta)

⚠ **Cannot Upgrade with Existing Functions**
    Major version upgrades can introduce breaking changes to languages and bindings. When upgrading major versions of the runtime, consider creating a new function app and migrate your functions to this new app.

You can learn more about Azure Functions runtimes at `https://github.com/Azure/azure-functions-host/wiki/Azure-Functions-Runtime-2.0-Overview`.

Deployment slots

The next setting that you can configure in the Functions app is Deployment Slots. At the time of writing (June 2018), it is still in **Preview** mode. Deployment Slots provide the ability for developers to slot or stage a version of a Function App to be the production version. That particular version of the Function app can be made the production version with a simple managed swap action within the Azure Function App platform. You can learn more about Deployment Slots at `https://docs.microsoft.com/en-us/azure/app-service/web-sites-staged-publishing`.

Hosting plan

While creating the Function App, you can choose between Consumption and App Service Hosting plans. For some runtimes and programming languages within an Azure Function App, you don't have the option to choose between the two hosting plans.

Consumption plan

With the Consumption plan for your Azure Function app, you will pay for each execution and the Azure Function app will automatically scale based on load. However, you won't have better predictability with the plan around scale and cost, as it is dynamic and you won't be able to set a limit around the usage of the Function app.

App Service plan

If you want better predictability for your Azure Function App, you will choose the App Service plan and set a limit on how much of the platform the Azure Function App can use. You will typically set this in gigabytes per second. Once the limit is reached, the Azure Function App will stop and you would have to increase the spending quota associated with the Consumption plan before it starts to work again within a given day:

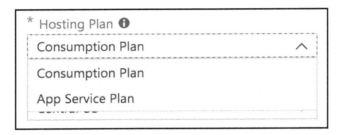

The Azure Functions Pricing page gives more details about these plans; you can access the page at http://azure.microsoft.com/pricing/details/functions/.

Authorization keys

An Azure Function app has HTTP triggers that let you use keys to add security to your Functions. There are multiple ways keys can be used within Azure Function apps. Webhooks can use these to add authorization to requests and you can enforce a HTTP trigger for a Function requiring these API keys. Keys are managed as part of your Azure Function app and are stored at rest.

There are two types of key that you can set on an Azure Function App:

- **Host keys**: These keys are shared by all functions within an Azure Function app. When these Host keys are used as an API key, they allow access to any function within the function app.
- **Function keys**: Function keys apply only to the specific functions under which they are defined. When Function keys are used as an API key, they only allow access to that one function instead of all the functions within Azure Function.

Each key is named for reference, and there is a default key (named `default`) at the function and host level. Function keys take precedence over host keys. When two keys are defined with the same name, the function key is always used.

The host key named `_master` cannot be deleted or revoked. It is used for administrative access to the Azure Functions runtime APIs and can be accessed by setting the `"authLevel": "admin"` header to the request that you make to the Azure Function HTTP trigger call.

At the Azure Functions App level (there could be multiple Azure Functions that are part of a single Azure Functions App), you can set and manage only the Host Keys:

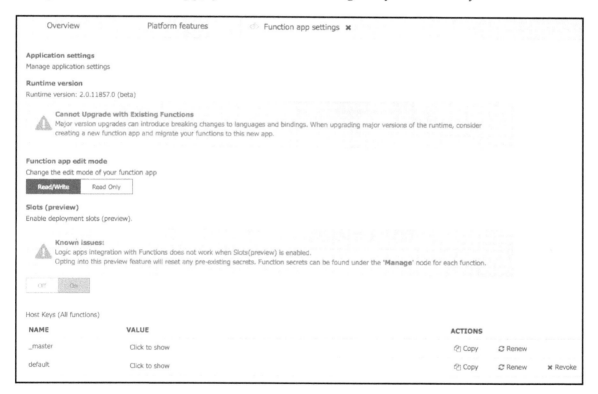

On a Function, you can configure both **Function Keys** and **Host keys** as shown next. If both Function keys and Host keys share the same name for the key, then at the Function level, the Function keys take precedence, and the key defined at the Function level will be used:

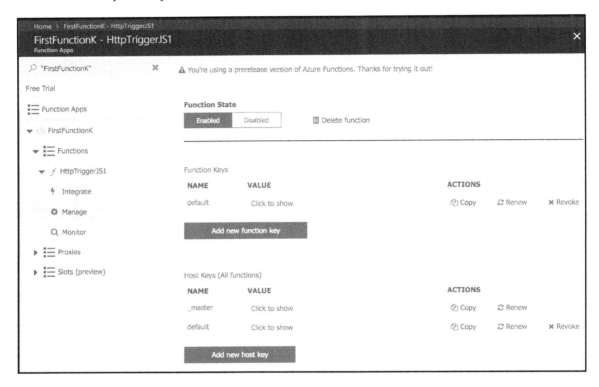

Platform features

Azure Function Apps are run and maintained with the Azure App Service platform, and they have access to many services that are part of the Azure App Service platform. The **Platform Features** tab in the Azure Function App is where you can see the features from the Azure App Service platform that you can leverage in your Azure Function apps:

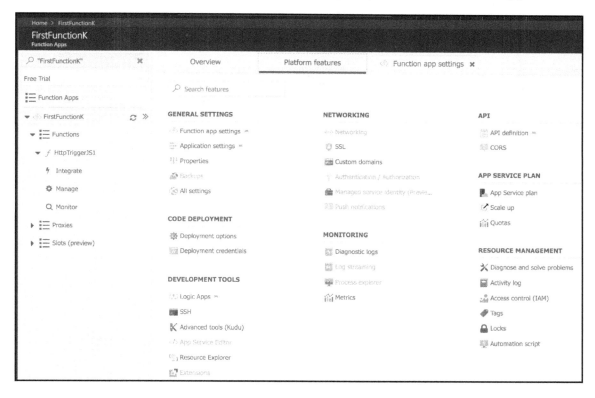

Let's look at some of the Platform Features that we can use.

Application settings

In the **Application settings** for Azure Function app, you can configure these settings:

- **Always On**
- **HTTP Version**
- **Affinity Cookie**
- App Settings
- Connection Strings:

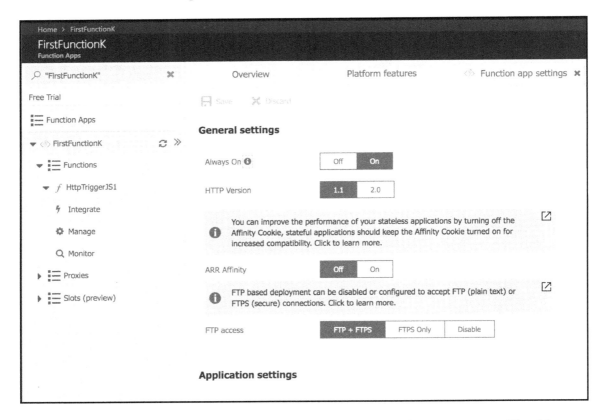

If you recall, we discussed cold start issues with FaaS in serverless computing. The **Always On** setting in the **Functions App Settings** helps to overcome this issue for Azure Functions. With that turned on, Azure will make sure to have the Function App always loaded, even when it is goes idle after a period of time. This should typically be turned on only when you know that the Azure Function App is going to get steady traffic.

SSH

The Azure Function App provides you with an option to work with your Function App by providing access to a command line shell. With the console, you have access to common command line tools to interact with file creation, navigation, and directory creation. You have access to execution scripts as well through the Console that the Azure Function App provides.

This works through the browser and you don't necessarily have direct access to the underlying system. Based on the type of OS you selected for the Azure Function when you created it, you will either get a Bash-based Linux shell or a PowerShell-based Windows Shell to interact with your function:

Kudu – Advanced tools

Azure App Service provides you with Kudu, which is a set of advanced tools for App Service that give you access to administer your Azure Function App. Using Kudu, you can:

- Manage app settings
- Get system information
- Manage Environment variables
- HTTP headers that are being used
- Site extensions
- Server variables

For any given Azure Function App (as an Azure Function app name is unique across all Azure Accounts), you can access Kudu using your browser by navigating to the SCM endpoint at `https://<yourfunctionappname>.scm.azurewebsites.net/`:

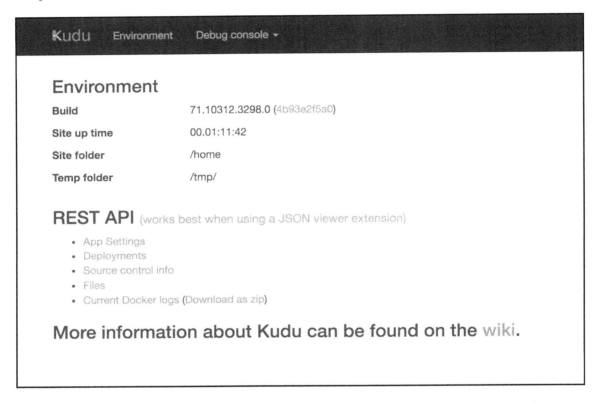

In Kudu, you also have access to the Debug Console using `Bash or Powershell`. Once you are inside the Bash Debug Console, you can debug and investigate why something is not working with your Azure App right from the browser itself. You can also upload files for further debugging and troubleshooting.

You can learn more about Kudu at `https://github.com/projectkudu/kudu/wiki`. It is an open source solution.

API Definition

An Azure Function App also provides you with an option to upload an API Definition using Swagger (`https://swagger.io/`) 2.0 metadata that describes your API. This is used for the HTTP triggers that are defined for each of your Functions which are part of the Azure Function App. You can also define a single Function Proxy that will work across all your Functions within the Function app. We will learn more about the Function Proxy in later chapters:

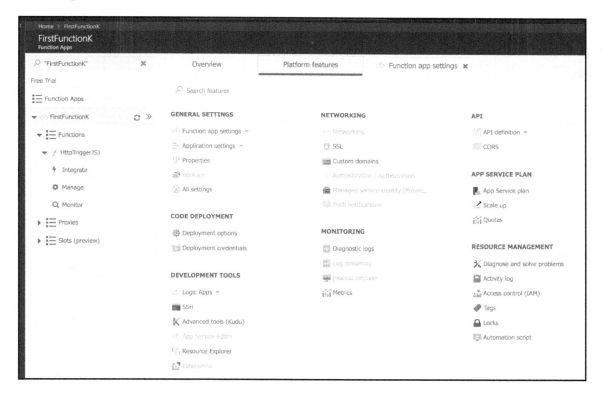

There are many other configuration settings that you can apply on the Azure Function App platform, such as specifying the amount of memory that is required for your Functions and the execution duration for the Functions. We will learn more about these during subsequent chapters, where we will be creating our first Serverless app on the Azure platform.

Summary

In this chapter, we learned what Azure Functions and an Azure Function App are. We looked at the features that Azure Function Apps provide, and we also learned about the integrations that it has with other Azure Service offerings. We then learned about how to create a free Azure account that we can use for our exercises. We explored the Azure portal, and we also learned a little bit about the Azure Function App console. We then learned about different configuration options that are available for Azure Functions, along with the tooling that Azure provides for debugging Azure Functions.

8
Triggers and Bindings for Azure Functions

In the previous chapter, we learned what Microsoft Azure Functions are. In this chapter, we will learn how to invoke Azure Functions from other Azure services and the different types of triggers that are available to invoke Azure Functions. We will also learn about the differences between Azure Function Triggers and Azure Function Bindings. We will then learn about Azure Blob storage integration with Azure Functions, HTTP, and Webhook Triggers for Azure Functions, and timer-based triggers.

In this chapter, we will cover these topics:

- How do Azure Functions get invoked?
- Azure Function triggers and bindings
- Azure Function integrations with Azure services
- Details of Azure Function integrations:
    - Azure Blob storage
    - Azure Cosmos DB
    - Azure Event Grid
    - HTTP and WebHook Triggers
    - Timer-based triggers

Azure Function triggers and bindings

Azure Function trigger outlines on how an Azure Function should be invoked or triggered. In Azure, a function can only have one trigger. Triggers in Azure Function have data, and that is usually the payload that invokes the Azure Function.

Bindings for an Azure Function are both input and output. They are a declarative way of sending and receiving data from an Azure Function. Your Azure Function can have multiple input bindings and output bindings. Bindings for Azure Functions are optional.

With the help of triggers and bindings, you don't have to hardcode any data or details of what you are going to interact with in your Azure Functions. With input binding, your Azure Function will receive the input data in the form of function parameters. Once you have processed the data within your Azure Function, you can send the data back, using output binding, with the `out` parameter object.

You can define triggers and bindings for an Azure Function using the `function.json` file. The Azure Portal provides a UI to modify and configure triggers and bindings, but you can also navigate to the Advanced editor and edit the `function.json` file yourself:

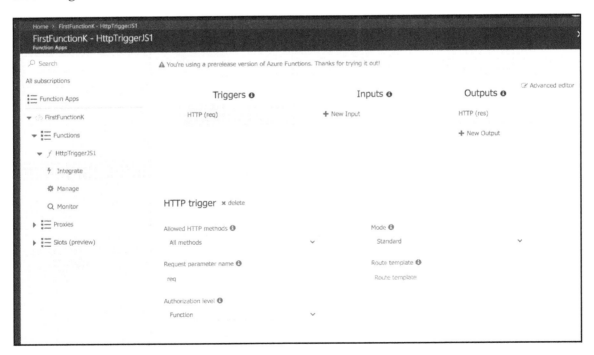

The preceding screenshot shows an option to edit the triggers and bindings, both as input and output. As mentioned earlier, if you click on the **Advanced** editor on the same page, you can edit `function.json` using an editor:

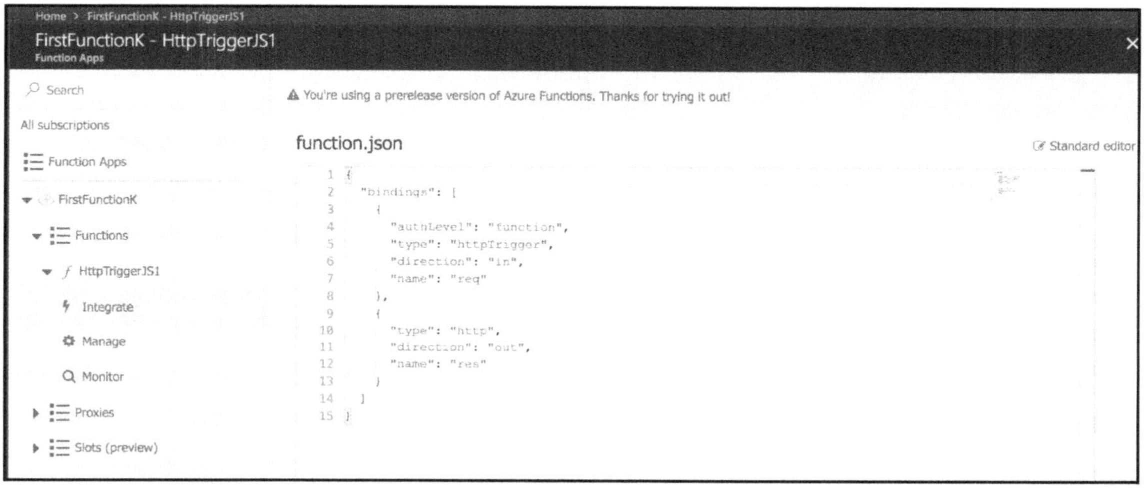

Example binding and trigger

Let's look at how a binding and trigger will look like in `function.json`. For this example, let's assume that your Azure Function will write a new row to Azure Table storage whenever a message is received in Azure Queue storage. The way to accomplish this is by creating a trigger on Azure Queue storage to call your Azure Functions and define an output binding for Azure Table storage so that the message from the queue is written to Azure Table storage.

Here, the `function.json` file for this example will be:

```
{
  "bindings": [
  {
  "name": "cart",
  "type": "queueTrigger",
  "direction": "in",
  "queueName": "cartItems",
  "connection": "MY_STORAGE_SETTING"
  },
  {
  "name": "$return",
```

```
"type": "table",
"direction": "out",
"tableName": "cartItems",
"connection": "MY_TABLE_STORAGE_SETTING"
 }
 ]
}
```

You can also find this `function.json` at `https://github.com/PacktPublishing/Hands-On-Serverless-Computing/blob/master/Triggers-and-Bindings-for-Azure-Functions/sample-function.json`.

Let's look at the content of this `function.json` file. The first element in it is the trigger from Azure Queue storage, along with the direction of the trigger, which, in this case, is `in`. Within the same element, you can also see the name of the queue, which, in this case, is `cartItems`. The second element in the bindings file is an output binding, which in this case is Azure Table storage, defined by `"type": "table"`, and then the name of the Azure Table storage, which, in this case, is `cartItems`.

Here is a sample Node.js—based Azure Function, which consumes the preceding `function.json` bindings file:

```
module.exports = function (context, cartItems) {
  order.PartitionKey = "Orders";
  order.RowKey = generateRandomCartId();

  context.done(null, cartItems);
};

function generateRandomCartId() {
  return Math.random().toString(40).substring(3, 18) +
  Math.random().toString(40).substring(3, 18);
}
```

You can also find this code at `https://github.com/PacktPublishing/Hands-On-Serverless-Computing/blob/master/Triggers-and-Bindings-for-Azure-Functions/sample.function-json-index.js`.

Now that we have learned what Azure Function triggers and bindings are, let's look at which Azure services support triggers and which Azure services support input and output bindings for Azure Functions.

For more information on triggers, visit `https://docs.microsoft.com/en-us/azure/azure-functions/functions-triggers-bindings`.

Azure services–triggers and bindings

Let's look at each Azure service that supports either triggers or bindings with Azure Functions. We will look at each Azure service one at time, and look at what it supports. Let's start with Azure Blob storage.

Azure Blob storage

Azure Blob storage is scalable storage for unstructured data. It can support storage capacities up to exabytes with massive amounts of scalability. Azure Blob storage can store billions of objects in different tiers, such as hot, cool, and archive. The tiers are determined by how often you access the data. You can store any type of data in Azure Blob storage, such as images, audio, videos, documents, and many more, all at cost-effective pricing.

You can learn more about Azure Blob storage at `https://azure.microsoft.com/en-us/services/storage/blobs/`.

Azure Blob storage supports triggers and input and output bindings for Azure Functions.

Trigger

The Azure Blob storage trigger for Azure Functions will start a function whenever a new or updated blob is detected in storage. Whatever changes happened in blob storage are provided as an input to the Azure Function.

You can also leverage Azure Event Grid's (`https://docs.microsoft.com/en-us/azure/event-grid/overview`) support for blob events and use that to start Azure Function whenever changes are detected with a publisher, which, in this case, is Azure Blob storage.

An example `function.json` binding for an Azure Blob storage trigger will look as follows:

```
{
"disabled": false,
"bindings": [{
```

```
"name": "kuldeepsBlob",
"type": "kuldeepsblobTrigger",
"direction": "in",
"path": "bookChapters/{chapter}",
"connection": "MyStorageSetting"
}]
}
```

On Azure Portal's **Azure Function App** page, you can add trigger integration for Azure Blob storage with the following steps:

1. Select your Azure Function from the **Function Apps** page
2. Navigate to **Integrate**
3. Click on **New Trigger**
4. Choose **Azure Blob Storage**

The preceding steps can be seen in the following screenshot:

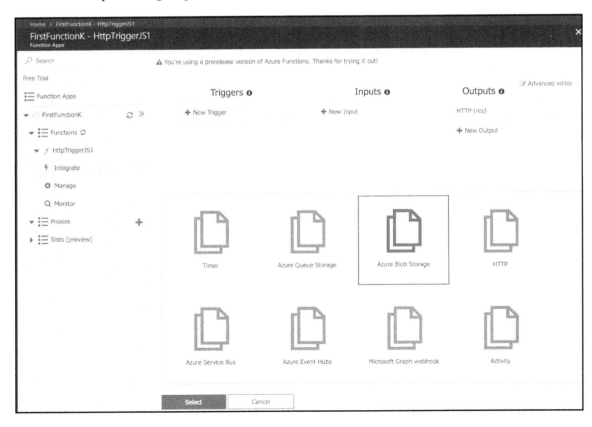

5. Click **Select** at the bottom
6. On the next page, add the details for your **Azure Blob Storage trigger**
7. Save the trigger settings for the Azure Function

The preceding steps can be seen in the following screenshot:

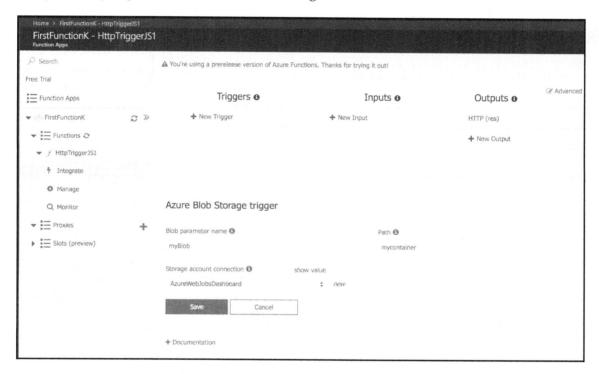

Bindings

Azure Blob storage supports both input and output bindings for Azure Functions. Let's look at an example of a bindings file that defines both input and output bindings. The following example has data coming from Azure Queue and Output Bindings as Azure Blob storage:

```
{
"bindings": [{
"queueName": "cartItems",
"connection": "MyStorageSetting",
"name": "cartItem",
"type": "queueTrigger",
```

```
      "direction": "in"
      },
      {
      "name": "kuldeepsInputBlob",
      "type": "blob",
      "path": "bookChapters/{queueTrigger}",
      "connection": "MyStorageSetting",
      "direction": "in"
      },
      {
      "name": "kuldeepsOutputBlob",
      "type": "blob",
      "path": "bookChapters/{queueTrigger}-Copy",
      "connection": "MyStorageSetting",
      "direction": "out"
      }
      ],
      "disabled": false
      }
```

This binding sample is also available at `https://github.com/PacktPublishing/Hands-On-Serverless-Computing/blob/master/Triggers-and-Bindings-for-Azure-Functions/azure-blob-storage-bindings.json`.

You can also use Azure Portal to add input and output bindings for Azure Functions. You can follow the steps listed here to add them through Azure Portal:

1. Select your Azure Function from the **Function Apps** page
2. Navigate to **Integrate**
3. Click on **New Input**
4. Choose **Azure Blob Storage**

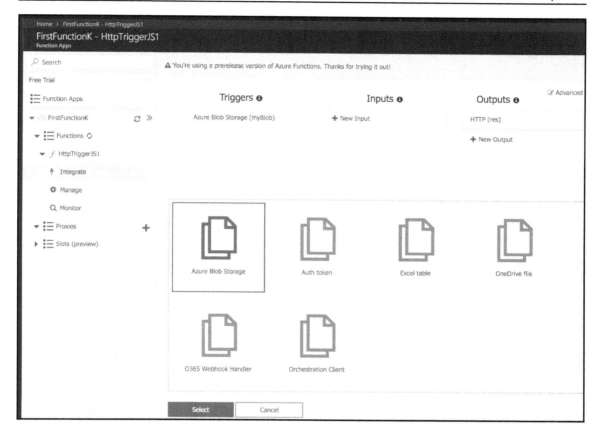

5. Click `Select` at the bottom

6. On the next page, add the details for your **Azure Blob Storage input**

7. Save the trigger settings for the Azure Function

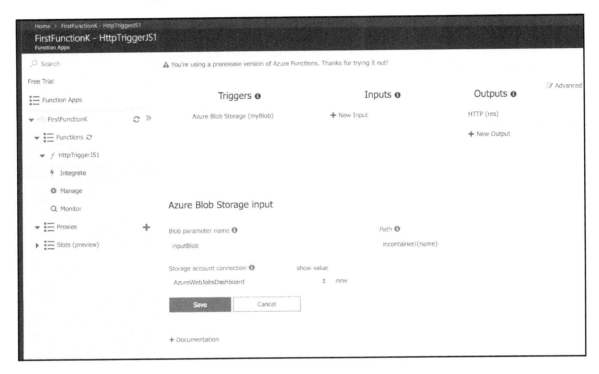

You can learn more about the Azure Blob storage triggers and bindings for Azure Functions at `https://docs.microsoft.com/en-us/azure/azure-functions/functions-bindings-storage-blob`.

Azure Cosmos DB

Azure Cosmos DB is a globally distributed, multi-model database service for massively scalable applications with low latency requirements, and has support for NoSQL natively. It has been built by Microsoft Azure from scratch, with global distribution and horizontal scaling in mind. It elastically scales the throughput that is required by these applications and also elastically scales the storage that is required globally. You will only pay for what you need with Azure Cosmos DB.

You can learn more about Azure Cosmos DB at `https://azure.microsoft.com/en-us/services/cosmos-db/`.

Azure Cosmos DB supports triggers and input and output bindings for Azure Functions.

Trigger

The Azure Cosmos DB Trigger listens to the messages sent to the Azure Cosmos DB change feed for inserts and updates to data across partitions. The change feed doesn't publish deletes; it only does inserts and updates.

Let's look at how we can create a trigger for Cosmos DB through Azure Portal:

1. Select your Azure Function from the **Function Apps** page
2. Navigate to **Integrate**
3. Click on **New Trigger**
4. Choose **Azure Cosmos DB**

The preceding steps can be seen in the following screenshot:

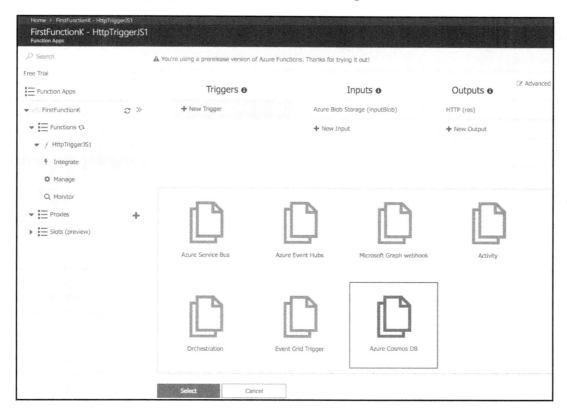

5. Click **Select** at the bottom
6. On the next page, follow the instructions to provide the necessary information for Cosmos DB:
   - Database name
   - Collection name
   - Collection name for lease

This can be seen in the following screenshot:

You can learn more about Azure Cosmos DB triggers and bindings for Azure Functions at https://docs.microsoft.com/en-us/azure/azure-functions/functions-bindings-cosmosdb-v2.

Have a look at this article as well, which talks about serverless database computing with Azure Cosmos DB using Azure Functions: https://docs.microsoft.com/en-us/azure/cosmos-db/serverless-computing-database.

Azure Event Grid

Azure Event Grid is an Azure service that sends HTTP requests as notifications, which contain events that happen in the publisher. In this case, this is an Azure service. Azure Event Grid allows you to choose the Azure service or resource that you want to be notified about, and you will need to provide a Webhook endpoint or some sort of event handler to notify you of the event that happened in the service you wanted to be notified about.

You can learn more about Event Grid at `https://docs.microsoft.com/en-us/azure/event-grid/overview`.

Event Grid only support triggers with Azure Functions. It doesn't support input or output bindings with Azure Functions.

A sample `function.json` binding file for Event Grid trigger will look like this. If you look at the content of the file, it has the `type` set as `eventGridTrigger`, along with the name of the Event Grid that is going to trigger the Azure Function:

```
{
  "bindings": [
  {
  "type": "eventGridTrigger",
  "name": "eventGrid10Event",
  "direction": "in"
  }
  ],
  "disabled": false
  }
```

Let's look at how we can create an Event Grid trigger from Azure Portal:

1. Select your Azure Function from the **Function Apps** page
2. Navigate to **Integrate**
3. Click on **New Trigger**
4. Choose **Event Grid Trigger**

The preceding steps can be seen in the following screenshot:

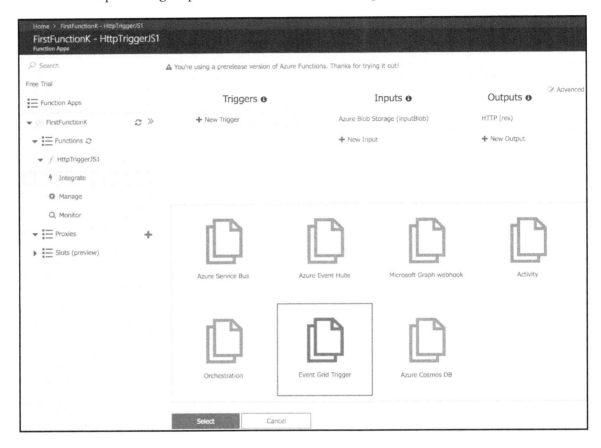

5. Click **Select** at the bottom
6. On the next page, enter the **Event Trigger parameter name**
7. Enter the **Event Grid Subscription URL**
8. Click on **Save**

The preceding steps can be seen in the following screenshot:

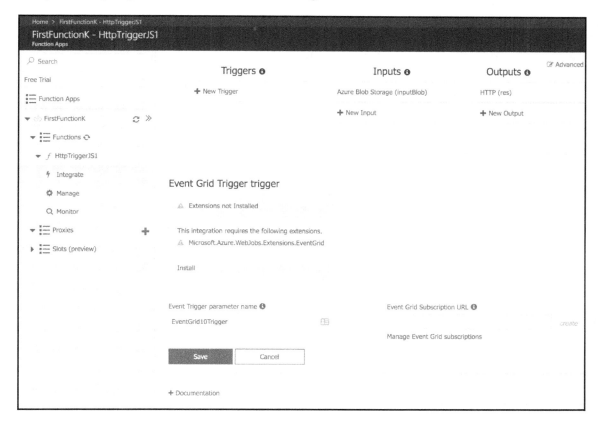

You can learn more about Azure Event Grid triggers for Azure Functions at `https://docs.microsoft.com/en-us/azure/azure-functions/functions-bindings-event-grid`.

HTTP and webhook bindings

Azure Functions support HTTP and WebHook bindings for both Triggers and Output Bindings. HTTP triggered Azure Functions doesn't support Input Bindings.

You can customize an HTTP trigger to respond to WebHooks. The Azure Functions webhook trigger will only accept a JSON payload and will only validate JSON. Azure Functions also support special versions of WebHook triggers, which make it easier to consume webhooks from providers such as Slack and GitHub.

HTTP trigger

Let's look at a sample `function.json` binding file for the HTTP trigger for Azure Functions. In the following bindings, you can see that the `type` is set to `httpTrigger`, which means that the trigger is HTTP, and the output binding is also set to HTTP, which means the output of the function is an HTTP request:

```
{
  "disabled": false,
  "bindings": [
  {
  "authLevel": "function",
  "name": "req",
  "type": "httpTrigger",
  "direction": "in",
  "methods": [
  "post"
  ]
  },
  {
  "name": "$return",
  "type": "http",
  "direction": "out"
  }
  ]
  }
```

Let's look at how to create an HTTP Trigger using Azure Portal:

1. Select your Azure Function from the **Function Apps** page
2. Navigate to **Integrate**
3. Click on **New Trigger**
4. Choose **HTTP**

The preceding steps can be seen in the following screenshot:

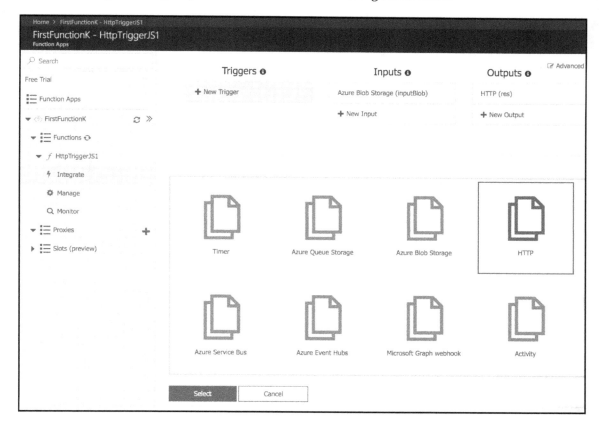

5. Click **Select** at the bottom
6. On the next page, select the HTTP methods that will be used to trigger the Azure Function
7. Enter the **Request parameter name**
8. Select **Standard** as the mode
9. Click **Save**

The preceding steps can be seen in the following screenshot:

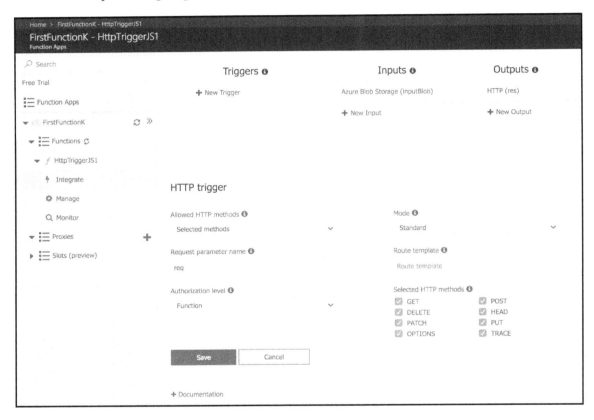

With this, an HTTP Trigger on the Azure Function will be available.

Webhook trigger

Let's look at a sample `function.json` binding file for the `webhook` trigger for Azure Functions. In the following bindings file, the type of trigger is set as `httpTrigger`. However, to denote that this trigger is a special type of HTTP trigger, the `webHookType` attribute is also added to the trigger definition in the bindings file. In the following example, the `webHookType` is set to `slack`:

```json
{
  "bindings": [
  {
  "type": "httpTrigger",
  "direction": "in",
  "webHookType": "slack",
  "name": "req"
  },
  {
  "type": "http",
  "direction": "out",
  "name": "res"
  }
  ],
  "disabled": false
  }
```

Let's look at how to create a `WebHook Trigger` using Azure Portal:

1. Select your Azure Function from the **Function Apps** page
2. Navigate to **Integrate**
3. Click on **New Trigger**
4. Choose **HTTP**
5. Click **Select** at the bottom
6. On the next page, select the HTTP methods that will be used to trigger the Azure Function
7. Enter the **Resource parameter name**
8. Select **WebHook** as the mode
9. Select **Slack** as the **WebHookType**
10. Click **Save**

The preceding steps can be seen in the following screenshot:

With this, a WebHook Trigger on the Azure Function will be available.

You can learn more about HTTP and WebHook Triggers for Azure Functions at `https://docs.microsoft.com/en-us/azure/azure-functions/functions-bindings-http-webhook`.

Timer trigger

You can set up Timer-based triggers for Azure Functions. The benefit of Timer-based Triggers is that they help you to ensure that you run an Azure Function on a fixed schedule that you define.

Let's look at a sample `function.json` binding file for the Timer trigger for Azure Functions. In the following bindings file, you can see that the schedule is set to run the Azure Function at 15:00 every day. The schedule utilizes the `cron` format, and you can learn more about this at `http://www.nncron.ru/help/EN/working/cron-format.htm`:

```
{
  "schedule": "0 */15 * * * *",
  "name": "my15thHourTimer",
  "type": "timerTrigger",
  "direction": "in"
}
```

Let's look at how to create a `Timer` trigger using Azure Portal:

1. Select your Azure Function from the **Function Apps** page
2. Navigate to **Integrate**
3. Click on **New Trigger**

4. Choose **Timer**

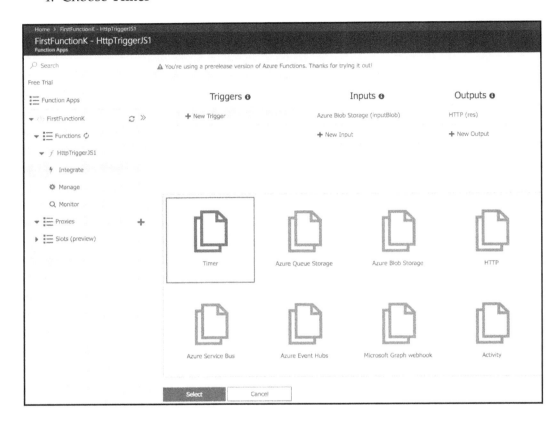

5. Click **Select** at the bottom
6. On the next page, enter the name of the parameter
7. Enter the cron format for the **Schedule** for the Timer Trigger
8. Click on **Save** to save the changes

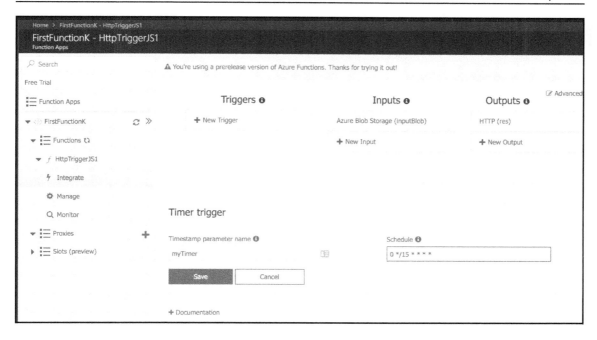

You can learn more about the Timer Trigger at `https://docs.microsoft.com/en-us/azure/azure-functions/functions-bindings-timer`.

Summary

In this chapter, we learned about Azure Function Triggers and Bindings, and the different triggers and bindings that are available for Azure Functions. We learned about the triggers and bindings for Azure Services such as Blob Storage, Cosmos DB, and Event Grid. We also learned about HTTP Triggers, Webhook Triggers, and Timer triggers for Azure Functions. In the next chapter, we will be writing our first serverless apps to be run in a Microsoft Azure environment.

9

Your First Serverless Application on Azure

In this chapter, we will learn how to write serverless applications that will run on Microsoft Azure using Node.js. We will learn about creating an HTTP trigger for Azure Functions. We will also learn about Azure Functions Core Tools so that you are able to create Azure Functions locally on your workstation and test the Azure Functions locally before we publish them to your Azure subscription.

There are multiple ways of creating serverless apps on the Azure Functions platform; I will cover two of those methods as part of this chapter:

- Azure portal
    - We will learn how to create an Azure Function App
    - We will learn how to create an Azure Function
    - We will learn how to create an HTTP trigger for the function
    - We will test the Azure Function through the Azure portal and also using Postman
    - We will configure the function through the Azure portal
- Local workstation
    - We will learn how to create an Azure Function app using Azure Functions Core Tools and Visual Studio Code
    - We will learn how to create an Azure Function locally using Azure Functions Core Tools
    - We will learn how to create an HTTP trigger for the function on your local workstation
    - We will test the Azure Function by making HTTP calls to the endpoint of the function that is running locally
    - We will publish the locally created Azure Function App to Azure Subscription

Technical requirements

For deploying and testing the serverless app that we will develop in this chapter, you will need an Azure account and a subscription. Microsoft Azure offers 12 months of free services (there are limits to how much you can use) and also gives you $200 credit (for 30 days) to get started with Microsoft Azure. The free account also provides you with 25+ always free services.

You can sign up for a Microsoft Azure account at `https://azure.microsoft.com/en-us/free/`.

To be able to create a Microsoft Azure account, you will need a Microsoft account as well. Once you have created the Azure account, a free plan subscription is automatically created for you so that you can start building apps to run in the Microsoft Azure Cloud environment.

Once you have access to the Azure portal, we can start building our serverless apps for the Azure environment. For this chapter, you also need to make sure you have installed the tools that are listed in `Chapter 2`, *Development Environment, Tools, and SDKs*.

For the code files, refer to the following GitHub link:

```
https://github.com/PacktPublishing/Hands-On-Serverless-Computing/blob/master/
Your-first-Serverless-application-on-Azure/first-azure-function.js
```

Your first serverless app (using the Azure portal)

In this section, we will be learning how to create an Azure function app through the Azure portal. We will explore some of the settings that are associated with Cloud Functions. We will learn about creating HTTP trigger-based Azure Functions through the portal. We will learn about proxies as well for Azure Functions. We will also look at the automation script associated with the Function app that you can use to create other functions using Azure Resource Manager. We will also look at the **Application Insights** services Microsoft Azure offers for Azure Functions.

Let's look at accessing the Azure Functions Console using the portal.

You can navigate to the Azure Functions Console in the Azure portal by:

1. Clicking on **All Services** in the left-hand menu
2. From the window that pops out, search for Functions in the text box
3. Select **Function Apps**
4. You will be taken to the home page of Azure Function Apps:

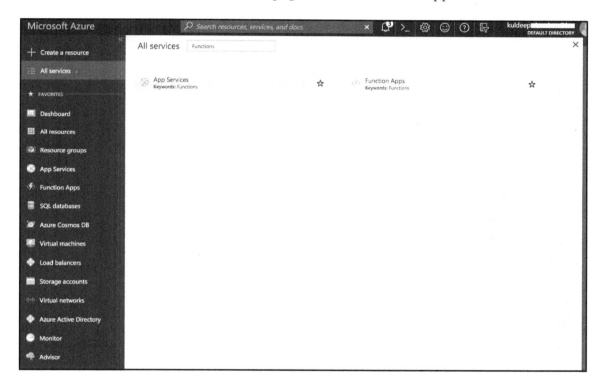

As we don't have any functions at the moment, you will not see any functions listed on that screen. If you had already created Azure Functions, then you would see them on the page, and you could select the function that you want to look in detail. We will come back to this again in later sections to see how this page looks when you have functions that have already been created. Once you have selected **Function Apps** from the list, it will automatically get added to the **Favorites** in the left-hand menu, as in the next screenshot:

If you already had Azure Function Apps, then the dashboard would include:

- A list of Function Apps
- Functions that are part of a Function App
- Proxies that are part of a Function App
- Slots that are part of a Function App

We will learn more about all of these in this chapter.

Let's look at creating our first Azure Function App.

You can create an Azure Function App in the Azure portal by:

1. Clicking on **Create a Resource** in the left-hand menu
2. From the window that pops out, selecting **Serverless Function App** as shown in the following screenshot:

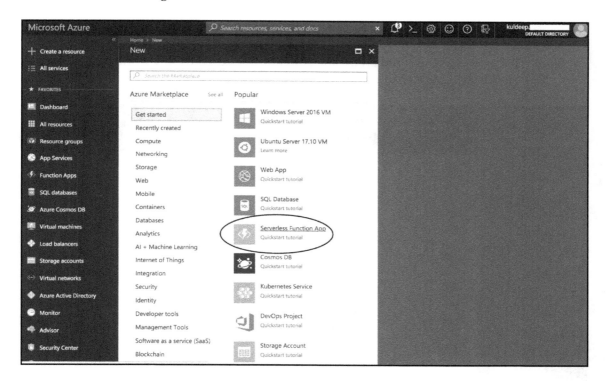

In the **Create Function App** dialog window:

1. Enter a name for your Azure Function App; the name has to be unique across all Azure accounts and the console will automatically tell you whether it is unique or not. For example, I entered the name of the function as FirstAzureFunctionByKuldeep so that the name will be unique. However, I wouldn't recommend naming production functions with your name in it, but rather map it to a business problem that you are trying to solve using functions.
2. Then, either choose **Use existing** resource group or choose **Create new** resource group.

3. For the **OS**, I chose **Linux**. You can choose **Windows** or **Docker** based on your preference. Keep in mind that the subsequent options might change while creating the Function app based on the operating system that you choose.

4. Either choose **Use existing** storage or **Create new** storage so that Azure Functions can use it to store artifacts, metadata, and other stuff.

5. You can turn on **Application Insights**. We will learn about **Application Insights** later in this chapter.

6. Once you have entered all the input fields, click on the **Create** button as shown in the following screenshot:

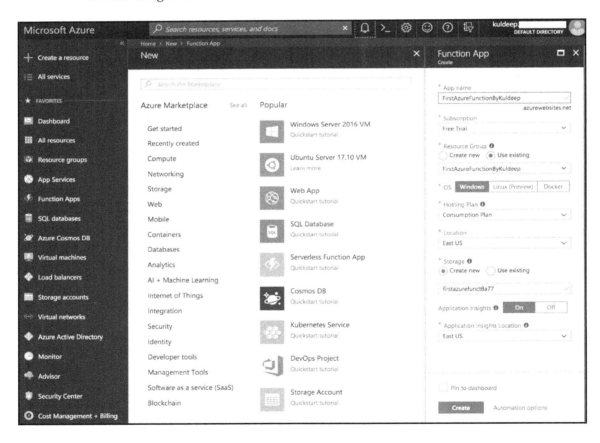

Once you have clicked on the **Create** button, the Azure Function App environment will take a few minutes to provision the resources that are needed. Once the app is created, you will be notified in the **Notifications** section and using that, you can access your resources as well.

Once the Function App is created, when you navigate to the Azure Function App console, you will automatically see the new Function App in there, as shown in the following screenshot:

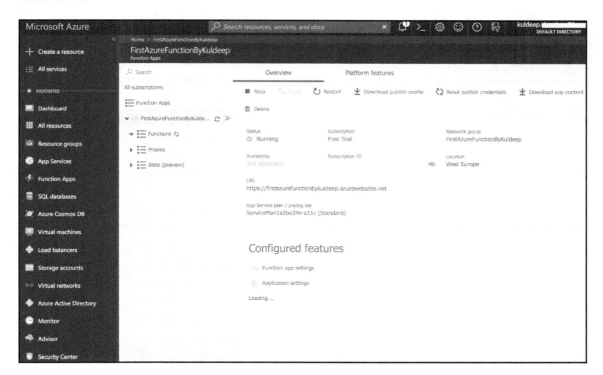

So far, we haven't created an Azure Function that performs a particular compute operation. We have created a Function App, not necessarily an Azure Function itself.

Let's look at how to create an Azure Function using the Azure portal.

Carry out the following steps in the Azure Function Apps console:

1. Select the Function App that you just created
2. Under **Functions** within the Function App, click on the + button or select **New function**:

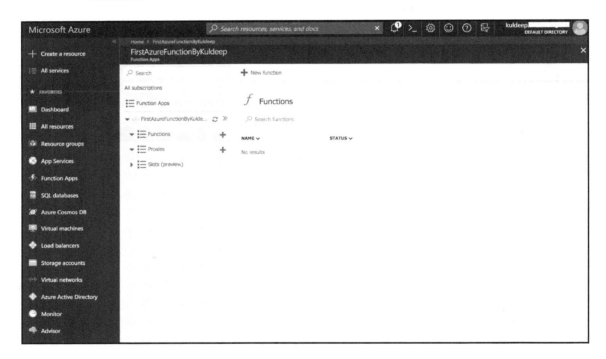

Creating an HTTP trigger-based function

So far, we have created an Azure Function app that could host multiple Azure Functions; let's look at creating an Azure Function with an HTTP trigger.

1. Select the Function App that you just created.
2. Under **Functions** within the Function App, click on the + button or select **New function**.

3. You will then be provided with options to create different types of Azure Function (**HTTP trigger**, **Timer Trigger**, and others).

4. Let's select **HTTP trigger** from the list of templates that are provided to you.
5. In the **New Function** dialog box, set the language as **JavaScript.**

6. Enter a **Name** for the Functio
7. Select **Authorization level** as **Anonymous** for now for ease of testing. However, I don't recommend this setting for your production functions. We will later learn about how to change this setting on the function.
8. Click on **Create** as shown in the following screenshot:

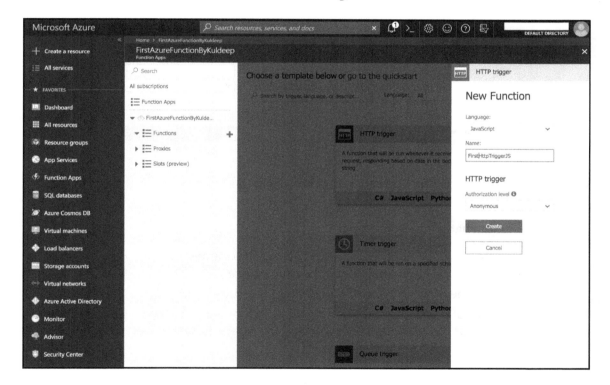

9. Once the function has been created, in the Function App console you will see the newly created function under the **Functions** list.

10. Once the function has been created, you will be automatically redirected to the index.js file that has been created for your function.

11. The source code in index.js will look like this:

```
module.exports = function (context, req) {
    context.log('HTTP trigger function is processing an incoming
request.');

    if (req.query.name || (req.body && req.body.name)) {
        context.res = {
            status: 200,
            body: "Hello World!, " + (req.query.name ||
req.body.name)
        };
    }
    else {
        context.res = {
            status: 400,
            body: "Please provide a name within the query string or
in the request body"
        };
    }
    context.done();
};
```

Once the function is created, you can make changes in the browser and test them in the browser itself.

Let's understand what the code is doing:

- The code is looking either for an HTTP query parameter named name, or it is looking for the name attribute in the request body
- If either one of them is found, it uses that to print Hello World!, <name>
- If neither of them is found, then it will print a message to the console stating that name needs to be sent in either through the query parameter or event body

Testing Azure Functions

Let's look at the how to make changes to the function that we just created and test the changes through the portal:

1. Navigate to the Azure Function App that we just created.
2. Select the Azure Function that we just created. It is an HTTP trigger-backed Azure Function.
3. From the list of functions, select the one to open the `index.js` file of your Azure Function.
4. Click on the **Run** button, shown in the following screenshot:

5. By clicking on the **Run** button, the Azure portal will automatically make an HTTP request to your Azure Function.

6. Once you click on the **Run** button, the test window opens up and shows the result of the test. In this case, you will see the following output as shown in the next screenshot :
   - 200 HTTP status code
   - "Hello World!, Azure"

There is also another way of testing an Azure Function with an HTTP trigger. You can get the URL to your Azure HTTP Function and with the URL in hand, you can use multiple HTTP test tools to send HTTP requests to that endpoint. Let's look at how we can do that using Postman.

Postman is a tool to test your HTTP-based APIs and is available for multiple operating systems. You can learn more about it and download the executable from https://www.getpostman.com/.

You can also use curl on your MacOS Terminal or on the Powershell terminal in Windows.

Let's look at how to get the URL of the function that we created:

1. Navigate to the Azure Function App that we just created.
2. Select the Azure Function that we just created. It is an HTTP trigger-backed Azure Function.
3. From the list of functions, select the function to open the `index.js` file of your Azure Function.
4. Click on the button with the name `</>` `Get function URL`, which is next to the **Run** button.
5. A window will pop up which will have the URL to your function.
6. Click on **Copy** to copy the URL, as follows:

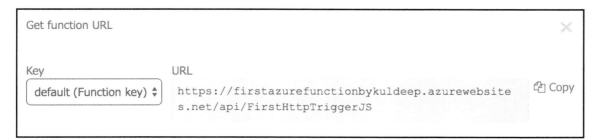

Once you have the URL, let's open Postman and send the request to the URL by appending `name` as a query string parameter. The URL that I was able to get for the function that I created is `https://firstazurefunctionbykuldeep.azurewebsites.net/api/FirstHttpTriggerJS`. To this URL, I will append a query string parameter, `?name=kuldeep`, and the response that I should see in Postman should be `Hello World!, Kuldeep`.

Let's test the Azure HTTP Function using Postman:

1. On your workstation, open the `Postman` app
2. Either select the **GET** or **POST** HTTP methods
3. Enter the copied URL into the **Enter request URL** text box
4. The URL in my case would be `https://firstazurefunctionbykuldeep.azurewebsites.net/api/FirstHttpTriggerJS?name=kuldeep`
5. Make sure you append `?name=<REPLACE WITH YOUR NAME>` to the URL that you copied from the Azure portal
6. Then, click on the **Send** button
7. In the response you get, you should receive a `200 HTTP` status code

8. You will see the response from the REST API with the message `Hello World!, <REPLACE WITH YOUR NAME>`

9. In my case, the response was `Hello World!, kuldeep`, as shown here:

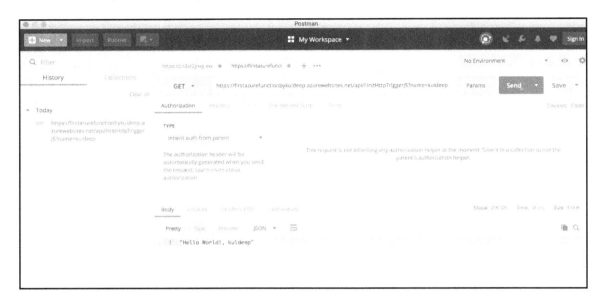

As mentioned earlier, you can also use `curl` on your MacOS Terminal or in the Powershell terminal on Windows to test the Azure HTTP function. There are many other tools that you can use to send HTTP requests.

Managing Azure Functions

In this section, let's look at configuring different settings that are available in Azure Functions and Azure Function App. We will look at triggers and bindings, and how to change the authorization level on the HTTP Trigger. We will also look at the function keys and host keys.

Triggers and bindings

If you recall, we learned about Azure Function's Triggers and bindings. You can manage the Triggers, and input and output bindings, for the function that we created earlier by click on the **Integrate** in the **Function** menu. As the function that we created is HTTP-based, the trigger is set to `HTTP(req)`.

An HTTP Triggered Azure Function won't have any input bindings; that is the reason it is left empty.

The output binding for the HTTP Triggered Azure Function is again HTTP with the `res` object.

You can change the parameter name for both `req` and `res` by clicking on a trigger or output bindings in the **Integrate** section, as shown in the following screenshot:

Authorization level

If you recall, when we were creating the function, we chose the **Authorization level** to be **anonymous** so that it will be easier for us to test the function. However, in practice using **anonymous** is not a recommended approach.

Let's look at how to change that setting to use the function keys and how the URL will change now we have set the **Authorization level** to **Function**:

1. Navigate to the Azure Function App that we just created.
2. Select the Azure Function that we just created. It is an HTTP trigger-backed Azure Function.
3. Click on the **Integrate** button, which is available in the Azure Function.
4. Select the HTTP trigger that was already created for the Azure Function.
5. In the HTTP trigger, there will be an option to change the authorization level and it will be currently set as **anonymous**.
6. We will change the authorization level to **Function** and save the trigger, as shown in the following screenshot:

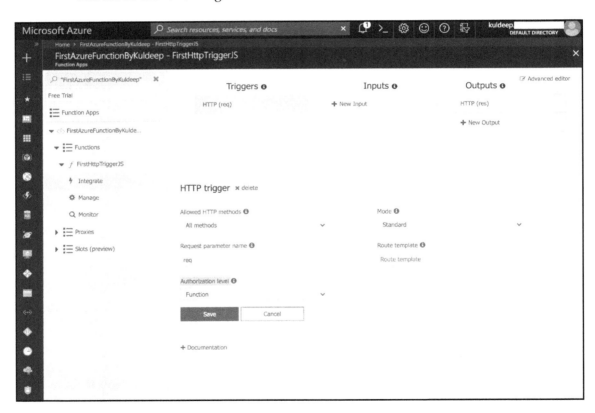

With the **Authorization level** set to **Function**, if you try to get the function URL, you will now see a new request parameter with `?code=` in it. The code here is the Function key defined for your Azure Function. We will learn about it in the next section.

Let's look at how the new URL looks by taking the following steps:

1. Navigate to the Azure Function App that we just created.
2. Select the Azure Function that we just created. It is an HTTP trigger-backed Azure Function.
3. From the list of functions, select the function to open the `index.js` file of your Azure Function.
4. Click on the button with the name **</> Get function URL**, which is next to the **Run** button.
5. A window will pop up, which will have the URL to your function.
6. Click on **Copy** to copy the URL.
7. The URL that I was able to get for the function that I created with the Function key added looks like this now:
   `https://firstazurefunctionbykuldeep.azurewebsites.net/api/FirstHttpTriggerJS?code=T9PTcZpcw1ouiEDa/KrxusxtbjSgjjJxFKH7/MsBPpAgRNPJ5WMRTA==.`

Function and host keys

In this previous chapter, we learned about function and host keys. Let's look at the values for the Function and Host keys for the function that we created just now. Host keys are set at the Azure Function app level, and function Keys are set at the Azure Function level itself.

You can access the function and host keys for the function using these steps:

1. Navigate to the Azure Function App that we just created.
2. Select the Azure Function that we just created. It is an HTTP trigger-backed Azure Function.
3. From the list of functions, select the function to open the `index.js` file of your Azure Function.
4. Click on the **Manage** button, which is available in the Azure Function.

5. Then, you will both see the function and host keys that are associated with the Azure Function, as shown in the following screenshot:

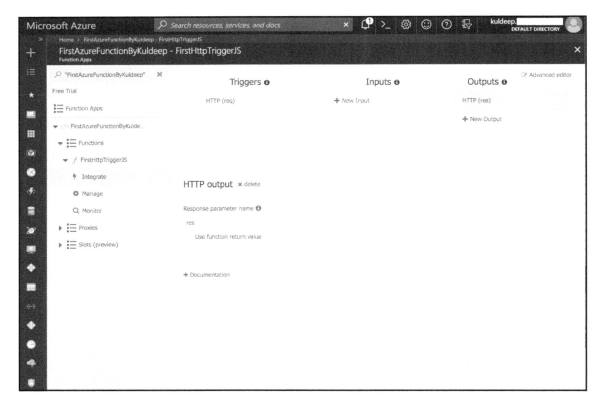

If you recall, when we set the **Authorization level** to **Function**, code was added to the Function URL. That code is nothing but the default Function Key that is available in your Function keys. Click on **Click to Show** and see the value that has been set for that key. In my case, it has been set as T9PTcZpcw1ouiEDa/KrxusxtbjSgjjJxFKH7/MsBPpAgRNPJ5WMRTA==, which is what was used earlier with the code query parameter in the URL that was generated: https://firstazurefunctionbykuldeep.azurewebsites.net/api/FirstHttpTrig gerJS?code=T9PTcZpcw1ouiEDa/KrxusxtbjSgjjJxFKH7/MsBPpAgRNPJ5WMRTA==

Note the following screenshot:

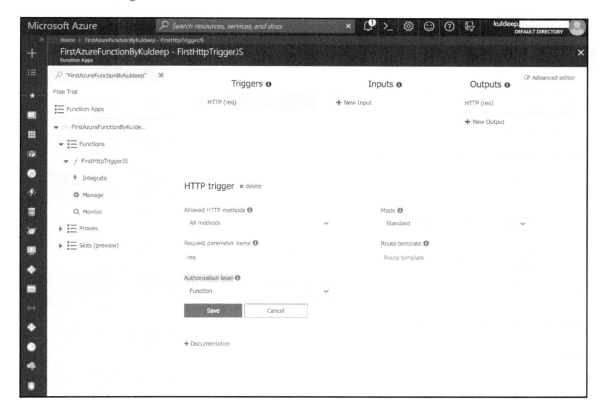

Monitoring your Azure Function

Microsoft Azure provides a service called Application Insights, through which you can gain insights into the applications through analytics and performance management. It can detect performance issues with your application. It can detect and diagnose errors and exceptions that are happening within your application. You can monitor any application that is running anywhere—public cloud, private cloud, and on-premises data centers. Application Insights has good integration built into Azure Function apps.

You can learn more about Application Insights at `https://azure.microsoft.com/en-us/services/application-insights/`.

If you recall, while creating the Azure Function App, I asked you to turn on Application Insights. That is the only thing that you need to turn on to integrate your Azure Function with Application Insights and to let it monitor and analyze your Azure Function.

Here's how you can access the Application Insights instance:

1. Navigate to the Azure Function App that we just created.
2. Select the Azure Function that we just created. It is an HTTP trigger-backed Azure Function.
3. From the list of functions, select the function to open the index.js file of your Azure Function.
4. Click on the **Monitor** button, which is available within the Azure Function.
5. In the page that renders after you click **Monitor**, you will see the last successful executions that happened for that Azure Function, along with links to navigate to the Application Insights instance that has been created for this Azure Function. note the following screenshot:

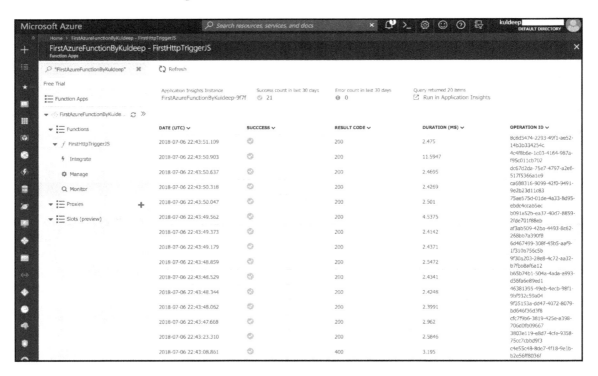

Click on the Application Insights instance and you will redirected to the Application Insights instance page, where you can find charts that have been created for your Azure Function. Some of the pre-built charts on the **Overview** dashboard are:

- Server Response Time
- Failed Requests
- Server Requests
- Availability

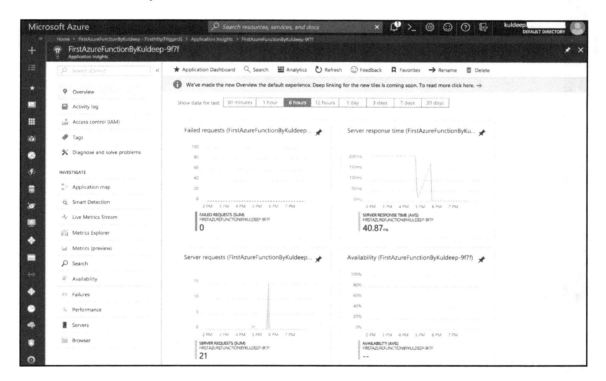

Application Insights also provides many other features that can help to better monitor, debug, and diagnose issues with your Azure Function. Application Insights also provides you with a Live Metrics Stream where you can see what is happening in real time with your application/Azure Function. Other features that Application Insights provides are:

- Application Map
- Smart Detection
- Analytics
- Metrics Explorer

- Performance
- Alerts
- Usage
- Search

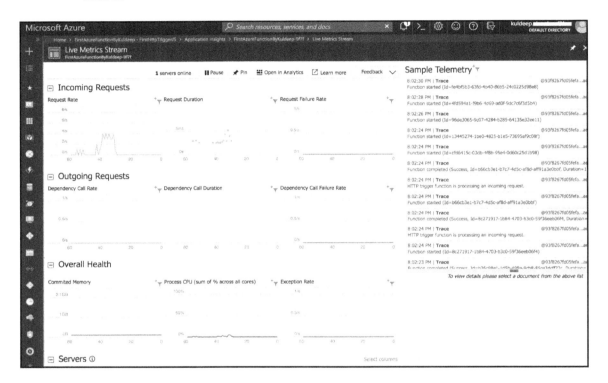

Function proxies

Azure Function proxies gives you the option to break your API into multiple endpoints and associate each endpoint to implement different Azure Functions so that your API also follows the microservice architecture pattern. For clients, you will still present one single API to interact with, but behind the scenes, different Azure Functions are operating at the same time.

You can create a function proxy like this:

1. Navigate to the Azure Function App that we just created within the Azure portal
2. Under **Proxies** within the Function App, click on the + button or select **New Proxy**
3. Specify the `Route template` and the associated HTTP methods
4. Give the Proxy a name
5. Click on **Create**

I'm not going to cover this topic in detail, as it is more advanced than just creating an Azure Function. You can learn more about Function Proxies at `https://docs.microsoft.com/en-us/azure/azure-functions/functions-proxies`.

Generating automation script

For the Azure Function App that we just created, we can generate the Automation script that you use to create or modify resources using Azure Resource Manager.

Let's quickly understand what Azure Resource Manager is. Typically, when we talk about an application, it involves multiple resources. It no longer represents just one resource. Azure Resource Manager gives you the capability to work with all the resources that your application needs as a group. With Azure Resource Manager, you can deploy, delete, and update all the resources for your application in a coordinated manner. You will be using a template that defines your resources and you will use that to create the resources. Azure Resource Manager has built-in capabilities for security, tagging, and auditing to help you manage your application resources.

You can learn more about Azure Resource Manager at `https://docs.microsoft.com/en-us/azure/azure-resource-manager/resource-group-overview`.

Let's look at how to generate the Automation script for the Azure app that we created. You can check this template into your source control and use Azure Resource Manager to deploy further updates to your Azure Function app using Continuous Integration and Continuous Deployment tools. The steps are as follows:

1. Navigate to the Azure Function App that we just created within the Azure portal.
2. By default, the **Overview** tab will be selected for the Azure Function App.
3. Click on the **Platform Features** tab for the Azure Function App.

4. Click on **Automation Script**, which is under Resource Management:

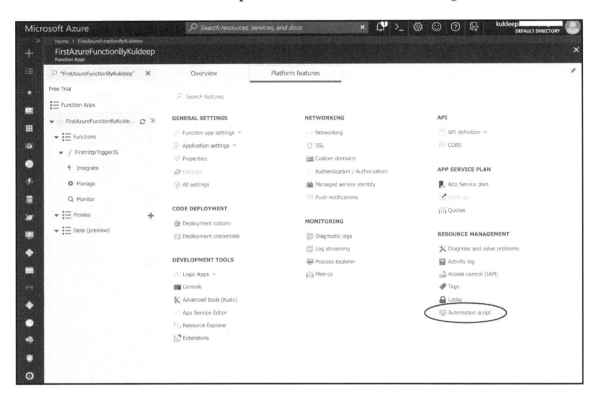

You will be automatically navigated to the Export Resource Group Template page where you can see the Azure Resource Manager template. The template code for the Azure Function App that we created looks like this (I have mentioned only a few lines, as the whole template is well over 300 lines):

```
{
"$schema":
"https://schema.management.azure.com/schemas/2015-01-01/deploymentTemplate.
json#",
"contentVersion": "1.0.0.0",
"parameters": {
"serverfarms_EastUSPlan_name": {
"defaultValue": "EastUSPlan",
"type": "String"
},
"sites_FirstAzureFunctionByKuldeep_name": {
"defaultValue": "FirstAzureFunctionByKuldeep",
"type": "String"
```

```
},
"storageAccounts_firstazurefunct8a77_name": {
"defaultValue": "firstazurefunct8a77",
"type": "String"
},
"storageAccounts_firstazurefunct8881_name": {
"defaultValue": "firstazurefunct8881",
"type": "String"
},
........
```

The resource template for the Azure app that we created is available at `https://github.com/PacktPublishing/Hands-On-Serverless-Computing/blob/master/Your-first-Serverless-application-on-Azure/automation-script.json`. You can generate your own resource template for the Azure app that you created as part of this chapter.

In this section, we learned about creating an Azure Function app and an Azure HTTP Function, configuring and managing Azure Functions, and doing this through the Azure portal. We also learned about testing an Azure Function through the portal and through an HTTP test client, Postman.

Your first Serverless app (using Azure Functions Core Tools)

In the previous section, we learned about creating Azure Functions using the Azure portal. In this section, we will learn about creating Azure Functions through Visual Studio Code and Azure Functions Core Tools. As part of Chapter 2, *Development Environment, Tools, and SDKs*, we learned about installing Visual Studio Code on your operating system (macOS or Windows). Please make sure Visual Studio Code is installed; if not, please refer to the instructions in Chapter 2, *Development Environment, Tools, and SDKs*, and install it.

Azure Functions Core Tools

Azure Functions Core tools provides you the ability to develop, deploy, debug, and manage Azure Functions directly from your workstation. After you have installed Azure Functions Core tools, you can connect to live Azure services from your local functions, and you can debug your functions on your workstation as you will have the full Functions runtime available on your workstation. With Azure Functions Core Tools, you can deploy your local function app to your Azure environment.

Azure Functions Runtime 2.x is the only one that is supported on all platforms, as it is built on .NET Core. Let's look at the installation instructions for macOS and Windows.

macOS

Here are the installation instructions on macOS for Azure Functions Core Tools:

- Install the .NET Core 2.0 runtime for macOS; installation instructions are available at `https://www.microsoft.com/net/download/macos`.
- If you haven't already installed Homebrew, please install it using the instructions at `https://brew.sh/`. Homebrew is a package manager for macOS.
- Once the .NET 2.0 runtime for macOS and Homebrew are installed, then you can install Azure Functions Core Tools using the following commands in your macOS Terminal:

```
brew tap azure/functions
```

With this, the installation of Azure Functions Core Tools is complete on macOS.

Windows

Here are the installation instructions on Windows for Azure Functions Core tools:

- Install the .NET Core 2.0 runtime for Windows; installation instructions are available at `https://www.microsoft.com/net/download/windows`.
- If your Windows installation doesn't already have Node.js (`https://docs.npmjs.com/getting-started/installing-node#osx-or-windows`) with `npm`, please install at least Node.js 8.5 or above, as those are the only versions that work with the Azure Functions 2.x runtime.
- Once the .Net 2.0 runtime for Windows and Node.js with npm are installed, then you can install Azure Functions Core Tools using the following command in your Windows Command prompt:

```
npm install -g azure-functions-core-tools@core
```

With this, the installation of Azure Functions Core Tools is complete on Windows.

Visual Studio Code

Before we start creating our local Azure Function, let's look at how we can install the Azure Functions runtime in Visual Studio Code so that we can develop, deploy, debug, and manage Azure Functions directly from Visual Studio Code. The installation instructions are the same across macOS and Windows:

1. Open **Visual Studio Code** on your operating system.
2. Click on **Extensions** in the left-hand menu.
3. Search for the `Azure Functions` extension.
4. Be sure to select the one that has been released by Microsoft.
5. Click **Install** for the extension, as shown in the following screenshot:

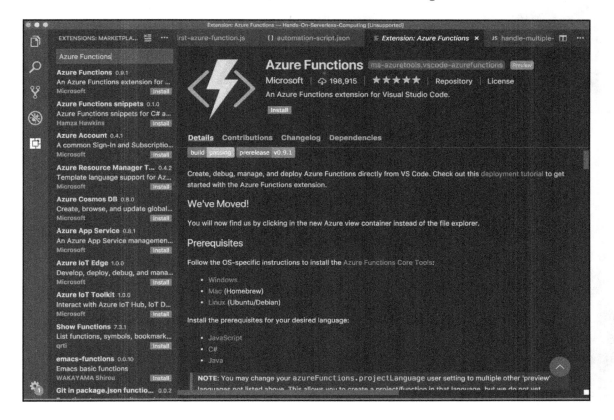

6. Once the installation is complete, click on **Reload** so that Visual Studio Code reloads with the plugin installed. The plugin won't be in effect until Visual Studio is either reloaded or restarted.

7. Once the plugin is installed, then in the left-hand menu you will now see Azure as well.

8. Select **Azure** in the left-hand menu.

9. Click on **Sign in** to Azure and follow the prompts to sign in to your Azure subscription that was created when we signed up for the free trial:

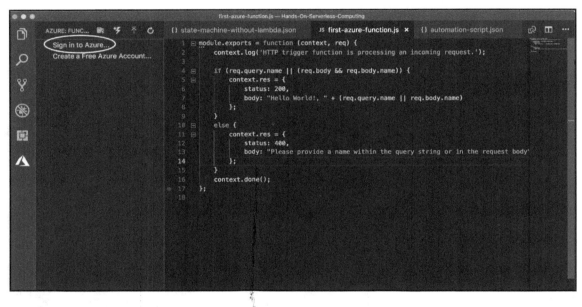

10. Once you have signed in to Azure, then in the Azure extensions window, you can view your Azure subscription and the associated resources.

11. You can view the list of Azure Function Apps, along with the functions and proxies that are associated with each Azure Function App, in the same left-hand menu.

12. For example, I created one Azure Function App and one Azure Function in that app. After I sign in to Azure, I can see them in the left-hand menu, shown as follows:

With this, we have successfully installed the prerequisites for us to create and deploy Azure Functions from our local workstation.

Create a local Azure Function app

Let's look at how we can create a local Azure Functions project and deploy that to the Azure environment, taking the following steps:

1. Navigate to a local working directory where you want to develop the local Azure Function project using Azure Functions Core Tools

2. Run the following command to initialize the local Azure Functions project:

   ```
   func init MyLocalFunctionProj
   ```

3. It will prompt you for the `worker runtime environment;` select the `node` option

4. Azure Functions Core Tools automatically creates a directory with the name `MyLocalFunctionProj` and initializes the directory with some files that are required to run the Azure Function locally

5. It also initializes a `.git` repository so that you can push the code to a remote git server such as `github.com`

6. Open the folder that Azure Functions Core Tools created in Visual Studio Code.
7. Once you open the folder, Visual Studio Code will automatically prompt you by stating that the project/folder looks like it has been created for Azure Functions, but has been created outside of Visual Studio, and it will prompt you to decide whether you want to initialize it for use with Visual Studio Code.
8. Select `Yes` in the prompt.
9. Visual Studio Code will prompt you to select the language for the project; select `JavaScript` and press **Enter.**
10. Visual Studio Code will automatically initialize it for use with Visual Studio Code:

Create a local Azure Function

Let's look at how we can create a local Azure Function. We will create a similar HTTP Trigger-based Azure Function locally to the one we created using the Azure portal:

1. In the `MyLocalFunctionProj` folder, run the following command:

   func new

2. Then, it will prompt you to select a template; select `HTTP Trigger` by entering 4
3. Give the function a name, such as `FirstLocalFunctionJS`
4. It will automatically create an `index.js` and a `function.json` for triggers and bindings, and a sample data file, as shown in the following screenshot:

```
~/src/MyLocalFunctionProj    master    func new
Select a language: Select a template:
1. Blob trigger
2. Cosmos DB trigger
3. Event Grid trigger
4. HTTP trigger
5. Queue trigger
6. SendGrid
7. Service Bus Queue trigger
8. Service Bus Topic trigger
9. Timer trigger
Choose option: 4
HTTP trigger
Function name: [HttpTriggerJS] FirstLocalFunctionJS
Writing /Users/kuldeepchowhan/src/MyLocalFunctionProj/FirstLocalFunctionJS/index.js
Writing /Users/kuldeepchowhan/src/MyLocalFunctionProj/FirstLocalFunctionJS/sample.dat
Writing /Users/kuldeepchowhan/src/MyLocalFunctionProj/FirstLocalFunctionJS/function.json
```

If you inspect the code that Azure Functions Core Tools has created, it is similar to what we created through the Azure portal. It takes a name as a request parameter, or as an attribute in the event body, and displays that name as output along with `Hello` appended to it.

Now that we have an Azure Function that has been created locally, let's look at how to run it locally:

- You can run the Azure Function locally by running this command:

   func host start

- Running the command will enable triggers that are associated with all the functions in the Azure Function App/project
- When the `func host` command's execution completes, then it will display the URL of the local HTTP Triggered Azure Function that we just created, shown as follows:

If you look closely at the output, the URL for my `FirstLocalFunctionJS` is mentioned as `http://localhost:7071/api/FirstLocalFunctionJS`. With this URL in place, I can use Postman to send the name as a request parameter and see if it responds successfully with a 200 HTTP status code and a Hello message with the name:

1. On your workstation, open the **Postman** app
2. Either select the **GET** or **POST** HTTP methods
3. Enter the copied URL into the **Enter request URL** text box
4. The URL in my case would be
   `http://localhost:7071/api/FirstLocalFunctionJS?name=kuldeep`

5. Make to sure to append `?name=<REPLACE WITH YOUR NAME>` to the URL that you copied from the Azure portal

6. Then, click on the **Send** button

7. In the response you get, you will received a `200 HTTP` status code

8. You will see the response from the REST API with the message `Hello <REPLACE WITH YOUR NAME>`

9. In my case, the response was `Hello kuldeep`, as shown here:

As mentioned earlier, you can also use the `curl` command on your MacOS Terminal or in your Powershell terminal on Windows to test the Azure HTTP function. There are many other tools that you can use to send HTTP requests.

Using this, we were successfully able to test the Azure function locally. We have only created an HTTP Triggered Azure Function, but with Azure Functions Core Tools, you can interact with other types of Azure Functions locally that are integrated with live Azure services.

Publishing the local Azure Function app

So far, we have learned how to create an Azure Function app locally, how to create an HTTP triggered Azure Function locally, and we also learned about testing the function locally. Now, lets's look at publishing the Azure Function App that we built locally to Azure Subscription.

To be able to publish the Azure Function App, you need to run the command `func azure functionapp publish <Existing Azure Function App>`. Publishing from your local workstation can only be done to an existing Azure Function App. To be able to publish the local Azure Function App to Azure, I already created an Azure Function App named `firstlocalfunctionkuldeep` using the instructions that we saw earlier in this chapter.

When you create the Azure Function app through the portal, it defaults to functions runtime 1.x. If you have built your local Azure Function app with runtime 2.x, then be sure to update the runtime of the Azure app that you created through the portal as well. You can do that by running the following Azure CLI command:

```
az functionapp config appsettings set --name <function_app> \
  --resource-group myResourceGroup \
  --settings FUNCTIONS_EXTENSION_VERSION=beta
```

In this section, we learned about installing Azure Functions Core Tools, creating an Azure Function app and Azure HTTP Function locally using Azure Functions Core Tools, and testing the locally developed Azure function by hosting the API on your local workstation. At the end, we also learned about publishing the locally built Azure app to Azure Subscription.

You can learn more about Working with Azure Functions Core Tools at `https://docs.microsoft.com/en-us/azure/azure-functions/functions-run-local`.

Summary

In this chapter, we learned about how to write a serverless applications to run on Microsoft Azure using Node.js.

We also learned about two ways of creating Serverless apps on the Azure Functions platform: one was using the Azure portal and the other was on a local workstation. In the *Your first Serverless app using Azure portal* section, we learned how to create an Azure Function App through the Azure portal. We learned how to create an HTTP trigger for the function, testing the Azure Function through the portal, and also using Postman to configure the Function through the Azure portal. In the local workstation, we learned how to create an Azure function App through Azure Functions Core Tools and Visual Studio Code, creating an Azure Function locally using Azure Functions Core Tools, and an HTTP trigger for the function on your local workstation. We also learned about testing the Azure Function by making HTTP calls to the endpoint of the function that is running locally and publishing the locally created Azure Function App to Azure Subscription.

In the next chapter, we will learn about Google Cloud Platform's serverless offerings, and we will learn more about their Functions as a Service, called Google Cloud Functions.

10
Getting Started with Google Cloud Functions

In this chapter, we are going to learn about Google Cloud Functions in depth, along with configuration options for Google Cloud Functions. We learned about how to create serverless apps in AWS and the Microsoft Azure environment. We also learned about how to test and deploy serverless apps to AWS and the Microsoft Azure environment. In previous chapters, we also looked at invoking AWS Lambda and Azure Functions using HTTP triggers; we will also do the same for Google Cloud so that you can learn how it works in a Google Cloud environment versus an AWS environment versus a Microsoft Azure environment. In the coming chapters, we will be focusing on Google Cloud Functions and we will recreate the same serverless apps that we created and deployed to the AWS and Microsoft Azure environments for the Google Cloud environment as well.

We will learn about the following topics in this chapter:

- Introduction to serverless on **Google Cloud Platform** (**GCP**)
- Learning about Google Cloud Functions in depth
- Google Cloud Platform Free Trial setup
- Learning about Google Cloud Shell
- Securing Google Cloud Functions using Google Cloud **Identity and Access Management** (**IAM**)
- Configuration options for Google Cloud Functions

Google Cloud Serverless Platform

Let's look at the Serverless Platform that Google Cloud Platform offers.

Google Cloud introduced Google App Engine back in 2008, which was its PaaS offering, used to deploy your applications to GCP without having to worry about the underlying infrastructure. You still had to choose the web server framework to deploy your application. This is similar to AWS Elastic Beanstalk. Google Cloud Platform has launched many other serverless offerings over the years, such as Google BigQuery in 2010, Google Pub/Sub in 2015, and an FaaS offering called Google Cloud Functions in 2016. Let's look at some of the different serverless offerings that Google Cloud Platform has built over the years in the Application Development and Analytics and Machine Learning areas.

Application development

The Google Cloud Serverless platform provides the following tools for efficient application development.

Google App Engine

Google App Engine (`https://cloud.google.com/appengine/`) provides a fully managed platform to build and deploy applications with Google App Engine. You can scale your applications seamlessly without having to worry about the infrastructure. With Google App Engine, you have zero sever management and do not need to worry about configuration deployments. Developers will not have any management overhead and they can focus on building great apps.

Google App Engine supports the following languages:

- Node.js
- Python
- Java
- Go
- .NET
- PHP
- Ruby
- Custom runtimes with a flexible environment—you can learn more at `https://cloud.google.com/appengine/docs/flexible/custom-runtimes/`

Google Cloud Functions

Google Cloud Functions (`https://cloud.google.com/functions/`) provides an interface to run your code with a choice of programming languages, without having to worry about infrastructure. It scales on demand, based on the load on your functions. We will learn more about this in the following sections. The different Google Cloud Functions are as follows:

- **Google Cloud Datastore**: Google Cloud Datastore (`https://cloud.google.com/datastore/`) is a highly available and scalable NoSQL database platform from Google Cloud Platform for your apps. Google Cloud Datastore automatically handles replication and sharing of your database, which, in turn, provides you with a highly durable and scalable database platform. It also automatically scales to handle the load on the database, which, in turn, has been put on the database by your application. Google Cloud Datastore has many capabilities, such as:
  - SQL queries
  - Indexes
  - ACID transactions
- **Google Cloud Storage**: Google Cloud Storage (`https://cloud.google.com/storage/`) is highly available, durable, and scalable storage that is built for developers to build cloud applications. It is similar to S3 from AWS. You can store structured data, unstructured data, and files in Google Cloud Storage. It constitutes geo-redundant data storage from Google.
- **Google Pub/Sub**: Google Pub/Sub (`https://cloud.google.com/pubsub/`) is a scalable, reliable, and simple streaming platform to perform analytics and event-driven computing. Google Cloud Dataflow, Google BigQuery, and Google Cloud Pub/Sub make up Google Cloud's stream analytics solution. Google Cloud Pub/Sub scales automatically, based on the load, and you pay only for the resources that you have used.
- **Google Endpoints**: Google Endpoints (`https://cloud.google.com/endpoints/`) is a solution from Google Cloud Platform to develop, manage, deploy, and monitor APIs on Google Cloud. Google Endpoints utilizes an NGINX proxy to provide superior performance and scalability. Google Endpoints supports the Open API specification (`https://github.com/OAI/OpenAPI-Specification`). Google Cloud Endpoints support user authentication using JSON web tokens. Google Endpoints also supports logging and monitoring your API endpoints using Stackdriver monitoring.

Google Endpoints is not the same as Amazon API Gateway, where you can invoke your AWS Lambda functions (FaaS). With Google Endpoints, you can't invoke Google Cloud Functions (FaaS).

Analytics and Machine Learning

Google BigQuery (https://cloud.google.com/bigquery/) is Google's serverless data warehouse service, which helps your data warehousing solutions to become more productive. It is a highly scalable and low-cost enterprise solution for data warehousing from Google. As it is a serverless solution, there is no infrastructure to manage, which means you have more time to focus on analyzing the data to gather insights. Google BigQuery provides you with an SQL-like interface to query the data that you have ingested into Google BigQuery.

Google Dataflow (https://cloud.google.com/dataflow/) is a serverless batch and stream data processing service from Google. You can use Google Dataflow to transform and enrich your data that is sent through Google Dataflow with high levels of reliability. As it is a serverless solution, you don't have to worry or manage the infrastructure. Google Dataflow also scales based on the data that you are processing through the system.

Google Machine Learning Engine (https://cloud.google.com/ml-engine/) is a serverless machine learning platform from Google Cloud. Google Machine Learning Engine scales automatically and it has been built on custom Google infrastructure (Tensor Processing Units) to run machine learning solutions.

An Introduction to Google Cloud Functions

Google Cloud Functions is a service that Google Cloud offers to running functions. Google Cloud Functions is Google's implementation of FaaS. Its main goal is to enable developers to run small pieces of software code or functions to be run in Google Cloud Platform. If you recall the benefits of FaaS that we learned in Chapter 1, *What is Serverless Computing?* one of them is that the developer is just focused on writing the code to solve the problem at hand, rather than worrying about the infrastructure on which it will run; they don't have to worry about the entire application that is required to run the code, nor do they have to worry about scaling the infrastructure when the function receives a lot of traffic. As developers simply focus on solving the problem at hand, development can be more productive.

As of June 2018, Google Cloud Functions only supported the Node.js language runtime.

Google Cloud Functions, like AWS Lambda, also charges the user for the duration of execution of your Google Cloud Function and automatically scales based on load. Google Cloud Functions are also integrated with many Google Cloud services, which makes developing intelligent apps easy, and you can build seamless connections with Google Cloud services very easily.

Let's break down the features of Google Cloud Functions:

- **Pay for what you use**: As Google Cloud Functions run on demand, based on the triggers, you only pay for the duration that your Google Cloud Function runs for. Google Cloud Functions rounds your execution time to the nearest 100 milliseconds and charges based on that. Once the execution of the function is complete, you will not be charged.
- **No infrastructure management**: Google Cloud Functions automatically scales your code execution. You don't have to worry about the management of the underlying infrastructure. You can focus on writing the code that is required to solve the business problem at hand and iterate faster than even before. Google Cloud Functions can scale from zero to planet scale with the load that your Cloud Function is being executed with, or without you having to worry about it at all.
- **Language support**: At the time of writing, Google Cloud Functions only supports the Node.js runtime environment. You don't have to learn any new language specific to Google Cloud Platform to be able to use Google Cloud Functions. All you need to do is to bring your Node.js code to the Google Cloud Functions platform.
- **Google Cloud Service Triggers**: Google Cloud Functions have triggers built to be invoked from Google Cloud Platform, Google Assistant, Firebase, invoked directly from any web, or through a backend application using HTTP.

Google Cloud Console

Before we start looking into the Google Cloud Functions Console, let's look at the process of getting a Google Cloud Platform account. Google Cloud Platform offers a 12 months' free trial and also gives you $300 credit to get started with Google Cloud Platform. If you spend $300 credit in the first 12 months, then you need to upgrade to a paid account in order to continue to use Google Cloud Platform services.

You can sign up for Google Cloud Platform using your Google Account at `https://console.cloud.google.com/freetrial`.

To be able to create a Google Cloud Platform account, you will need a Google account. Once you have created the Google Cloud Platform account, a new project needs to be created so that you can start building apps to run in the Google Cloud Platform environment:

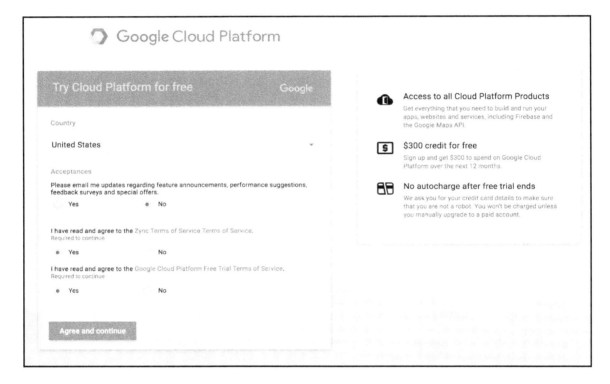

Once you have submitted all the details that are required to create the Google Cloud Platform account, you will receive a notification stating that your account is now active and you can start using Google Cloud Platform to build your solutions and deploy them into the environment:

Creating a Google Cloud project

To get started, you will need to create an empty project. Once you have signed up for the account, on Google Cloud Platform's **Getting Started** page, select **Create an empty project**. The getting started page also includes **TOUR CONSOLE**, showing the most popular Google Cloud Platform services. You can also tour Google Cloud Platform before you start creating an empty project:

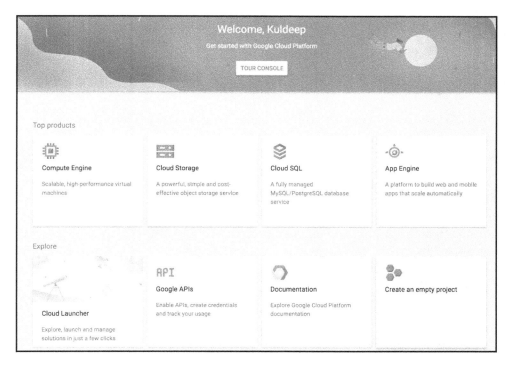

On the **New Project** page, enter a name for your Google Cloud Platform project. If you already have an organization in your Google Cloud Platform, then choose it; if not, then you can leave the default option of **No Organization**. Organizations in Google Cloud Platform let you organize Google projects. Once you have entered the name and selected the organization, click on **CREATE**:

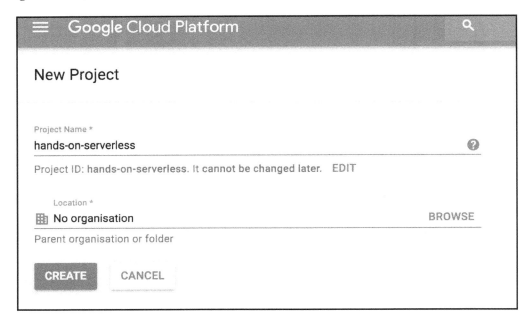

After you have created the project, you are all set to start building and deploying applications to Google Cloud Platform.

Google Cloud Project Dashboard

The home page for Google Cloud Project is **Dashboard**. Google Cloud Platform automatically creates a dashboard for each project with default widgets, as seen in the following screenshot:

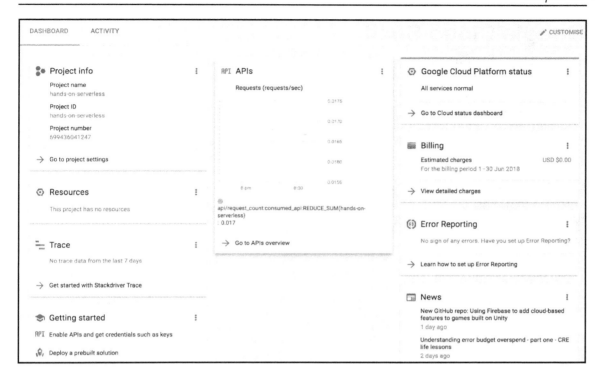

You can see information about your Google Cloud Project features:

- **Project Info**: Name, Project ID, and Project number
- **Resources**: Google Cloud Platform resources that you are using
- **Trace**: Stackdriver Distributed Tracing for your resources
- **APIs**: API request/sec across Google Cloud Platform resources that you are using
- **Google Cloud Platform status**
- **Billing**: It shows the estimated costs for the current billing period

You can customize the **Dashboard** by adding additional widgets for:

- Google Compute Engine
- Google App Engine
- Storage

Google Cloud Shell

Google Cloud Platform also provides you with a browser-based shell that runs in Google Cloud Platform, which you can access using a browser to run interactive commands against your Google Cloud environment. It provides you with the capability to administer your Google Cloud Project from anywhere using a browser, through a shell called **Cloud Shell**. You can use common tools and programming languages to control your Google Cloud Project. Cloud Shell has the Cloud SDK gcloud (`https://cloud.google.com/sdk/gcloud/`) already installed so that you can start using it.

Cloud Shell is managed and maintained by Google, which means it gets regularly patched and updated with the latest tools to interact with your Google Cloud Project. Google Cloud Shell already has the following tools pre-installed. The tools are also regularly updated by Google:

- Bash command-line tools
- vim, emacs, and sh
- MySQL client
- Kubernetes client
- Docker

You can access Cloud Shell from the top-right menu. Click on the Shell icon and you will be prompted to activate Cloud Shell for the first time:

Once you click on **Activate Google Cloud Shell** from the top-right corner, Google Cloud Platform will set up the shell and install all the tools, clients, and SDKs for you to get started. Once all the installations are complete, click on **Start Cloud Shell** from the dialog window:

Google Cloud Shell

Free, pre-installed with the tools that you need for the Google Cloud Platform. Learn more

Real Linux environment

- Linux Debian-based OS
- 5 GB persisted home directory
- Add, edit and save files

Configured for Google Cloud

- Google Cloud SDK
- Google App Engine SDK
- Docker
- Git
- Text editors
- Build tools
- View more ↗

Popular language support

- Python
- Java
- Go
- Node.js

CANCEL   START CLOUD SHELL

Once Cloud Shell is provisioned for you, you can start to run `gcloud` commands, deploy your favorite web applications in them, and test them from the browser before you push your web application code to your source control. Google Cloud Shell comes with 5 GB of persistent disk, which is mounted to your `$HOME` directory on your Cloud Shell. This persistent disk ensures that your files under `$HOME` are persisted across sessions:

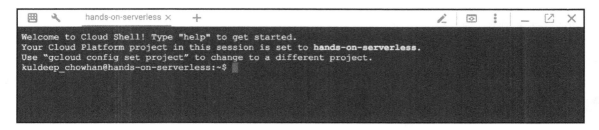

We will be utilizing this Google Cloud Shell in subsequent chapters.

Google Cloud Functions Console

You can navigate to the Google Cloud Functions Console in the Google Cloud Console by selecting **Cloud Function** under **Compute** in the navigation menu, which is on the left-hand side of the page. If you are accessing Google Cloud Functions for the first time, then Google Cloud Console will prompt you to enable the Google Cloud Functions API. Google Cloud Platform works in a similar way for other Google Cloud services:

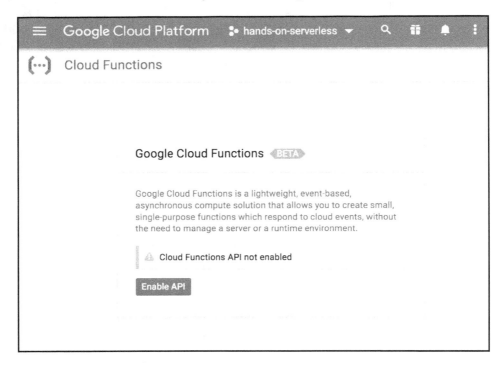

Once the API is enabled, then the screen changes to **CREATE FUNCTION**. If you already have Google Cloud Functions created, then the home screen of Google Cloud Functions will show you the list of functions. Once you select a particular Google Cloud Function, then you see the **LABELS** of that Google Cloud Function:

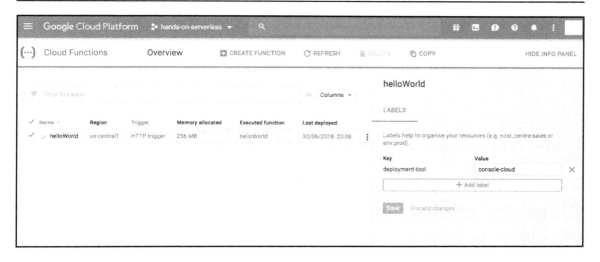

Access Control using IAM

Using Google IAM, you can control access to your Google Cloud project. You can create roles in Google IAM and control access to your Google Cloud project. When you create a new Google Cloud project, whoever has created the project automatically gets an account created and they are the only ones who can access the Google Cloud project. No one else has access to the Google Cloud project until new users are created and given access to the resources in the Google Cloud project console.

To be able to access the Google Cloud console, users need a Google account. Once they have a Google account, then you can add them as team members to your Google Cloud Project.

Google IAM provides three built-in roles:

- Editor
- Owner
- Viewer

Both Editor and Owner have full read and write access to all Google Cloud function resources. They have access to deploy, delete, and update Google Cloud Functions.

Viewer only has read-only access to Google Cloud Functions. They can list the functions that are in the Google Cloud console and look at Google Cloud function details.

You can learn more about roles in IAM at `https://cloud.google.com/iam/docs/understanding-roles`.

If you want someone to just see the Google Cloud functions that you are building, just giving them Viewer access is sufficient. However, if you want to collaborate with someone on building these Google Cloud Functions, start with the Editor role and, if needed, then upgrade them to the Owner role.

Cloud Functions runtime service account

Behind the scenes, the Google Cloud Functions service uses a runtime service account to interact with Google Cloud projects. The service account is in the form of `PROJECT_ID@appspot.gserviceaccount.com` and it has an Editor role in your Google Cloud project. If you want to limit the permissions, then you need to change the permissions of the Google Cloud Functions service account.

You can learn more about Google Service accounts at `https://cloud.google.com/iam/docs/understanding-service-accounts`.

Cloud Functions Service account

Google Cloud Functions has its own service account in the form of the `PROJECT_NUMBER@gcf-admin-robot.iam.gserviceaccount.com` service, used to perform administrative actions on the Google Cloud project.

In the following screenshot, you can see the list of users in the Google Cloud project that I created for this book. You can see me (Kuldeep Chowhan) listed as **Owner**, along with a Cloud Functions Service account and runtime service account with the **Editor** role. Additionally, you can see that there is another service account for Google APIs:

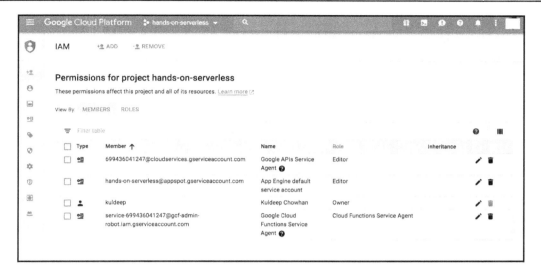

Creating a Google Cloud Functions user

Let's look at creating a Google Cloud project user who will be a developer for Google Cloud Functions only.

From the Google Cloud IAM console, click on the **Add** button. It will open up an overlay window with options to create new users and assign them roles:

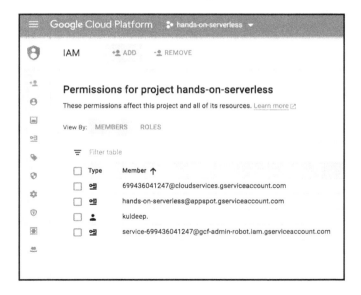

In the overlay window that opens up, select the new members that you want to create users for in your Google Cloud project. Please note that the email address that you can enter in the new members, text box needs to have a Google Account associated with it. Once you enter the email address, then Google Cloud console will automatically try to establish whether the user has a Google Account or not, and will let you know right away.

Once the user information is entered correctly:

1. In the select role dropdown, select **Cloud Functions**
2. From the list that is made available to you, select **Cloud Functions Developer**
3. Click on **Save:**

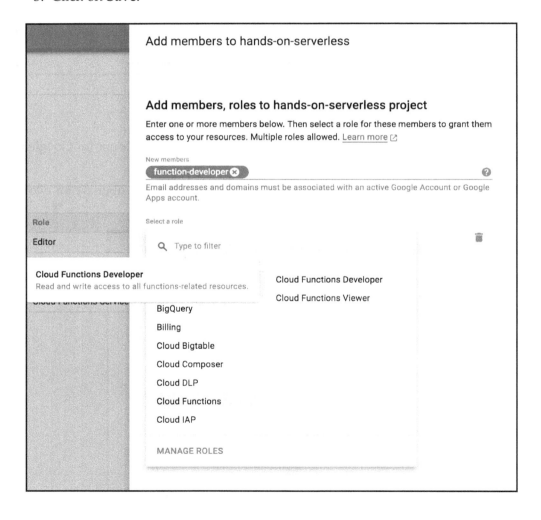

Once the user is created, then they will be shown in the list of IAM users along with their role set as Cloud Functions Developer. You can edit their permissions and give them additional roles based on the resources that they are going to work on. A Google Cloud project also provides you with options to create custom roles, where you can give access to multiple services within Google Cloud and use that custom role to grant access for multiple users to your Google Cloud project:

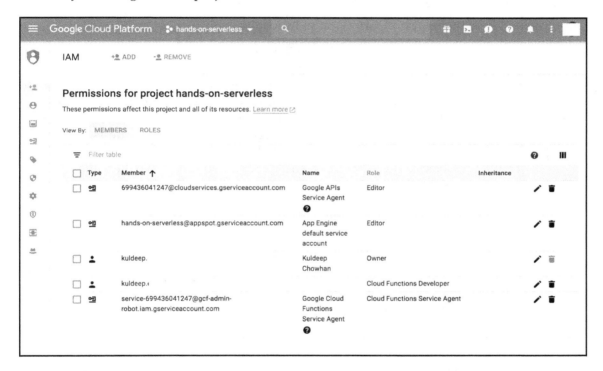

Configuring Google Cloud Functions

So far, we have learned about the Google Cloud Serverless platform, looked at the features that Google Cloud Functions offer, and we have also looked at the Google Cloud Console along with Google Cloud Console. In this section, we will learn about different configuration options that are available for Google Cloud Functions. We will be creating Google Cloud Functions in later chapters, but, for this section, I will be focusing on the different configuration options that are available for Google Cloud Functions.

Google Cloud Functions only support the Node.js runtime environment. At the time of writing this book (June 2018), the Google Cloud Functions Node.js execution environment was using the Node.js v6.14.0 runtime environment.

Types of Google Cloud Functions

Google Cloud Functions support two types of function:

- **HTTP Functions**: HTTP Functions will let you invoke your Google Cloud Function using standard HTTP(s) requests. These requests wait for the HTTP response and they support common HTTP request methods such as `PUT`, `GET`, `DELETE` and `POST`. Google Cloud Functions automatically provisions a TLS certificate, which lets you invoke your HTTP Google Cloud Functions using a secure connection. To allow seamless integration with HTTP requests, HTTP-based Google Cloud Functions allows HTTP semantics such as `request` and `response` objects. These `request` and `response` objects have the same properties as the Express.js (`https://expressjs.com/`) Node.js framework.

  An example HTTP Google Cloud Function looks like this:

  ```
  exports.helloHttpFunction = (req, res) => {
    res.send(`Hello ${req.body.name || 'World from Google Cloud HTTP
  Function'}!`);
  };
  ```

  You can learn more about writing HTTP functions at `https://cloud.google.com/functions/docs/writing/http`. We will be writing HTTP-based Google Cloud Functions in later chapters.

- **Background functions**: Background Functions will let you invoke your Google Cloud Function from your Google Cloud infrastructure. This lets your function be invoked by messages from a Google Cloud Pub/Sub topic, or based on events that are happening within a Google Storage bucket. Background functions take two parameters, an `event` object and a second optional `callback` function. The event object that Background functions take as the first parameter holds the event data that triggered the Background Google Cloud Functions; it also contains the metadata about that event trigger itself. The event's data is available in the `data` property of the event.

An example Background Google Cloud Function looks like this:

```
exports.helloBackgroundFunction = (event, callback) => {
    callback(null, `Hello ${event.data.name || 'World from Background
Function'}!`);
};
```

You can learn more about writing Background functions at `https://cloud.google.com/functions/docs/writing/background`. We will be writing Background Google Cloud Functions in later chapters.

Configuration options

Google Cloud Functions lets you configure a few settings on the Functions. Let's look at those settings:

- **Memory allocated**: For each Google Cloud Function that you create, by default, 256 MB of memory is allocated. However, you can modify the memory allocated to Cloud Functions with these values:

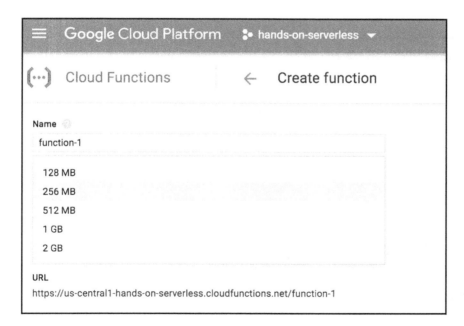

- **Region**: You can configure your Google Cloud Function to be deployed to four different Google Cloud Platform regions (as of June 2018). You can deploy to many more regions than four for AWS Lambda. The difference here is that Google Cloud Platform takes a region-agnostic approach in relation to these services and you need to specify the region you want your resources to run in. However, with AWS, you need to select a region in the AWS Console to see the resources that are available in that region. The following screenshot shows the Google Cloud Functions – supported regions:

- **Timeout**: Google Cloud Functions lets you specify the amount of time your Function can execute for. The default value for the timeout is 60 seconds and the maximum amount of time is 540 seconds. After 540 seconds, your Google Cloud Function execution will be terminated by the Google Cloud Function runtime.

Summary

In this chapter, we learned about different serverless platform offerings from Google Cloud Platform, created a free trial account for Google Cloud Platform, looked into Google Cloud Console and Google Cloud Shell, and secured Google Cloud Functions using Google Cloud IAM. We also learned about the Google Cloud Functions Console, its different types, and the configuration options for Google Cloud Functions.

In the next chapter, we will learn about the different events and triggers that are available in the Google Cloud Functions platform.

11
Triggers and Events for Google Cloud Functions

In the previous chapter, we learned about Google Cloud Functions. In this chapter, we will learn how to invoke Google Cloud Functions from other Google Cloud services. We will learn about the different types of events and triggers that are available for Google Cloud Functions. We will then learn about Google Cloud Pub/Sub triggers, HTTP triggers for Google Cloud Functions, Firebase, and Google Storage triggers.

In this chapter, we will cover the following topics:

- How Google Cloud Functions get invoked
- Google Cloud Function triggers and events:
    - HTTP
    - Google Cloud Pub/Sub
    - Google storage

Technical requirements

You can find the source code in the GitHub repository at `https://github.com/PacktPublishing/Hands-On-Serverless-Computing/blob/master/Triggers-and-Events-for-Google-Cloud-Functions/handle-multiple-http-methods.js`.

Events

Let's learn how to create and assign events to Google Cloud Functions. Associating these triggers with Google Cloud Functions will execute a function when an event is fired on the Google Cloud services. Within a Google Cloud Platform, such as AWS and Azure, cloud events are emitted when there is a change in the data in the storage system or database when new files are added to Google Cloud Storage or messages that are being sent to Google Cloud Pub/Sub. At the time of writing (July 2018), Google Cloud Functions only supported the following four event types:

- HTTP
- Google Cloud Storage
- Google Pub/Sub
- Firebase (`https://firebase.google.com/`)

Let's learn more about the event parameter and triggers for Google Cloud Functions in the next sections.

Event parameter

The event parameter, which is the first parameter that Google Cloud Functions accepts, holds the data associated with the event that triggered the execution of Google Cloud Functions. The actual event data is available within the `data` property of the event object.

Let's look at the properties of the event parameter:

- **Data**: This is the property where the event data is available for the Google Cloud Function
- **Context**: The context object for the event that triggered the Google Cloud Function
- `context.eventId`: This is a unique ID that has been generated for the event that triggered the Google Cloud Function
- `context.timestamp`: This is the date timestamp on which the event was triggered from the source
- `context.eventType`: This holds the type of event that triggered the Google Cloud Function
- `context.resource`: This holds the resources from the Google Cloud Platform that triggered the Google Cloud Function

As we learned in the previous chapter, there are different types of triggers that can invoke a Google Cloud Function. As each one is a different service that invokes the Cloud Function, each one of those types has it's own schema for the data property within the event parameter. Let's look at the different schema of each type of event used for their data property:

- The HTTP trigger uses the Express.js request (`http://expressjs.com/en/4x/api.html#req`) object for data property within the event

- Google Cloud Storage uses the Cloud Storage Object (`https://cloud.google.com/storage/docs/json_api/v1/objects`) for the data property within the event

- Google Cloud Pub/Sub uses `PubsubMessage` (`https://cloud.google.com/pubsub/docs/reference/rest/v1/PubsubMessage`) for the data property within the event

Triggers

Let's learn about Google Cloud Function triggers. Whenever you create a response to an event that was invoked when new files are added to Google Cloud Storage or whenever a new message is published to Google Cloud Pub/Sub, it is called a **trigger**. A trigger on a Google Cloud Function is a declaration/definition stating that you want the Google Cloud Function to be invoked in response to a certain set of events. You need to associate the Google Cloud Function to a trigger, which allows you to act upon the events that invoked the Google Cloud Function.

Triggers and Functions are associated with each other on a many-to-one basis. You can only have one trigger on a Google Cloud Function. However, you can have multiple Google Cloud Functions invoked from the same cloud event within the Google Cloud Platform.

Let's take a look at different triggers that are available for Google Cloud Functions, beginning with Google Cloud Storage.

Google Cloud Storage

Google Cloud Storage is a highly available, durable, and scalable storage, built for developers to build cloud applications. It is similar to S3 from AWS. You can store structured data, unstructured data, and files in Google Cloud Storage. It is a geo-redundant data storage from Google.

You can learn more about Google Cloud Storage at `https://cloud.google.com/storage/`.

Google Cloud Storage triggers to Google Cloud Functions are based on Pub/Sub notifications from Google Cloud Storage. The triggers are available for these types of events:

- **Finalize**: This event gets triggered when a successful write of an object happens within Google Cloud Storage and when it is finalized. This trigger is fired whenever there is a new object or existing objects get updated. Metadata updates and archive operations on objects are not handled by this trigger, as we have specific triggers for those.

- **Delete**: This event gets triggered when an old version of an object is deleted from Google Cloud Storage. These events are also triggered whenever an old version of an object is overwritten. This behavior is very useful in non-versioned Google Cloud Storage accounts. For versioned buckets, the event is triggered whenever an object is permanently deleted from the Cloud storage account.

- **Archive**: This event gets triggered when an old version of an object is archived. These events are only triggered for versioned Google Cloud Storage buckets. What this means is that whenever an object is deleted or overwritten in a versioned bucket, an archive event is triggered.

- **Metadata update**: This event gets triggered whenever metadata of an existing object is updated within a Google Cloud Storage bucket.

We will be learning more about configuring Cloud Pub/Sub notifications for Google Cloud storage and invoking Google Cloud Functions in the next chapter.

You can learn more about the Pub/Sub notifications for Google Cloud Storage at `https://cloud.google.com/storage/docs/pubsub-notifications`.

Let's look at the configuration options that you have while creating cloud storage-based Google Cloud Functions in the Google Cloud Console. In creating the function from the Console you should:

1. Give a **Name** to the Google Cloud Function.
2. Select the memory you want to allocate to the Function.

3. Select the trigger type as **Cloud Storage bucket**.
4. Choose an associated event type from the list; for example, select **Finalise/Create**.
5. From the **Bucket** text box, browse and select the `Google Cloud Storage Bucket` that you want the trigger to run from.
6. Click on **Create** and wait for the function to be created. This function will be invoked whenever you upload a file to that bucket.
7. As you can see in the below screenshoot, the event that triggers the function will get the name of the file that changed in the Google Cloud Storage bucket.

The following screenshot illustrates the implementation of these steps:

Google Cloud Pub/Sub

Google Pub/Sub is a scalable, reliable, and simple streaming platform to perform analytics and event-driven computing. Google Cloud Dataflow, Google BigQuery, and Google Cloud Pub/Sub make up the Google Cloud's stream analytics solution. Google Cloud Pub/Sub scales automatically, based on the load, and you pay only for the resources that you have used.

 You can learn more about Google Cloud Pub/Sub at `https://cloud.google.com/pubsub/`.

Google Cloud Functions get invoked with Google Cloud Pub/Sub triggers (`https://cloud.google.com/functions/docs/calling/pubsub`). Google Cloud Functions get invoked for each message that gets published to a Google Cloud Pub/Sub topic.

We will be learning more about configuring Cloud Pub/Sub notifications to trigger Google Cloud Functions in the next chapter.

Let's look at the configuration options that you have while creating Cloud Pub/Sub-based Google Cloud Functions in the Google Cloud Console. In creating the function from the Console:

1. Give a name to the Google Cloud Function.
2. Select the memory you want to allocate to the function.
3. Select the trigger type as **Cloud Pub/Sub topic**.
4. In the **Topic** list box, select the Pub/Sub topic that you want the trigger to run from.
5. Click on **Create** and wait for the function to be created. This function will be invoked whenever you upload a file to that bucket. We will explore this further in the next chapter.

The following screenshot illustrates the implementation of these steps:

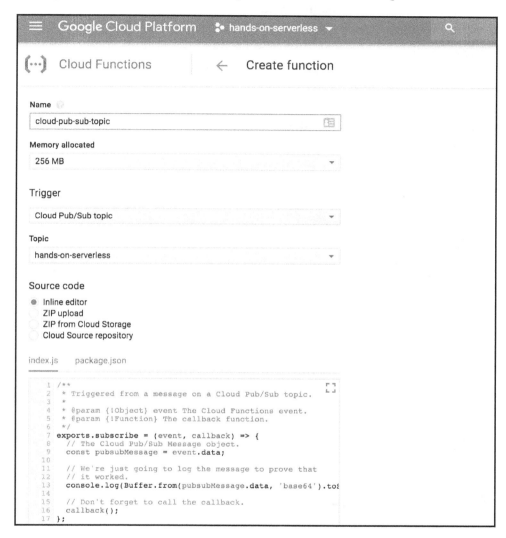

HTTP triggers

As we have learned in the earlier chapter about HTTP Google Cloud Functions, they will let you invoke your Google Cloud Function using standard HTTP(s) requests. These requests wait for the HTTP response and they support common HTTP request methods, such as PUT, GET, DELETE, and POST.

Let's look at the configuration options that you have while creating HTTP trigger-based Google Cloud Functions in the Google Cloud Console. In creating the function from the Console you should:

1. Give a name to the Google Cloud Function.
2. Select the memory you want to allocate to the function
3. Select **Trigger** type as the **HTTP trigger**
4. Click on **Create** and wait for the function to be created. This function will be invoked whenever you send a HTTP request to the URL displayed in the below screenshot.

The following screenshot illustrates the implementation of these steps:

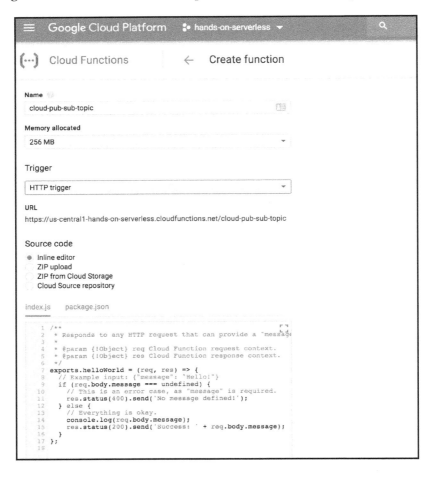

Once your Function has been created and deployed successfully, you can directly invoke your HTTP Google Cloud Function using an HTTP endpoint. An example is shown in the following code:

```
curl -X POST https://<YOUR_REGION>-
<YOUR_PROJECT_ID>.cloudfunctions.net/<FUNCTION_NAME> -H "Content-
Type:application/json" --data '{"name":"Kuldeep"}'
```

Handing different HTTP methods

If your Google Cloud Function needs to handle multiple HTTP methods, such as PUT, GET or POST, you can add code to your Cloud Function to check the method property of the HTTP request object and act accordingly. In AWS Lambda functions, the HTTP-based trigger on the Lambda function is not directly available and you need to use Amazon API Gateway to add HTTP triggers to your Lambda function. Within Amazon API Gateway, you can specify the HTTP methods that are allowed and configure the Amazon API Gateway to call the Lambda function when only certain HTTP methods are matched. Because of this, you don't have to check within your Function code for the HTTP method.

Let's look at a sample Google Cloud Function code on how to handle this scenario:

```
function handleGET(req, res) {
    res.status(200).send('Hello from HTTP Google Cloud Function!');
}

function handlePUT(req, res) {
    res.status(403).send("Forbidden, you don't have access");
}

exports.helloHttpFunction = (req, res) => {
    switch (req.method) {
        case 'POST':
            handlePOSTMethod(req, res);
            break;
        case 'PUT':
            handlePUTMethod(req, res);
            break;
        case 'PUT':
            handleGETMethod(req, res);
            break;
        default:
            res.status(500).send({
                error: 'Something went wrong in the function!'
            });
            break;
```

```
    }
};
```

Summary

In this chapter, we have learned about invoking Google Cloud Functions and triggers and events. Regarding triggers, we learned about HTTP, Google Cloud Pub/Sub, and Google storage.

In the next chapter, we will create our first serverless app to be deployed on the Google Cloud Platform using Google Cloud Functions. We will build three types of Google Cloud Functions: HTTP, Google Cloud Pub/Sub, and Google Storage.

12
Your First Serverless Application on Google Cloud

In this chapter, we will learn how to write serverless applications that will run on the Google Cloud Platform using Node.js. We will learn about creating Google Cloud Functions from the Google Cloud Console. We will also learn about how to deploy Google Cloud Functions from your local workstation using the `gcloud` command-line interface.

In this chapter, we will learn about creating Google Cloud Functions using the following:

- The Google Cloud Console:
    - We will learn how to create a Google Cloud Function
    - We will learn how to create HTTP types of Google Cloud Functions
    - We will learn about testing the Google Cloud Function through the Console and also using Postman
    - We will learn about viewing logs for the Google Cloud Function
- Local workstation:
    - We will learn how to create a Google Cloud Function on your local workstation
    - We will learn how to deploy Google Cloud Functions on your local workstation to the Google Cloud Platform using the `gcloud` CLI

Technical requirements

For deploying and testing the serverless app that we will develop in this chapter, you will need a Google Cloud Project. Let's look at the process of setting up a Google Cloud Platform account. The Google Cloud Platform offers a 12-month free trial and also gives you $300 credit to get started. If you spend the $300 credit in the first 12 months, then you will need to upgrade to a paid account to continue to use Google Cloud Platform services.

You can sign up for the Google Cloud Platform using your Google account at `https://console.cloud.google.com/freetrial`.

To be able to create a Google Cloud Platform account, you will need a Google account. Once you have created the Google Cloud Platform account, a new project needs to be created so that you can start building apps to run on the Google Cloud Platform environment.

Once you have submitted all the details that are required to create the Google Cloud Platform account, then you will receive a notification stating that your account is now active and you can start using the Google Cloud Platform to build your solutions and deploy them into the environment.

Your first serverless app (using the Google Cloud Console)

In this section, we will learn about creating a Google Cloud Function through the Google Cloud Console. We will explore some of the settings that are associated with Google Cloud Functions. We will also learn about creating two types of Google Cloud Functions, HTTP and Background, through the Google Cloud Console. We will learn about how to test Google Functions through the Console. We will also learn how to look at logs for the Google Cloud Functions.

Let's look at accessing the Google Cloud Function Console.

You can navigate to the Google Cloud Function Console by performing the following steps:

1. Open the Navigation menu in the Google Cloud Console.
2. Select **Cloud Functions** under **Compute** within the Navigation Menu.
3. If you are accessing Google Cloud Functions for the first time, then the Google Cloud Console will prompt you to enable Google Cloud Functions API.

4. The home page of the Google Cloud Functions Console will show the list of Google Cloud Functions.
5. Selecting one of them will provide details about the Google Cloud Function.
6. If there are no Google Cloud Functions that have been already created, it will prompt you to create a new Google Cloud Function as shown in the following screenshot:

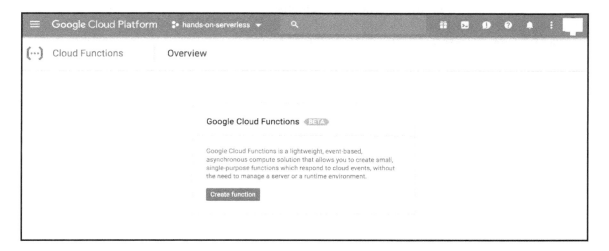

Creating a Google Cloud Function

Let's look at creating a Google Cloud Function through the Console. As we have learned in the earlier chapters, Google Cloud Functions support two types of functions—HTTP and Background. Let's first look at creating HTTP Google Cloud Functions and then we will look into the Background Function.

Google Cloud Functions support only Node.js within there Google Cloud Functions platform.

Perform the following steps:

1. Open the Navigation Menu in the Google Cloud Console.
2. Select **Cloud Functions** under **Compute** within the Navigation Menu.
3. From the homepage of Google Cloud Functions, click on **Create function**.

4. On the **Create function** page, enter a name for the function.
5. Select the memory that you want to allocate to the function. By default, **256 MB** will be allocated.
6. You can change the memory settings anywhere between **128 MB** and **2 GB**.
7. For the trigger, select **HTTP trigger**.
8. Leave the **Source code** as **Inline editor** and leave the source code of index.js intact as shown in the following screenshot:

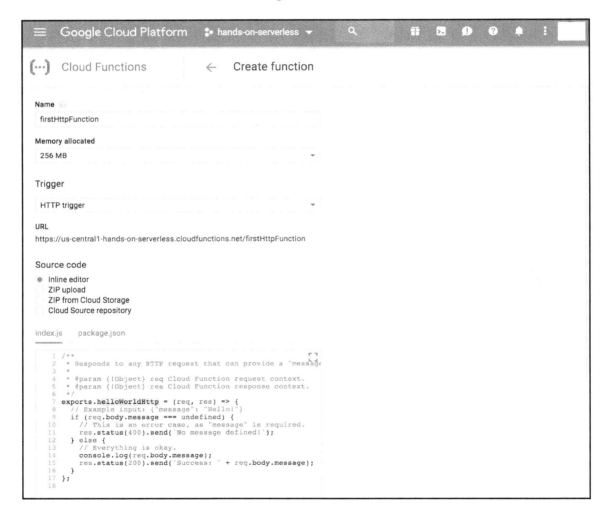

9. Leave the **Function to execute** intact as well.
10. Click on the **More** button if you want to change the **Region** and the **Timeout** for the Google Cloud Function.
11. I would just leave the defaults for now.
12. Click on **Create** button as shown in the following screenshot:

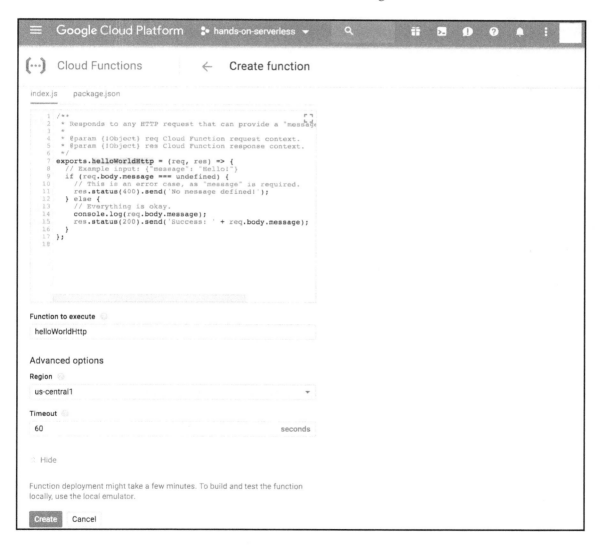

13. Wait for the function to be created.
14. Once it has been created, you will see the function in the Google Cloud Functions homepage.
15. Select the Function that we just created from the list and you can see the labels associated with the Google Cloud Function as per the next screnshot:

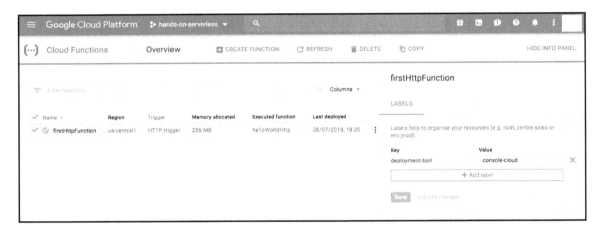

Let's take a look at the Google Function code that was auto-generated for us by the Console within the `index.js` file. There are two files that have been created automatically. One is `index.js`, where our Function's source code resides and the other one is `package.json`, where the `npm` package manifest exists:

```
exports.helloWorldHttp = (req, res) => {
  if (req.body.message === undefined) {
    res.status(400).send('No message defined in the request body!');
  } else {
    console.log(req.body.message);
    res.status(200).send('Hello World!, ' + req.body.message);
  }
};
```

You can find the preceding source code at `https://github.com/PacktPublishing/Hands-On-Serverless-Computing/blob/master/Your-first-Serverless-application-on-Google-Cloud/first-http-function.js`.

Let's understand what the code is doing here:

1. The `index.js` exports a function name: `helloWorld` or `helloWorldHttp`.
2. It takes in `req` and `res` parameters, which are Express.js (`https://expressjs.com/`) `HTTP request` and `HTTP response` objects.
3. The exporting of the function is required so that Google Cloud Function's runtime can invoke it when an event occurs.
4. The function is checking for an existence of a message attribute within the request body.
5. If it is not there, then it responds with the HTTP status code `400`.
6. If the message attribute exists, then it writes to the console the message that it received through the request body.
7. It also responds back to the caller with `Hello World` and the value of the message attribute from the request body.
8. It also responds back to the caller with the HTTP status code `200`.

Testing a Google Cloud Function

In the previous section, we created a Google Cloud Function of the HTTP type. We also looked at the source code that was automatically created by the Google Cloud Console. Let's learn on how to test the Function that we created through the Google Cloud Console:

1. Open the Navigation Menu in the Google Cloud Console.
2. Select **Cloud Functions** under **Compute** within the Navigation Menu.
3. The homepage of the Google Cloud Functions Console will show the list of Google Cloud Functions.
4. Click on the Google Cloud Function that we just created.

5. The console will navigate to the details page of the Function that we just created shown as follows:

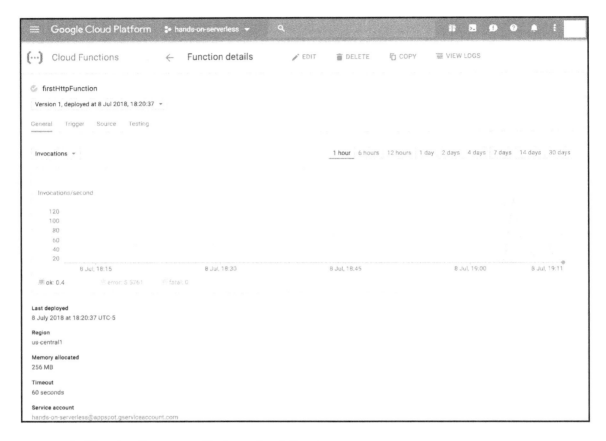

6. The details page will show the following:
   - **Invocations/second**
   - Execution time—milliseconds per call
   - **Memory allocated**—MB per call

7. To test the HTTP Google Cloud Function, select the **Testing** tab within the details page.

8. The **Testing** page contains the trigger event that you can send in to the Google Cloud Function for testing, which in this case is an HTTP request body object.

9. The page also has the **Output** that we will get from the function.

10. If you recall, when we walk through the function's code, the code is looking for an attributed called `message` in the request body object.
11. The page also displays the **Logs** from the execution of the function.
12. To test the successful execution of the Function that we created, let's send the request body as `{"message": "kuldeep"}`.
13. The **Output** section in the page should display a `Success` or `Hello World!` message.
14. The status code in the response logs should also be `200` as shown in the following screenshot:

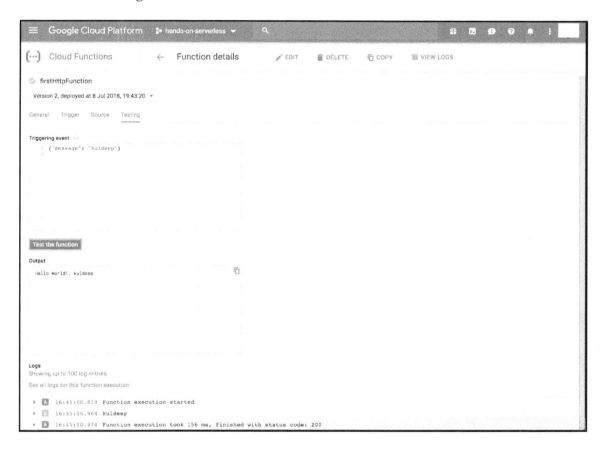

15. Let's also send an invalid request body and see what the function's output looks like.

16. To test this case, let's send the request body as `{"nomessage": "kuldeep"}`.

17. The **Output** section on the page should display a message stating that `message` attribute is missing in the request body.

18. The status code in the response logs should also be `400` as shown in the next screenshot:

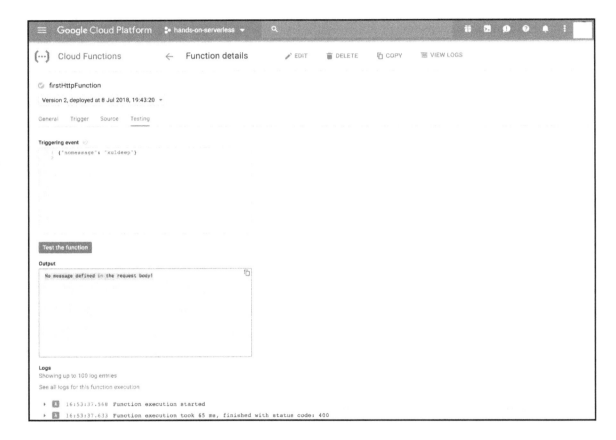

Testing using Postman

Postman is a tool to test your HTTP-based APIs and is available for multiple operating systems. You can learn more about it and download the executable from `https://www.getpostman.com/`.

Let's look at how to get the URL of the function that we created so that we can test using Postman:

1. Open the Navigation Menu in the Google Cloud Console.
2. Select **Cloud Functions** under **Compute** within the Navigation Menu.
3. The home page of the Google Cloud Functions Console will show the list of Google Cloud Functions.
4. Click on the Google Cloud Function that we just created.
5. The console will navigate to the details page of the Function that we just created.
6. Click on the **Trigger** tab. This will display the type of the trigger ,which in our case is HTTP. It will also display the URL to the Function that we use and send the request in as shown in the following screenshot:

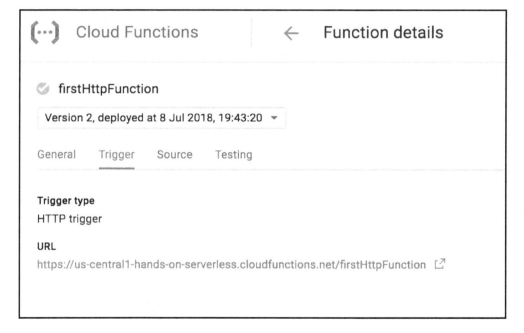

7. Copy the URL from the Function details page.
8. The URL that I was able to get for the Function that I created is https://us-central1-hands-on-serverless.cloudfunctions.net/firstHttpFunction.

Let's test the Google Cloud HTTP Function using Postman:

1. On your workstation, open the **Postman** app.
2. Select the **POST** HTTP method.
3. Enter the copied URL into the **Enter request URL** text box.
4. The URL, in my case, would
   be `https://us-central1-hands-on-serverless.cloudfunctions.net/f
   irstHttpFunction`.
5. Click on the **Body** tab and the select raw checkbox.
6. Enter the request body as `{"message": "kuldeep"}`.
7. Then click on the **Send** button.
8. Click on the **Headers** tab and add the following header in key value format.
9. Key: `Content-Type` and Value: `application/json` as shown in the following screenshot:

10. In the response you get, you should receive a `200` HTTP status code.
11. You will see the response from the REST API with the message as `Hello
    World! REPLACE WITH YOUR NAME` or `Success` message.
12. In my case, the response was `Hello World!, kuldeep`, as shown in the following screenshot:

Viewing logs for Google Cloud Functions

The Google Cloud Functions Console provides you with a way to view the execution logs of the Google Cloud Functions that you have created. Let's look at how you can view the logs for the Google Cloud Function that we created earlier:

1. Open the Navigation Menu in the Google Cloud Console.
2. Select **Cloud Functions** under **Compute** within the Navigation Menu.
3. The homepage of the Google Cloud Functions Console will show the list of Google Cloud Functions.
4. Click on the Google Cloud Function that we just created.
5. The console will navigate to the details page of the Function that we just created.

6. On the **Function details** page, there is a button called **VIEW LOGS**:

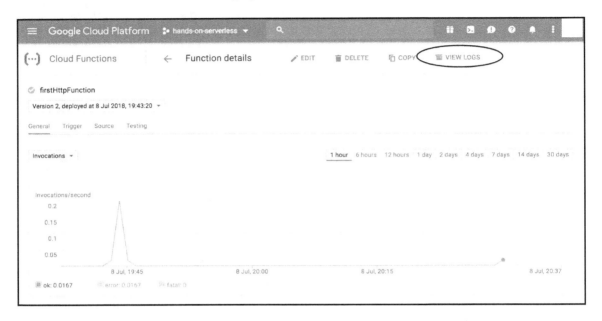

7. Clicking on `VIEW LOGS` will take you to a page that displays the logs for your Google Cloud Function.
8. Within the log viewer page for your function, you can search for a particular text or label within the logs.
9. You can also specify the time frame to search for the logs within the UI, as shown in the following screenshot:

Your first serverless app (on a local workstation)

In the previous section, we learned about creating Google Cloud Functions using the Google Cloud Console. In this section, we will learn about creating Google Cloud Functions on your local workstation using Visual Studio Code and uploading the code to the Google Cloud Platform with `gcloud` CLI.

As part of `Chapter 2`, *Development Environment and SDKs*, we learned about installing Visual Studio Code on your operating system (macOS or Windows). Please make sure Visual Studio Code is installed. If it is not installed, please refer to the instructions in `Chapter 2`, *Development Environment and SDKs*, and install it.

gcloud CLI

Before we start creating Google Cloud Functions on your local workstation, let's learn about the following:

- What is gcloud?
- How to install gcloud CLI
- Configuring gcloud CLI

What is gcloud?

The `gcloud` is a command-line interface designed to interact with the Google Cloud Platform. You can use `gcloud` to perform lots of administrative tasks associated with the Google Cloud Platform from your local workstation (macOS, Windows, and Linux).

Some of the tasks that you can perform using gcloud CLI include:

- **Google Kubernetes Engine** (**GKE**) clusters
- Google Cloud SQL instances
- Google Compute Engine instances
- Google Cloud DNS

The `gcloud` is part of Google Cloud SDK. In order to use `gcloud`, you need to first download Google Cloud SDK and initialize it. You can learn more about Google Cloud SDK at `https://cloud.google.com/sdk/docs/`.

Installing gcloud

You can install `gcloud` on your operating system by downloading the binary targeted for your operating system. The installation instructions for your operating system are listed at `https://cloud.google.com/sdk/docs/#install_the_latest_cloud_tools_version_ cloudsdk_current_version`.

Let's look at the installation instructions for macOS and Windows.

macOS

Let's look at the Google Cloud SDK installation instructions for macOS:

1. Make sure that your operating system already has Python 2.7 installed.

2. You can run the `python -v` command to check the version of Python that has been installed on your operating system.

3. Download the right installation package based on your processor type (32-bit versus 64-bit) from this page: `https://cloud.google.com/sdk/docs/quickstart-macos`.

4. Extract the archived package onto your local filesystem.

5. Navigate to the extracted folder and run the following command:
`./google-cloud-sdk/install.sh`

6. You can add the path of gcloud CLI to your `%PATH%` automatically during the installation process.

7. Once the installation is complete, restart your Terminal so the changes take effect as shown in the following screenshot:

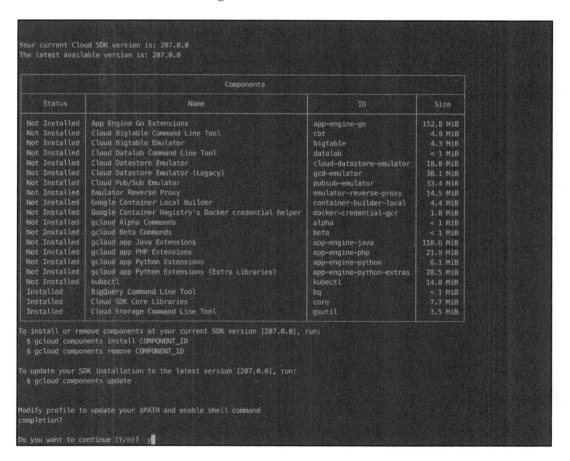

We will learn about initializing the gcloud CLI in the subsequent sections.

Windows

Let's look at the Google Cloud SDK installation instructions for Windows:

1. Download the installer from `https://dl.google.com/dl/cloudsdk/channels/rapid/GoogleCloudSDKInstaller.exe`.
2. Follow the prompts from the installer and install it on your local workstation.
3. After the installer has completed installing the executables on your local workstation, it will prompt you to select different options.
4. Be sure to select the following two:
   - Start Google Cloud SDK Shell
   - Run `gcloud init`
5. This completes the installation on Windows.
6. A new Command Prompt will be opened and the `gcloud init` command will be run waiting for prompts from you.
7. We will look at initializing `gcloud` in the next section.
8. More information about installation on Windows can be found at `https://cloud.google.com/sdk/docs/quickstart-windows`.

gcloud beta commands

Google Cloud Functions are still in beta. Because of that you need to install `gcloud beta` commands so that we can interact with Google Cloud Functions from our local workstation using `gcloud` CLI.

The installation instructions for `gcloud beta` commands is `gcloud components install beta` as shown in the following screenshot:

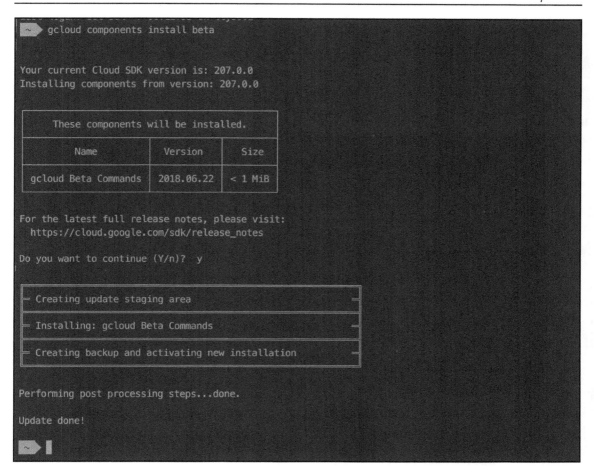

Initializing the gcloud CLI

After installation of the gcloud CLI, you need to initialize it so that it will interact with your Google Cloud Project resources.

Running the `gcloud init` command will perform many setup tasks for gcloud Cloud SDK.

Let's look at configuring the gcloud CLI:

1. In your Terminal or Command Prompt, run the following command: `gcloud init`.

2. It will prompt you to log into your Google user account. Enter `Y` to the prompt and enter your Google Cloud account; see the following screenhot:

```
~  gcloud init
Welcome! This command will take you through the configuration of gcloud.

Your current configuration has been set to: [default]

You can skip diagnostics next time by using the following flag:
  gcloud init --skip-diagnostics

Network diagnostic detects and fixes local network connection issues.
Checking network connection...done.
Reachability Check passed.
Network diagnostic (1/1 checks) passed.

You must log in to continue. Would you like to log in (Y/n)?  Y

Your browser has been opened to visit:
```

3. It will open a browser window. Log in to your user account.

4. Once successfully logged in, it will prompt you to select your default project:

```
Pick cloud project to use:
 [1] [my-project-1]
 [2] [my-project-2]
 ...
 Please enter your numeric choice:
```

5. It will prompt you to set the default compute zone:

```
Which compute zone would you like to use as project default?
 [1] [asia-east1-a]
 [2] [asia-east1-b]
 ...
 [14] Do not use default zone
 Please enter your numeric choice:
```

6. Confirm that the `gcloud init` is complete and see if it responds back as a successfully configured message.

Now that we have the gcloud CLI installed and configured, let's look at creating the Function locally and deploying to the Google Cloud Platform.

Creating a Google Cloud Function

Let's look at how to create a Google Cloud Function on your local workstation with the following steps:

1. Create a working directory on your workstation.
2. Run the `mkdir local-google-function` command on your Terminal (macOS) or Command Prompt (Windows).
3. Navigate to the directory that we just created by running the following command:

   ```
   cd local-google-function
   ```

4. Run the following command to create an empty file touch: `index.json`.
5. Run the following command to create another empty file touch: `package.json`, as shown in the following screenshot:

The required folder and the folder structure are all available now for us to create a Google Cloud Function. Let's look at how to add content to the files using Visual Studio Code with the following steps:

1. Open Visual Studio Code on your operating system.
2. Open the `local-google-function` folder that we just created.
3. On the left hand side, you will see **Functions** as an option.
4. We need to add content to both the files so that we can upload them to the Google Cloud Platform using `gcloud`.
5. For `index.js`, let's reuse the same code that we used earlier while we were creating the Google Cloud Function using the console:

```
exports.helloWorldHttp = (req, res) => {
  if (req.body.message === undefined) {
    res.status(400).send('No message defined in the request
body!');
  } else {
    console.log(req.body.message);
    res.status(200).send('Hello World!, ' + req.body.message);
  }
};
```

6. The preceding source code is also available at `https://github.com/ PacktPublishing/Hands-On-Serverless-Computing/blob/master/Your-first- Serverless-application-on-Google-Cloud/first-http-function.js`.
7. NPM manages installing the dependencies that you need for your Node.js application based on what's defined in the file called as `package.json`.
8. Add the following code to `package.json`.

```
{
 "name": "httpLocalFunction",
 "version": "0.0.1"
}
```

6. The source code for both `index.js` and `package.json` for the local Google Cloud Function is located at `https://github.com/PacktPublishing/Hands-On- Serverless-Computing/tree/master/Your-first-Serverless-application-on- Google-Cloud/local-google-function`.

Deploying a Google Cloud Function

Now that we have the content for the Google Cloud Function ready to go, let's look at the command that we need to run on our workstation so that we can deploy it to the Google Cloud Platform.

The command would look like this:

```
gcloud beta functions deploy <NAME> <TRIGGER>
```

In my case, I will be running the following command:

```
gcloud beta functions deploy firstlocalFunction --trigger-http --entry-point helloWorldHttp
```

You can see at the end I appended `--entry-point` as well to the command. By default, the `gcloud` CLI expects the same name of the Function be used in the module export for `index.js`. However if you prefer to use a different name than the Function, then you need to specify the argument.

The following screenshot shows the execution of the preceding command on my local workstation:

The CLI `gcloud` was able to successfully package up my files and create a Google Cloud Function name: `firstlocalFunction`.

Let's learn more about what `gcloud` does behind the scenes when you run that command:

1. If there are any dependencies listed in `package.json`, `gcloud` will automatically download them before it creates the ZIP file.
2. Once the ZIP file is created, it will upload it to a Google Cloud Storage bucket.
3. Once the ZIP file is available in a Google Cloud Storage bucket, it will call the Google Cloud Function API to create the Google Cloud Function and upload the ZIP file to that Google Cloud Function.

Let's look at the following screenshot of the Google Cloud Functions Console to verify if the Function was indeed created:

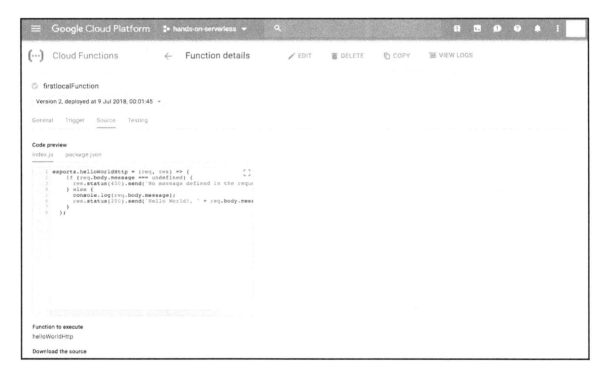

As you can see, the Function was successfully created with the name `firstlocalFunction` and with the same source code from the local workstation. The Function has been also created with `HTTP Trigger`.

Summary

In this chapter, we learned how to write serverless applications that will run on the Google Cloud Platform using Node.js. We learned about creating Google Cloud Functions using two methods namely The Google Cloud Console and Local workstation. In the Google Cloud Console we learned how to create a Google Cloud Function and how to create an HTTP type of Google Cloud Function. We also learned how to test the Google Cloud Function through the console and also using Postman and how to view logs for the Google Cloud Function. In Local workstation we learned how to create a Google Cloud Function on your local workstation and how to deploy a Google Cloud Function on your local workstation to the Google Cloud Platform using the gcloud CLI

In the next chapter, I will walk you through a reference architecture for a serverless web application that runs on AWS.

13
Reference Architecture for a Web App

In this chapter, we will be covering how to build a serverless web application in an AWS environment. The previous chapters only touched upon the FaaS offering, which was AWS Lambda + Amazon API Gateway. However, in reality, you would need a database to store your data and retrieve it, and many resources besides that are required to run your application in production.

In this chapter, we will look into:

- A reference architecture for building a serverless web app in the AWS environment.
- An example AWS **Serverless Application Model** (**SAM**) template to create the required AWS resources. We learned about AWS SAM in `Chapter 5`, *Your First Serverless Application on AWS*; if you want a refresher on this, please refer to that chapter.

Technical requirements

For the reference SAM template file, refer to this GitHub link: `https://github.com/ PacktPublishing/Hands-On-Serverless-Computing/blob/master/Reference- Architecture-for-a-web-App/template-hotels-search.yaml`.

Reference architecture

Let's look at what a reference architecture for a web app will look like using the serverless resources that AWS offers. Let's look at two use cases for a travel website that lets customers search for hotels and book them. Let's look at the resources that we need for the website. You can also look at AWS Well Architected Framework for reference at `https:// d1.awsstatic.com/whitepapers/architecture/AWS_Well-Architected_Framework.pdf`

Friendly domain name

With the travel website being a customer-facing site, you need a friendly domain name that your customers can easily remember. Once you have decided on a name for your travel website, you can use Amazon's Managed Cloud DNS, called Route 53, to register your domain name.

 You can learn more about Route 53 at
`https://aws.amazon.com/route53/`.
You can also learn about the pricing around Route 53 at `https://aws. amazon.com/route53/pricing/`.

SSL/TLS certificate

It is recommended to run your website on the HTTPS protocol. To be able to run your website on the HTTPS protocol, you will need an SSL/TLS certificate. AWS gives you the ability to create and manage SSL/TLS certificates through a service called **AWS Certificate Manager** (**ACM**). You can request a new certificate for your domain name and manage it in ACM. Public certificates are also free if you are going to use these certificates with ACM integrated services, such as Elastic Load Balancer or Amazon API Gateway resources. For the serverless web app, we will be using Amazon API Gateway and ACM will provide you with a free public certificate.

You can learn more about ACM at `https://aws.amazon.com/ certificate-manager/`.

You can request a public certificate by navigating to the AWS Certificate Manager console and clicking on provision new public certificates, and you will be taken to the following page:

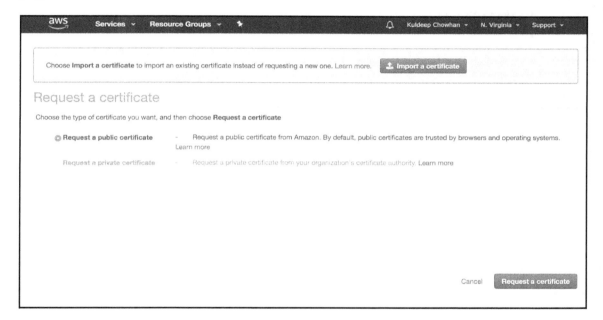

Amazon API Gateway + AWS Lambda

API Gateway + AWS Lambda allows you to invoke Lambda functions over HTTP(S). With API Gateway, you get a custom REST endpoint, and you can configure API Gateway to invoke AWS Lambda on different HTTP methods, such as PUT, GET, DELETE, and other HTTP methods. With this integration in place, when you invoke the custom REST endpoint that has been configured by API Gateway, API Gateway will invoke the configured AWS Lambda function. API Gateway facilitates proxying the information that it receives on the custom REST endpoint directly over to AWS Lambda functions, without any need for transformations. Within the AWS Lambda function, you can respond with valid HTTP status codes so that the caller of the custom REST endpoint will see those same HTTP status codes, as shown in the following screenshot:

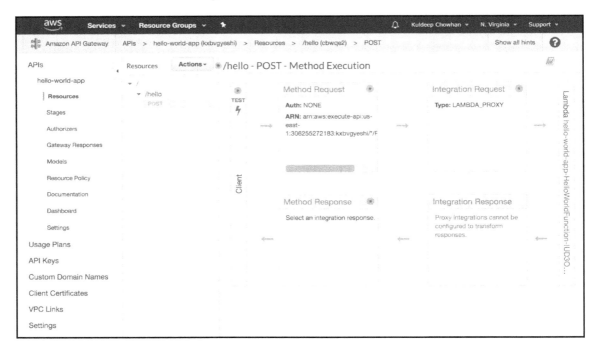

For the travel hotel website that we want to build, we will have both API Gateways.

Prior to the Lambda proxy integration feature in API Gateway, the way to integrate AWS Lambda was to use custom mapping templates within API Gateway. This document talks about how you can do that with custom Lambda integration: https://docs.aws.amazon.com/apigateway/latest/developerguide/getting-started-lambda-non-proxy-integration.html. It is highly recommend to use the Lambda proxy integration feature in API Gateway.

Amazon DynamoDB

Amazon DynamoDB is a fast NoSQL database for all applications that are looking for single-digit millisecond latency at scale. It is a fully managed cloud database provided by AWS. You can learn more about it at `https://aws.amazon.com/dynamodb/`. With DynamoDB in place, you can store data in the database and retrieve data from the database when searching for hotels to book them. We will look at the AWS SAM template to create this table as well, later in the chapter.

Combining all these resources that we talked about so far, let's look at a reference architecture for searching the hotels and adding requests to cart for the hotel travel website. For both use cases, we will be using the same type of resources:

- Amazon Route 53
- Amazon API Gateway
- AWS Lambda function
- Amazon DynamoDB Table

Hotel search

Let's look at the use case of searching hotels first. What I'm going to walk through is a very slimmed down version of what a hotel travel website will look like. In reality, it is a very complex system to build and operate. As mentioned, we use the following resources for this use case:

- Amazon Route 53 for storing the domain name of our hotel travel website
- Amazon API Gateway for handling the HTTP(S) that come to our hotel website in search of hotels
- The AWS Lambda function for handling the search calls to find hotels that are available in a city during a particular time frame
- The Amazon DynamoDB table, which actually holds the available inventory of hotels that can be displayed in the search results

The reference architecture of how the system works is shown in the following diagram. The flow for the system is:

1. The user searches for your website's domain name in their browser.
2. It resolves to Route 53 DNS servers.

3. It resolves to an API Gateway Endpoint URL.

4. As it resolves to an API Gateway URL, the request that was made in the browser reaches API Gateway.

5. API Gateway is acting as a proxy for the Lambda function and it forwards the request to the Lambda function.

6. The Lambda function makes a call to DynamoDB to get the available hotels and sends that information back through API Gateway to the user, as demonstrated in the following diagram:

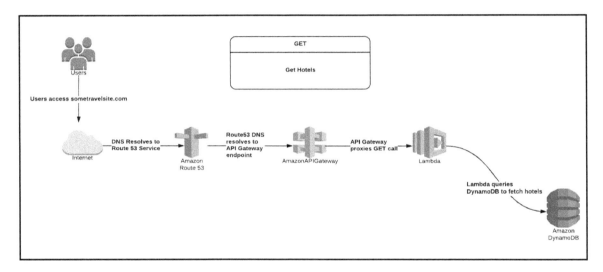

To create the resources that we need, we will use the AWS SAM. The template for creating the resources that we talked about earlier would look like this one. Keep in mind that this is just a reference, not the actual design of the system:

```
AWSTemplateFormatVersion: '2010-09-09'
Transform: AWS::Serverless-2016-10-31
Description: >
    Reference Hotels Web App

    AWS SAM Template for Hotels Web App
Globals:
    Function:
        Timeout: 10

Resources:

    SearchHotelsIngestionFunction:
      Type: AWS::Serverless::Function
```

```
        Properties:
            CodeUri: .
            Handler: index.handler
            Runtime: nodejs8.10
            Policies:
              - DynamoDBCrudPolicy:
                  TableName: !Ref HotelsListDynamoDB
            Events:
                SearchHotelsIngestion:
                    Type: Api
                    Properties:
                        Path: /hotels
                        Method: get
    HotelsListDynamoDB:
      Type: AWS::DynamoDB::Table
      Properties:
        AttributeDefinitions:
          -
            AttributeName: "hotelName"
            AttributeType: "S"
          -
            AttributeName: "hotelId"
            AttributeType: "N"
....
Outputs:

    SearchHotelsIngestionApi:
      Description: "API Gateway endpoint URL for Prod stage for Search
Hotels function"
      Value: !Sub
"https://${ServerlessRestApi}.execute-api.${AWS::Region}.amazonaws.com/Prod
/"

    SearchHotelsIngestionFunction:
      Description: "Search Hotels Lambda Function ARN"
      Value: !GetAtt SearchHotelsIngestionFunction.Arn

    SearchHotelsIngestionFunctionIamRole:
      Description: "Implicit IAM Role created for Search Hotels Lambda
function"
      Value: !GetAtt SearchHotelsIngestionFunctionRole.Arn
```

For the entire code, refer to the GitHub link provided in the *Technical requirements* section.

Let's walk through the template and look at the resources it has created.

Lambda Function + API Gateway

The following SAM template creates AWS Lambda Function and Amazon API Gateway resources. API Gateway is configured to proxy `GET` requests on the `/hotels` endpoint to the Lambda function. The template also gives the Lambda access to write to the DynamoDB table that gets created. It gives it CRUD access:

```
SearchHotelsIngestionFunction:
    Type: AWS::Serverless::Function
    Properties:
        CodeUri: .
        Handler: index.handler
        Runtime: nodejs8.10
        Policies:
          - DynamoDBCrudPolicy:
              TableName: !Ref HotelsListDynamoDB
        Events:
            SearchHotelsIngestion:
                Type: Api
                Properties:
                    Path: /
                    Method: get
```

Amazon DynamoDB

The following SAM template creates an Amazon DynamoDB with two keys to the table. Keep in mind this is just a reference, not the schema for the entire table to hold the hotel inventory:

```
HotelsListDynamoDB:
  Type: AWS::DynamoDB::Table
  Properties:
    AttributeDefinitions:
      -
        AttributeName: "hotelName"
        AttributeType: "S"
      -
        AttributeName: "hotelId"
        AttributeType: "N"
    KeySchema:
      -
        AttributeName: "hotelName"
        KeyType: "HASH"
      -
        AttributeName: "hotelId"
```

```
        KeyType: "RANGE"
      ProvisionedThroughput:
        ReadCapacityUnits: 5
        WriteCapacityUnits: 5
```

Add to cart

Let's look at the use case of adding a hotel to the cart. What I'm going to walk through is a very slimmed down version of what an e-commerce, add to cart functionality, will look like. In reality, it is a very complex system to build and operate. As mentioned, we need the following resources for this use case:

- Amazon Route 53 for storing the domain name of our hotel travel website, as discussed in the previous use case
- Amazon API Gateway for handling the HTTP(S) that come to our hotel website to add a hotel to their cart
- The AWS Lambda Function for handling the addition of hotels to carts
- The Amazon DynamoDB table that stores the cart items, along with information such as hotel details, trip start date and end date, and the number of adults and children

The reference architecture of how the system works is shown in the following diagram. The flow for the system is as follows:

1. The user adds a hotel to the cart; the request will again go back to our hotel travel website's Domain Name in the browser.
2. It resolves to Route 53 DNS servers.
3. It resolves to an API Gateway Endpoint URL.
4. As it resolves to an API Gateway URL, the request that was made in the browser reaches the API Gateway.
5. As the request is to add a hotel to the cart, it involves sending a JSON payload to the server to store the cart details in the DynamoDB table.
6. As part of the **add to cart** call, the JSON payload is attached to the HTTP request.
7. API Gateway is acting as a proxy for the Lambda function and it will also forward the JSON payload as a request body to the Lambda function.

8. The Lambda function will process the JSON payload and make a call to DynamoDB to store the cart details in the cart items DynamoDB table:

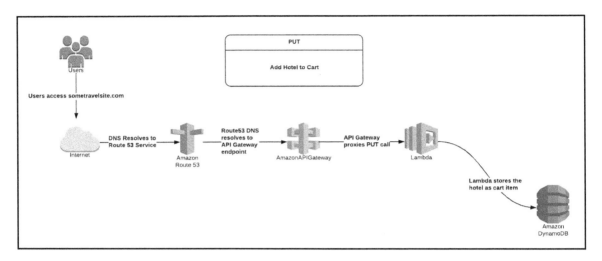

To create the resources that we need, we will use the AWS SAM. The template for creating the resources that we talked about earlier would look like this one. Keep in mind that this is just a reference, not the actual design of the system:

```
AWSTemplateFormatVersion: '2010-09-09'
Transform: AWS::Serverless-2016-10-31
Description: >
    Reference Add to Cart Web App

    AWS SAM Template for Add to Cart
Globals:
    Function:
        Timeout: 10

Resources:

    AddToCartIngestionFunction:
      Type: AWS::Serverless::Function
      Properties:
          CodeUri: .
          Handler: index.handler
          Runtime: nodejs8.10
          Policies:
            - DynamoDBCrudPolicy:
                  TableName: !Ref CartItemsDynamoDB
          Events:
```

```
                  AddToCartIngestion:
                      Type: Api
                      Properties:
                          Path: /cart
                          Method: post
    ...
```

For the entire code, refer to the GitHub link provided in the *Technical requirements* section.

Here is the output for the preceding code:

```
Outputs:

    AddToCartIngestionApi:
        Description: "API Gateway endpoint URL for Prod stage for Add to Cart
function"
        Value: !Sub
"https://${ServerlessRestApi}.execute-api.${AWS::Region}.amazonaws.com/Prod
/"

    AddToCartIngestionFunction:
        Description: "Add to Cart Lambda Function ARN"
        Value: !GetAtt AddToCartIngestionFunction.Arn

    AddToCartIngestionFunctionIamRole:
        Description: "Implicit IAM Role created for Add to Cart Lambda
function"
        Value: !GetAtt AddToCartIngestionFunctionRole.Arn
```

Let's walk through the template and look at the resources it has created.

Lambda Function + API Gateway

The following SAM template creates AWS Lambda Function and Amazon API Gateway resources. The API Gateway is configured to proxy POST requests on the /cart endpoint to the Lambda function. The template also gives the Lambda access to write to the DynamoDB table that gets created. It gives it CRUD access:

```
AddToCartIngestionFunction:
    Type: AWS::Serverless::Function
    Properties:
        CodeUri: .
        Handler: index.handler
        Runtime: nodejs8.10
        Policies:
          - DynamoDBCrudPolicy:
```

```
                    TableName: !Ref CartItemsDynamoDB
           Events:
               AddToCartIngestion:
                   Type: Api
                   Properties:
                       Path: /cart
                       Method: post
```

Amazon DynamoDB

The following SAM template creates an Amazon DynamoDB instance with multiple keys to the table. Bear in mind that this is just a reference, not the schema for the entire table to hold a cart item with a hotel:

```
CartItemsDynamoDB:
  Type: AWS::DynamoDB::Table
  Properties:
    AttributeDefinitions:
      -
        AttributeName: "cartId"
        AttributeType: "S"
      -
        AttributeName: "hotelId"
        AttributeType: "N"
      -
        AttributeName: "customerId"
        AttributeType: "N"
      -
        AttributeName: "tripStartDate"
        AttributeType: "N"
      -
        AttributeName: "tripEndDate"
        AttributeType: "N"
      -
        AttributeName: "adults"
        AttributeType: "N"
      -
        AttributeName: "children"
        AttributeType: "N"
    KeySchema:
      -
        AttributeName: "cartId"
        KeyType: "HASH"
      -
        AttributeName: "hotelId"
        KeyType: "RANGE"
```

```
ProvisionedThroughput:
  ReadCapacityUnits: 5
  WriteCapacityUnits: 5
TableName: "cart-items"
```

Summary

In this chapter, we learned about a reference architecture for building serverless web apps in the AWS environment. We also looked at two reference architectures for web apps: one was focused on searching for hotels, while the other was focused on adding a hotel to a cart. Also, for both use cases, we looked at the architecture diagram, along with the AWS SAM templates.

In the next chapter, we will look into a reference architecture for a file processing serverless app.

14
Reference Architecture for a Real-time File Processing

By this point, we have learned what serverless computing is, and we've also learned how to build serverless apps using three public cloud providers: AWS, Microsoft Azure, and Google Cloud Platform. We learned about creating FaaS offerings in all three public cloud providers, along with the creation of an HTTP trigger for each of the different FaaS offerings the three public cloud providers offer.

In this chapter, I want to cover how to build a serverless application in the AWS environment that processes files. The reference architecture that I want to cover as part of this chapter concerns creating different resolutions for a photo as soon as it gets uploaded to an S3 bucket. The end result of different sets of resolutions for the same photos is that they will all end up in an S3 bucket.

In this chapter, we will look into:

- A reference architecture for building a real-time serverless photo processing app in the AWS environment.
- An example AWS SAM template to create the required AWS resources. We learned about AWS SAM in `Chapter 5`, *Your First Serverless Applications on AWS*; if you want a refresher on this, please refer to that chapter.

Technical requirements

For the reference SAM template files, refer to the following link: `https://github.com/PacktPublishing/Hands-On-Serverless-Computing/blob/master/Reference-Architecture-for-File-Processing-App/template.yaml`.

Reference architecture

Let's look at what a reference architecture for a real-time photo processing app will look like using the serverless resources that AWS offers. Let's look at one use case for an app that creates different types of resolution for a photo as soon as it gets uploaded to an Amazon S3 bucket. The end result will also be stored in an S3 bucket. You can also look at AWS Well Architected Framework for reference at `https://d1.awsstatic.com/whitepapers/architecture/AWS_Well-Architected_Framework.pdf`

S3 bucket

We need an Amazon S3 bucket to which the photos can be uploaded for further processing. Let's learn about S3 first.

Amazon S3 is object storage built to store and retrieve any amount of data from any location. You can learn more about Amazon S3 at `https://aws.amazon.com/s3/`:

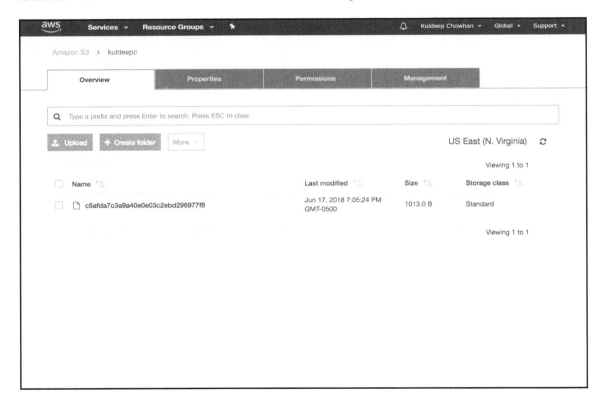

You can have AWS Lambda functions invoked to process Amazon S3 events, such as object created or object deleted events. You can have the AWS Lambda function invoked whenever a new photo is created in an Amazon S3 bucket, which will automatically create a thumbnail for the photo that was uploaded to the S3 bucket.

Here is a screenshot of an AWS Lambda configuration to invoke all **Object Created (All)** events:

Bucket
Please select the S3 bucket that serves as the event source. The bucket must be in the same region as the function.

binv2

Event type
Select the events that you want to have trigger the Lambda function. You can optionally set up a prefix or suffix for have multiple configurations with overlapping prefixes or suffixes that could match the same object key.

Object Created (All)

Prefix
Enter an optional prefix to limit the notifications to objects with keys that start with matching characters.

e.g. images/

Filter pattern
Enter an optional filter pattern.

e.g. .jpg

Lambda will add the necessary permissions for Amazon S3 to invoke your Lambda function from this

☑ Enable trigger
Enable the trigger now, or create it in a disabled state for testing (recommended).

However, with our use case of creating multiple types of resolution for the same photo in real time, if we had only one Lambda invoked whenever a file gets created in S3, then we won't be able to process a photo that has been uploaded and create three types of resolution at the same time. For that, we need a fan out - approach, where we need to have multiple AWS Lambda functions working on the photo to create different resolutions at the same time. To be able to achieve this, we will need a solution that can be used with the publisher and subscriber model. Amazon offers a solution for this problem, and it is called Amazon Simple Notification Service.

Amazon Simple Notification Service

Amazon **Simple Notification Service** (**SNS**) is a fully managed pub/sub (`https://aws.amazon.com/pub-sub-messaging/`) messaging and mobile notification service, that coordinates the delivery of messages to subscribers. With SNS, you can send messages to a wide variety of subscribers, including services such as AWS Lambda, along with distributed systems and mobile devices. You can learn more about Amazon SNS at `https://aws.amazon.com/sns/`.

You can invoke one or more AWS Lambda functions to process Amazon SNS notifications. When a message is published to an Amazon SNS topic, the message is sent to the AWS Lambda function as a payload parameter, as can be seen in the following screenshot:

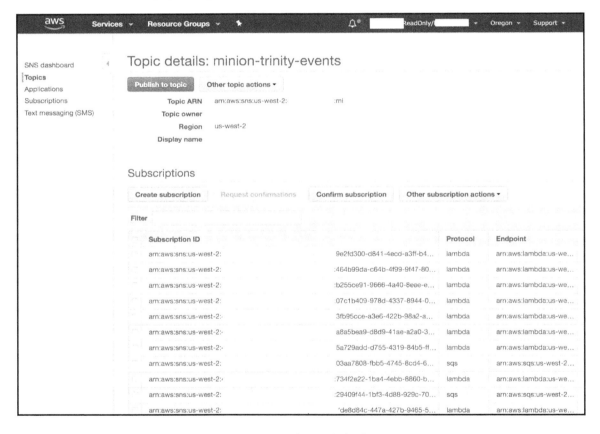

With this integration, you can trigger an AWS Lambda function in response to Amazon CloudWatch alarms and many other AWS services that leverage Amazon SNS.

Here is a screenshot of AWS SNS configuration with the AWS Lambda console:

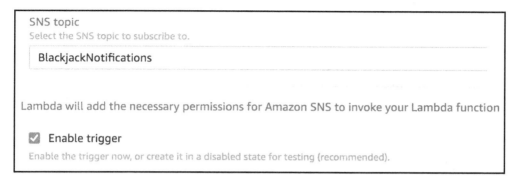

AWS Lambda

AWS Lambda is a compute service through which you can run your functions. It will run your functions without the need for you to provision or manage any compute infrastructure. AWS Lambda can not only execute your functions, but can also easily scale to thousands of executions per second. As server management is abstracted away from the developer, the latter can just focus on solving the business problem rather than having to also focus on server management and scaling the solution. The other big benefit in terms of cost is that you only pay the compute cost for the time AWS Lambda is executed, which provides you with a higher utilization of resources at a significantly lower price than what you would typically be paying if you were to run the compute infrastructure all the time.

In our case, we will be creating three AWS Lambda to process a photo that gets uploaded to an S3 bucket, and, once it is processed, the three AWS Lambda functions will again store it back in the S3 bucket in different folders.

Photo processing application

The three AWS services that we just learned about will make up our serverless app for photo processing. To recap, the three AWS services are:

- Amazon S3
- Amazon SNS
- AWS Lambda functions

The reference architecture for the photo processing application is shown next. Let me break down what is going on here:

1. The user uploads a photo to an S3 bucket
2. The upload of the photo to the S3 bucket could happen in multiple ways:
   - AWS S3 Console
   - Application that acts as a layer in front of S3
   - AWS CLI
3. However, the files get uploaded to the S3 bucket, due to the configuration that we have on the S3 bucket, and a notification is sent to Amazon SNS as soon as a file gets created in the S3 bucket
4. The notification is sent to an SNS topic that has three subscribers:
   - A Lambda function that creates thumbnails for the photo that was uploaded
   - A Lambda function that creates icons for the photo that was uploaded
   - A Lambda function that creates high resolution photos for the photo that was uploaded
5. Once each Lambda processes the uploaded photo and creates the required resolution for the photo, it stores it back in the same S3 bucket, under different prefixes/folders, as can be seen in the following diagram:

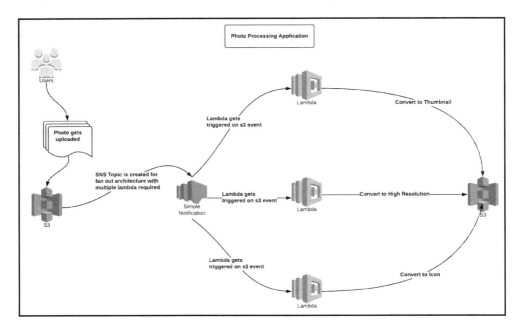

To create the resources that we need, we will use the AWS SAM. The template for creating the resources that we talked about earlier would look like this one. Bear in mind, this is just a reference, not the actual design of the system:

```
AWSTemplateFormatVersion: '2010-09-09'
Transform: AWS::Serverless-2016-10-31
Description: >
    Reference Photo Processing Application with fan out architecture

    AWS SAM Template for Photo Processing Application
Globals:
    Function:
        Timeout: 10

Resources:

    ThumbNailGenerationFunction:
      Type: AWS::Serverless::Function
      Properties:
          CodeUri: .
          Handler: index.handler
          Runtime: nodejs8.10
          Policies:
            - AmazonS3FullAccessPolicy
          Events:
            SNS1:
              Type: SNS
              Properties:
                Topic:
                    Ref: PhotoUploadTopic
    IconGenerationFunction:
      Type: AWS::Serverless::Function
      Properties:
          CodeUri: .
          Handler: index.handler
          Runtime: nodejs8.10
          Policies:
            - AmazonS3FullAccessPolicy
  ...
Outputs:

    ThumbNailGenerationFunction:
      Description: "ThumbNail Generation Lambda Function ARN"
      Value: !GetAtt ThumbNailGenerationFunction.Arn

    IconGenerationFunction:
      Description: "Icon Generation Lambda Function ARN"
      Value: !GetAtt IconGenerationFunction.Arn
```

```
HighResolutionGenerationFunction:
    Description: "High Resolution Generation Lambda Function ARN"
    Value: !GetAtt HighResolutionGenerationFunction.Arn
```

For the entire code, refer to the GitHub link provided in the *Technical requirements* section.

Let's walk through the template and look at the resources it has created.

Three Lambda functions

The following SAM template creates three AWS Lambda functions that generate different resolutions for the photo that was uploaded to the S3 bucket. If you look at the template, all three AWS Lambda function events are configured to the same Amazon SNS topic:

```
ThumbNailGenerationFunction:
    Type: AWS::Serverless::Function
    Properties:
        CodeUri: .
        Handler: index.handler
        Runtime: nodejs8.10
        Policies:
            - AmazonS3FullAccessPolicy
        Events:
            SNS1:
                Type: SNS
                Properties:
                    Topic:
                        Ref: PhotoUploadTopic
IconGenerationFunction:
    Type: AWS::Serverless::Function
    Properties:
        CodeUri: .
        Handler: index.handler
        Runtime: nodejs8.10
        Policies:
            - AmazonS3FullAccessPolicy
        Events:
            SNS1:
                Type: SNS
                Properties:
                    Topic:
                        Ref: PhotoUploadTopic
HighResolutionGenerationFunction:
    Type: AWS::Serverless::Function
    Properties:
        CodeUri: .
```

```
Handler: index.handler
Runtime: nodejs8.10
Policies:
  - AmazonS3FullAccessPolicy
Events:
  SNS1:
    Type: SNS
    Properties:
      Topic:
        Ref: PhotoUploadTopic
```

S3 Bucket + Amazon SNS

The following SAM template creates an S3 bucket that we use to upload the photo, and the SNS topic on which the notifications are sent to as soon as a photo is uploaded to the S3 bucket:

```
PhotoUploadTopic:
  Type: 'AWS::SNS::Topic'
PhotosUpload:
  Type: AWS::S3::Bucket
```

Summary

In this chapter, we looked into a reference architecture for building a serverless application in the AWS environment that would create multiple resolutions of the same photo that was uploaded to an S3 bucket. Also, we looked at the architecture diagram, along with the AWS SAM template.

This is the end of the book. I hope it proved useful in enabling you to learn how to build serverless applications on Amazon Web Services, Microsoft Azure, and Google Cloud Platform.

Other Books You May Enjoy

If you enjoyed this book, you may be interested in these other books by Packt:

Docker for Serverless Applications
Chanwit Kaewkasi

ISBN: 978-1-78883-526-8

- Learn what Serverless and FaaS applications are
- Get acquainted with the architectures of three major serverless systems
- Explore how Docker technologies can help develop Serverless applications
- Create and maintain FaaS infrastructures
- Set up Docker infrastructures to serve as on-premises FaaS infrastructures
- Define functions for Serverless applications with Docker containers

Azure Serverless Computing Cookbook
Praveen Kumar Sreeram

ISBN: 978-1-78839-082-8

- Develop different event-based handlers supported by serverless architecture supported by Microsoft Cloud Platform – Azure
- Integrate Azure Functions with different Azure Services to develop Enterprise-level applications
- Get to know the best practices in organizing and refactoring the code within the Azure functions
- Test, troubleshoot, and monitor the Azure functions to deliver high-quality, reliable, and robust cloud-centric applications
- Automate mundane tasks at various levels right from development to deployment and maintenance
- Learn how to develop statefulserverless applications and also self-healing jobs using DurableFunctions

Leave a review - let other readers know what you think

Please share your thoughts on this book with others by leaving a review on the site that you bought it from. If you purchased the book from Amazon, please leave us an honest review on this book's Amazon page. This is vital so that other potential readers can see and use your unbiased opinion to make purchasing decisions, we can understand what our customers think about our products, and our authors can see your feedback on the title that they have worked with Packt to create. It will only take a few minutes of your time, but is valuable to other potential customers, our authors, and Packt. Thank you!

Index

www.ingramcontent.com/pod-product-compliance
Lightning Source LLC
Chambersburg PA
CBHW080618060326

40690CB00021B/4734